S0-BFD-225

# WEAPONS OF
# THE WEALTHY

# WEAPONS OF THE WEALTHY

Predatory Regimes and Elite-Led Protests in Central Asia

**Scott Radnitz**

**CORNELL UNIVERSITY PRESS**   **ITHACA AND LONDON**

Cornell University Press acknowledges receipt of a grant from the University of Washington, which aided in the publication of this book.

Copyright © 2010 by Cornell University

All rights reserved. Except for brief quotations in a review, this book, or parts thereof, must not be reproduced in any form without permission in writing from the publisher. For information, address Cornell University Press, Sage House, 512 East State Street, Ithaca, New York 14850.

First published 2010 by Cornell University Press
Printed in the United States of America

Library of Congress Cataloging-in-Publication Data

Radnitz, Scott, 1978–
   Weapons of the wealthy : predatory regimes and elite-led protests in Central Asia / Scott Radnitz.
      p. cm.
   Includes bibliographical references and index.
   ISBN 978-0-8014-4953-6 (cloth : alk. paper)
   1. Kyrgyzstan—Politics and government—1991–   2. Uzbekistan—Politics and government—1991–   3. Demonstrations—Kyrgyzstan.   4. Demonstrations—Uzbekistan.   5. Political participation—Kyrgyzstan.   6. Political participation—Uzbekistan.   7. Elite (Social sciences)—Kyrgyzstan.   8. Elite (Social sciences)—Uzbekistan.   I. Title.
   DK918.8757.R33   2010
   958.4308'6—dc22            2010024646

Cornell University Press strives to use environmentally responsible suppliers and materials to the fullest extent possible in the publishing of its books. Such materials include vegetable-based, low-VOC inks and acid-free papers that are recycled, totally chlorine-free, or partly composed of nonwood fibers. For further information, visit our website at www.cornellpress.cornell.edu.

Cloth printing            10  9  8  7  6  5  4  3  2  1

# Contents

# Figures and Tables

# Acknowledgments

When I started this project in 2001, Central Asia was not yet on the West's "map." It is somewhat more prominent now thanks to the war in Afghanistan, but it is still terra incognita to many, and it suffers from numerous misconceptions and stereotypes. I hope, with this book, to help readers gain a better understanding of Central Asia and to demonstrate how it can be incorporated fruitfully into comparative analysis.

The research for and writing of this book took me across three continents. I would not have completed it without the indulgence and assistance of many people at various stages. Prior to visiting Central Asia, I studied Uzbek with Gulnora Aminova. John Schoeberlein's Central Asia and the Caucasus Working Group at Harvard University gave me insight into the region. My first visit to Uzbekistan was funded by the Mellon-MIT Program on NGOs and Forced Migration and a Foreign Languages and Area Studies grant. A later trip was funded by ACTR/ACCELS. Ruslan Ikramov in Tashkent helped me improve my conversational Uzbek. John Payne and Marc DeVore inspired me to seize the yak by the horns.

Along the way, Christoph Zuercher and Jan Koehler organized an ambitious collaborative project at the Free University in Berlin and made me a part of it. Christoph provided valuable feedback as I fumbled my way toward a manageable project and shared his wisdom from the Caucasus while I was in the field. Jan helped me to flesh out and refine my ideas, with a social anthropologist's eye for the interesting and unexpected. The other researchers—Alexey Gunya, Bahodir Sidikov, Azamat Temirkulov, Gunda Wiegmann, and Jonathan Wheatley—provided many hours of intellectual stimulation in Berlin, Bishkek, and Baku. Julia Larycheva and Sarah Riese helped keep things running. The Volkswagen Foundation provided financial support while I was in Berlin and during two follow-up visits to Kyrgyzstan.

During my year of fieldwork, the Fulbright program provided financial and logistical support in Kyrgyzstan and Uzbekistan. In the field, I benefited from the assistance of many people, only some of whom I can name here. In Osh, I was affiliated with the Kyrgyz-Uzbek University. The Adyshev family generously provided shelter and food. My fieldwork and cultural education benefited immensely from the assistance of Almaz Kalet and Ilhom Melibaev. I have also enjoyed the help and support of Kiyal Tuksonbaev, Azizkin Soltobaev, Galina Nikolaevna, and Edil Baisalov in Bishkek; Aslambek Buriev in Tashkent; Saparbek Narkeev and the UN Development Programme in Aksy; Alisher Saipov and Zalkar Jumabaev in Osh; Bekzod, Ali, Timur Khakberdiev, and CHF International in Karshi; Jurabek and Gulnora in Namangan; and Jusupjon Ajibaev, Maqsad, Aibek, and the National Democratic Institute in Jalalabad. Abdulla and Mavjuda always gave me a home in Tashkent—and much more.

Back home, my mentors were always responsive and provided vital constructive criticism. Roger Petersen was encouraging yet tough, and he steered me toward the big picture. Chappell Lawson provided amazingly quick and detailed comments on my dense and verbose early drafts—and then on my somewhat improved later chapters—and helped me develop and broaden my ideas. Pauline Jones Luong's research significantly influenced my thinking about Central Asia. Her advice on early drafts marked a critical juncture in this book's development. Lily Tsai made insightful critiques of my writing, helping me to refine concepts and strengthen my arguments.

I received postdoctoral fellowships from the Belfer Center for Science and International Affairs at Harvard in 2006–07 and the Kennan Institute at the Woodrow Wilson International Center for Scholars in 2007. Robert Rotberg and Blair Ruble invited me into their respective scholarly circles. I presented parts of the manuscript at the Belfer Center, the Kennan Institute, UC Berkeley, Georgetown, the School of Advanced International Studies, and the U.S. Department of State.

I have used material from several previously published articles with permission from the publishers: "Networks, Localism, and Mobilization in Aksy, Kyrgyzstan," *Central Asian Survey* 24, no. 4 (2005): 405–24, from Taylor and Francis; "What Really Happened in Kyrgyzstan?" *Journal of Democracy* 17, no. 2 (2006): 132–46, © 2006 National Endowment for Democracy and the Johns Hopkins University Press; and "A Horse of a Different Color: Revolution and Regression in Kyrgyzstan," in *Democracy and Authoritarianism in the Postcommunist World,* ed. Valerie Bunce, Michael A. McFaul, and Kathryn Stoner-Weiss (New York: Cambridge University Press, 2010).

At the University of Washington, Dan Chirot, Steve Hanson, Sunila Kale, Wolf Latsch, Tony Lucero, Joel Migdal, Robert Pekkanen, Saadia Pekkanen, and Steve Pfaff read all or parts of the manuscript. Anand Yang was especially supportive as the book neared completion. I was assisted at various stages of the project by Kelly McMann, Dmitry Gorenburg, Regine Spector, Rachel Gisselquist, Laura Adams, Ed Schatz, Boaz Atzili, Cory Welt, Neema Noori, Erica Chenoweth, Tammy Smith, Noor O'Neill Borbieva, Zamir Borbiev, Matteo Fumagalli, Morgan Liu, Larry Markowitz, Audrey Sachs, Elena Erosheva, Chris Adolph, and Fredrik Sjoberg. I thank Roger Haydon at Cornell University Press for supporting and helping to improve the book manuscript. Josef Eckert drew the maps.

Jeff Broude started me on my figurative journey to Central Asia at about age ten by introducing me to Tamerlane and Chinggis Khan. I am indebted to my family—my parents Alan and Rena, and my brother Todd—who supported me during this project, including long stretches spent on the other side of the world. And finally, Rahima Niyazova emerged as an unexpected reward during the course of my research. I learned more about life in Central Asia through her than from any other source. She gave me a reason to keep coming back to the region and turned my journey, which eventually led us both to Seattle, into an adventure.

# Note on Transliteration

For transliteration of Russian words I use the Library of Congress system with some exceptions. Where a word appears frequently in the text, I leave out diacritical marks for the reader's convenience (e.g., oblast); and for Russian words that commonly appear in English with a different transliteration, I use the more familiar spelling (intelligentsia, not intelligentsiia, and Moscow instead of Moskva). I transliterate plural forms of most words in the original Russian (e.g., sportzaly), but use the English plural style by adding an "s" if a word is used frequently, as in "raions."

For Central Asian words and place names, I generally transliterate from the Russified/Cyrillic spelling (e.g., aksakal) but make exceptions for proper names that typically appear in English with an alternative spelling (e.g., Tajikistan, Jalalabad, or Bayaman). For the plural forms of Central Asian words, I use the English plural, as in "mahallas."

# WEAPONS OF
# THE WEALTHY

# PUZZLES OF PEOPLE POWER

In a dusty corner of Jalalabad Province in southern Kyrgyzstan, poor farmers in the village of Vin-Sovkhoz tilled the soil, herded their sheep, drank tea, and gossiped about village life, as they often tend to do. They had never taken part in a protest, had contact with a nongovernmental organization (NGO), or met an American with the exception of a Peace Corps volunteer who had once lived in a neighboring village. The monotony of village life for these people would be briefly interrupted in March 2005 when they would take part in bringing about the first peaceful change in government in Central Asia's fourteen-year history of independent statehood. Following parliamentary elections that many believed were rigged, some of these villagers would congregate in Jalalabad's central square, forcibly enter and seize the governor's office, and appear on Russian and Western television broadcasts defacing a portrait of Kyrgyz president Askar Akaev.

Over a period of weeks, similarly ordinary citizens took part in mass demonstrations in other central squares across the country. Most would follow similar routines: call for a rerun of local elections, storm the governor's office, decry the president to the local and international media, establish committees to maintain order, appoint a "shadow government" to take over in case the current one fell, negotiate with police who were charged with guarding government buildings, and finally declare themselves the new authorities in the region. These simultaneous protest actions around the country would culminate later that month in the convergence of thousands of citizens on the capital, Bishkek, as they forced a final showdown with the president.

1

On the surface none of this may have seemed surprising, for the Kyrgyz had sufficient motivation to rise up. Since the collapse of the Soviet Union in 1991, people had suffered a significant decline in well-being. Already one of the least developed republics in the Soviet Union, Kyrgyzstan's economy was devastated by the cessation of subsidies from Moscow and the severance of Soviet-era trade and distribution networks. To make matters worse, the privatization of collective farms in the early 1990s was botched, enriching a small elite and reducing many to subsistence farming. By 2005, the "losers" from the postindependence economic reforms could not be faulted for vocalizing their dissatisfaction. Kyrgyzstan thus appears a classic case of "people power," with disillusioned masses taking matters into their own hands.

And yet the massive upheaval caught many observers off guard. Kyrgyz villagers were not prone to rebelliousness. Like many people in the former Soviet Union, they had adapted to the new and difficult reality through patience and resourcefulness, quietly tending their home gardens and relying on neighbors to help them through difficult times. They are apolitical and focused on solving immediate and mundane problems. They rarely leave their villages, traveling outside only to visit relatives or obtain administrative documents in the district capital. Few households own telephones, yet this poses no problems since they can visit most acquaintances on foot.[1] Relying on their communities, ordinary Kyrgyz citizens focused their energies on gradually restoring their quality of life rather than seeking someone to blame. Far from a boiling cauldron, Kyrgyzstan was a placid lake.

Thus we have a contradictory picture of the dramatic events in Kyrgyzstan. On one hand, thousands of people came out into the streets following the 2005 election, in numbers beyond any the Central Asian region had seen since the 1920s.[2] What is more, the demonstrators exhibited a high level of coordination across regions in their timing, organizational tactics, and common slogans. On the other hand, there were few precedents for the sudden and politically charged reaction of these impoverished farmers to tainted elections, and little basis to expect that they would have the wherewithal to carry out mobilization on such a large scale.

---

1. In 2002, Kyrgyzstan had 7.7 telephone lines for every 100 inhabitants. "Country Profile: Kyrgyzstan," Library of Congress, Federal Research Division, 2007, 11.

2. The Basmachi revolt, an uprising in present-day Uzbekistan and Tajikistan against Communist rule that ended in 1931, probably involved twenty thousand people. Monica Whitlock, *Land beyond the River: The Untold Story of Central Asia* (New York: St. Martin's Press, 2002), 55. Central Asian republics experienced the fewest nationalist demonstrations in the Soviet Union from 1987 to 1991. See Mark R. Beissinger, *Nationalist Mobilization and the Collapse of the Soviet State* (New York: Cambridge University Press, 2002), 210–11. The 2005 Tulip Revolution is estimated to have involved forty to fifty thousand people, out of a population of five million.

Theories about the breakdown of authoritarian regimes have traditionally viewed the process of political transition as a "top down" or "bottom up" phenomenon. The events in Kyrgyzstan at first appeared to exemplify the latter, in which the mobilization of civil society—parties, civic groups, labor, and other social organizations—puts pressure on regime elites to concede power. Regime change from below, it is argued, tends to force a wholesale replacement of the old elite and the inauguration of new, more democratic, rules of the game.[3] This mode typifies the post-1989 transitions in Eastern Europe and the people power movement that overthrew Philippine president Ferdinand Marcos in 1986.

However, closer scrutiny of Kyrgyzstan's "revolution" reveals some discrepancies from the conventional narrative. The putative agent of change, mobilized civic groups, were not the primary vehicle for mass participation. Civil society is weak across the former Soviet Union, and ordinary citizens, preoccupied with their own problems and generally distrustful of one another, are not likely to be members of civic organizations.[4] Also, instead of being centered in the capital, where civic groups and the middle class are usually concentrated, the earliest and largest protests took place in provincial areas far from Bishkek.

Other conventional theories of social movements have trouble accounting for the distribution of protesters across Kyrgyzstan. Theories of protest in repressive settings emphasize how small episodes can rapidly expand as previously hidden antiregime sentiment is revealed.[5] Contact among individuals or organizations can cause mobilization to diffuse, resulting in spatial patterns analogous to biological contagion processes.[6] Yet, as table 0.1 illustrates, variation in participation rates by oblast (province) was highly uneven, being high in Jalalabad and Osh but not Batken, in the south; and high in Bishkek and Talas, but not Chui, in the north. Even within oblasts, participation rates by village did not correspond to geography, as chapter 6 will show in detail.

Structural factors, moreover, cannot account for where protests took place. Some may surmise that the poorest would be the angriest, and therefore the

3. Valerie Bunce, "Rethinking Recent Democratization: Lessons from the Postcommunist Experience," *World Politics* 55, no. 2 (2003): 167–92; Michael McFaul, "The Fourth Wave of Democracy and Dictatorship," *World Politics* 54, no. 2 (2002): 212–44.

4. Marc Morjé Howard, *The Weakness of Civil Society in Post-Communist Europe* (New York: Cambridge University Press, 2002).

5. Timur Kuran, "Now Out of Never: The Element of Surprise in the East European Revolution of 1989," *World Politics* 44 (1991): 7–48.

6. On spatial diffusion, see Peter Hedstrom, "Contagious Collectivities: On the Spatial Diffusion of Swedish Trade Unions, 1890–1940," *American Journal of Sociology* 99, no. 4 (1994): 1157–79; Daniel J. Myers, "Racial Rioting in the 1960s: An Event History Analysis of Local Conditions," *American Sociological Review* 62, no. 1 (1997): 94–112; Dingxin Zhao, "Ecologies of Social Movements: Student Mobilization during the 1989 Prodemocracy Movement in Beijing," *American Journal of Sociology* 103, no. 6 (1998): 1493–1529.

**Table 0.1**  Election-related protests and demographic indicators by oblast, Kyrgyzstan, 2005

| REGION | LOCATION WITHIN KYRGYZSTAN | ESTIMATED NUMBER OF PROTESTERS[a] | GROSS REGIONAL PRODUCT, \$US[b] | HIGHER EDUCATION (AS PERCENT OF POPULATION 15 YEARS AND OVER)[c] | PERCENT URBAN[d] |
|---|---|---|---|---|---|
| Jalalabad | South | 15,000 | 1,421 | 6.3 | 23.1 |
| Bishkek | North | 10,000 | 4,340 | 21.8 | 99.5 |
| Osh | South | 10,000 | 1,024 | 7.6 | 23.2 |
| Talas | North | 5,000 | 1,718 | 8.3 | 16.8 |
| Naryn | North | 3,000 | 2,218 | 8.4 | 18.3 |
| Issyk Kul | North | 2,500 | 3,517 | 10.8 | 30.4 |
| Chui | North | 500 | 3,776 | 8.8 | 22.0 |
| Batken | South | 0 | 1,039 | 5.4 | 19.2 |
| **Kyrgyzstan** | **N/A** | **46,000** | **2,374** | **10.5** | **34.8** |

[a]This figure refers to the total number of protesters at all protest sites in the oblast. Sources include akipress. kg and Radio Free Europe/Radio Liberty. For an explanation of estimates of protest numbers, see the methodological appendix.
[b]Data is adjusted for purchasing power parity (PPP). *Kyrgyzstan: National Human Development Report for 2000* (Bishkek: United Nations Development Program, 2000), 86, 100–107.
[c]*Population of Kyrgyzstan: Results of the First National Population Census of the Kyrgyz Republic of 1999 in Tables* (Bishkek: National Statistical Committee of the Kyrgyz Republic, 2000), 125–130.
[d]Ibid., 14.

most enthusiastic, participants. Alternatively, wealthier, educated people may have greater wherewithal and more confidence in challenging authority. Or perhaps urban citizens, who have the greatest access to media and inhabit dense social networks, would be the drivers of change.[7] Yet the evidence casts doubt on such attempts to find patterns: as the table indicates, variation in the number of protesters did not correspond to the oblast's per capita income, education, or urbanization. These facts suggest that other forces were at work.

## Mobilization as a Weapon

In this book I argue that mass mobilization can result from the aggregate decisions of numerous self-interested actors, and as a by-product of the institutional incentives endemic to nondemocratic political systems. Wealthy actors and political aspirants who are not part of the regime are vulnerable to government harassment and expropriation, and have an incentive to seek out various means to protect their interests and assets. Strategies such as building political

---

7. Karl W. Deutsch, "Social Mobilization and Political Development," *American Political Science Review* 55, no. 3 (1961): 493–514; Mark R. Beissinger, *Nationalist Mobilization and the Collapse of the Soviet State* (New York: Cambridge University Press, 2002).

parties or relying on the courts are unlikely to be effective, since power holders are prone to subvert or ignore formal state institutions, thus pushing insecure elites to pursue informal means of self-protection. One of these strategies is to create a social support base by making material and symbolic investments in local communities, which I call *subversive clientelism*. If challenged from above, elites who have cultivated a support base can mobilize loyal supporters in their defense.

Mobilization through subversive clientelism is likely to occur if several conditions hold. First, formal institutions must be weak. Rational individuals will be reluctant to stake their wealth, status, or freedom on institutions that are politicized and personalistic. Second, there must be economic opportunities that allow actors who are not part of the regime to earn and dispose of wealth. Third, there must be a deficit of public goods in society. Ordinary people must be desirous of, or receptive to, the provision of targeted goods that satisfy their everyday needs. If these conditions hold, then elites who have invested in communities can defend themselves from the regime by mobilizing supporters. Mobilization can rapidly spread across regions if independent elites under threat have previously collaborated on the basis of common interests, enabling them to confederate to strengthen their position.

To explain Kyrgyzstan's revolution, it is necessary to go back a decade and a half, to crucial decisions made in the aftermath of its independence from the Soviet Union. Kyrgyzstan developed the preconditions for subversive clientelism as a result of the Akaev government's implementation of political and economic reforms. These reforms resulted in a wider dispersion of resources than during the Soviet era, or contemporaneously in countries that underwent less dramatic reforms, such as Belarus and Uzbekistan. Although many members of the Soviet-era elite still occupied the highest positions of the executive branch in Kyrgyzstan through the early 2000s, a new set of elites also emerged that was not loyal to, or dependent on, the regime. Their ability to act independently would prove crucial in the country's political development.

As time went by, the interests of the regime and of independent elites increasingly diverged. Akaev backtracked on his early reforms in the mid-1990s and worked to preserve his power and weaken potential opposition. Independent elites, seeking to protect their property and influence, responded to the uncertainty engendered by the regime in two ways: by forming subversive clientelist ties in society and establishing informal contacts with similarly insecure elites in other regions of the country. These two sets of networks—vertical and horizontal—could be activated to resist encroachments by the regime.

The overthrow of the government in 2005 was thus the aggregate result of rational decisions made by insecure elites who had embedded themselves in society and established informal links with one another. In the final analysis, regime change was inadvertent—a result of tentative adaptations to political and economic insecurity and hastily improvised responses to the regime's attempt to steal an election.

## Mobilization and Its Discontents

This explanation yields several ironic implications for the study of politics in nondemocratic states and the forms of opposition that arise. First, illiberal regimes may end up sowing the seeds of their own destruction in the course of crafting policies intended to sustain their rule. When a regime liberalizes its economy—a vital step for economic growth—resources can fall into the hands of potential future oppositions.[8] If it is unable to shield poorer citizens from economic shocks, it engenders mass discontent. These two effects of its policy choices invite the rich to form strategic alliances with the poor, enabling the creation of formidable cross-class coalitions. A regime can prevent a consolidation of opposition by limiting economic opportunities—at the expense of economic growth—or by providing sufficient public goods to retain the support of the poor—but at the risk of overstretching its budget. This was the dilemma Akaev faced in Kyrgyzstan. By contrast, states such as Uzbekistan, which maintain control over the economy, avoid such predicaments.

A second irony is that a ruler who tries to stifle the opposition can inadvertently provoke disparate rivals to coalesce against him. The poor tend to mobilize more frequently for parochial and material concerns than for abstract principles. By its nature, then, mobilization tends to be limited in size and narrow in geographic scope, and therefore not threatening to regime survival. It is therefore unsurprising that authoritarian leaders are often willing to tolerate localized protests, many of which go unreported in the press and expire on their own. However, when multiple protests merge and unite in their demands, the regime faces a greater threat. Protest leaders ordinarily seek quick restitution and may not see a need to confederate, but they might do so if the regime precipitated a crisis that simultaneously affected multiple groups. Hence, in trying to neutralize its adversaries by cracking down preemptively, the regime may counterproductively (from its point of view) turn localized disputes into widespread opposition.

---

8. However, growth can take a long time to materialize, especially if the reform process is flawed. It took Kyrgyzstan several years to show positive rates of growth, and by 2003 its GDP had not yet returned to 1989 levels. Richard Pomfret, *The Central Asian Economies since Independence* (Princeton: Princeton University Press, 2006).

Third, material deprivation makes opposition to a regime more likely, but not in ways predicted by conventional theories.[9] When a state neglects to provide public goods to its citizens, the immediate effect is to starve society of resources. Although this is likely to generate dissatisfaction, it has the countervailing effect of hindering the ability of societal groups to organize and articulate their grievances.[10] I demonstrate that the limited provision of public goods has a more significant unanticipated consequence: it weans people from dependence on the state and makes them more susceptible to appeals by nonstate (economic and political) entrepreneurs. This shift of allegiance has major implications for citizen compliance, threatening to undermine the legitimacy of the state while providing opportunities for new actors to win popular support.

This book explores these ironies by specifying the conditions that give rise to subversive clientelism and then demonstrating how it can result in mobilization. I demonstrate the theory, first, by comparing Kyrgyzstan with its neighbor, Uzbekistan—which did not experience mass mobilization—and then through an analysis of protest dynamics in Kyrgyzstan, which illustrates the mechanisms implied by the theory. Although most of the action of this book takes place in Central Asia, similar underlying patterns of political interaction can be found in other settings around the world. The theory therefore contributes more broadly to the study of informal politics and political change in hybrid and authoritarian regimes worldwide.

This book also contributes to the study of postcommunist politics and society. Richard Rose and others have argued that, whereas there was a relatively egalitarian distribution of resources in communist countries, economic reforms have caused society to bifurcate into distinct classes, in which the rich benefit from abundant social capital, while the poor struggle to make ends meet.[11] I show that there is in fact redistribution through vertical channels, which has helped to alleviate the worst aspects of postcommunist economic decline and created common interests across classes. However, although it improves the material lives of

---

9. On deprivation and protest, see James C. Davies, "Toward a Theory of Revolution," *American Sociological Review* 27 (1962): 5–19; Ted Robert Gurr, *Why Men Rebel* (Princeton: Princeton University Press, 1970).

10. This insight comes from theories of resource mobilization and civil society. See J. Craig Jenkins, "Resource Mobilization Theory and the Study of Social Movements," *Annual Review of Sociology* 9 (1983): 527–53; Bob Edwards and John D. McCarthy, "Resources and Social Movement Mobilization," in *The Blackwell Companion to Social Movements*, ed. David A. Snow, Sarah Anne Soule, and Hanspeter Kriesi (Malden, Mass.: Blackwell, 2004), 116–52; Grzegorz Ekiert and Jan Kubik, "Contentious Politics in New Democracies: East Germany, Hungary, Poland, and Slovakia, 1989–93," *World Politics* 50, no. 4 (1998): 547–81.

11. Richard Rose, "Russia as an Hourglass Society: A Constitution without Citizens," *East European Constitutional Review* 4, no. 3 (1995): 34–42.

the poor, this largesse often comes with strings attached, as reliance on the state is replaced by implicit obligations to independent elites.

At the same time, just as privatization creates incentives for the rich and the poor to ally, it also produces fissures among the wealthy and powerful. Economic actors have a tendency to develop their own interests, which may put them at loggerheads with the ruling elite. Theorists of democratization in western Europe have argued that capitalists secured a permanent counterweight to executive power and the protection of property rights in exchange for their contributions to the state budget.[12] In contrast, in modern times the business class is just as likely to support autocratic governments in the interests of stability or to partake in rent-seeking.[13] If the interests of capitalists are transgressed, under the right circumstances they may be impelled to challenge—or support challengers to—the status quo.[14] Yet this transition will not necessarily lead toward democracy, especially if the challengers, upon securing power, are primarily interested in self-enrichment, have short time horizons, and face little pressure from below.

The evidence in this book also has implications for the study of people power, a phenomenon brought to prominence in Eastern Europe in 1989, which came back into vogue in the 2000s.[15] Advocates of democracy promotion initially rejoiced at the postcommunist "color revolutions" in Georgia, Ukraine, and Kyrgyzstan as a remedy for stunted democratic transitions. Yet over time, the initial

---

12. Barrington Moore, *Social Origins of Dictatorship and Democracy* (Boston: Beacon Press, 1966). Douglass North and Barry Weingast, "Constitutions and Commitment: The Evolution of Institutions Governing Public Choice in Seventeenth-Century England," *Journal of Economic History* 49, no. 4 (1989): 803–32.

13. Guillermo A. O'Donnell, *Modernization and Bureaucratic-Authoritarianism: Studies in South American Politics* (Berkeley: Institute of International Studies, 1973); John Waterbury, "Democracy without Democrats? The Potential for Political Liberalization in the Middle East," in *Democracy without Democrats? The Renewal of Politics in the Muslim World,* ed. Ghassan Salame (London: I. B. Taurus, 1994), 23–47; Kellee S. Tsai, "Capitalists without a Class: Political Diversity among Private Entrepreneurs in China," *Comparative Political Studies* 38, no. 9 (2005): 1130–58.

14. Leigh Payne, *Brazilian Industrialists and Democratic Change* (Baltimore: Johns Hopkins University Press, 1994); Stephan Haggard and Robert R. Kaufman, *The Political Economy of Democratic Transitions* (Princeton: Princeton University Press, 1995); Eva Bellin, "Contingent Democrats: Industrialists, Labor, and Democratization in Late-Developing Countries," *World Politics* 52 (2000): 175–205.

15. On the people power phenomenon, see Timothy Garton Ash, *The Magic Lantern: The Revolution of '89 Witnessed in Warsaw, Budapest, Berlin, and Prague* (New York: Random House, 1990); Samuel P. Huntington, *The Third Wave: Democratization in the Late Twentieth Century* (Norman: University of Oklahoma Press, 1993), 146; Peter Ackerman and Jack DuVall, *A Force More Powerful: A Century of Nonviolent Conflict* (New York: St. Martin's Press, 2000); Grzegorz Ekiert and Jan Kubik, *Rebellious Civil Society: Popular Protest and Democratic Consolidation in Poland, 1989–1993* (Ann Arbor: University of Michigan Press, 2001).

euphoria in all three cases gave way to the realization of the new leaders' striking propensity to continue old practices in the political arena.

The tendency of people power to end in disappointment highlights the importance of looking inside a movement to understand why it occurred and what to expect in terms of governance if it succeeds. Close inspection may reveal that elites alone possess the resources to overcome problems of free riding and can benefit from mobilization.[16] Ordinary participants, even if personally invested in the movement, will have difficulty influencing its trajectory. If this is the case, then a putative revolutionary insurrection may simply be a consequence of the inability of the regime and nonregime elites to come to terms. A change in government that results from defensive mobilization by elites is not likely to be a democratic breakthrough or even a break with prevailing political trends, but may simply be the replacement of one set of elites by another.

## Studying Informal Politics in Central Asia

To demonstrate the theory, I conduct a controlled comparison of Kyrgyzstan and Uzbekistan along with two in-depth case studies of protest. The post-Soviet Central Asian states lend themselves to generating and testing theories because their similar cultural characteristics and legacies of Soviet rule make it possible to isolate and identify causal variables. All were exposed to the same economic policies, political institutions, and cultural influences as part of the Soviet Union, thus reducing the number of variables that could credibly account for visible divergences occurring after the Soviet collapse. Yet Kyrgyzstan stands out from its neighbors—particularly Uzbekistan—in its tendency toward instability, having experienced extra-constitutional changes of government as a result of protests in 2005 and 2010. To explain this variation, I contrast the political and economic decisions that the leaders of Kyrgyzstan and Uzbekistan made after gaining independence. I then detail how this divergence led to the emergence in Kyrgyzstan of an autonomous elite class and clientelist politics, and the absence of both in Uzbekistan.

To show how early reforms later translated into clientelist mobilization, I use ethnographic methods, including participant-observation and interviews, in two cases of mobilization in Kyrgyzstan. I trace the process of mobilization from its origins, follow the actions of the protagonists and participants, and reconstruct the sequence of recruitment and expansion. This two-part research design

---

16. Samuel L. Popkin, *The Rational Peasant* (Berkeley: University of California Press, 1979); Mark Irving Lichbach, *The Rebel's Dilemma* (Ann Arbor: University of Michigan, 1995).

enables me to detail both the medium-term origins and the proximate causes of mobilization through clientelist ties.[17]

Chapter 1 elaborates the theory that structures the book. It explains how, under certain conditions, autonomous elites have an incentive to cultivate ties to local communities—a process I call subversive clientelism—and collaborate with other elites. I use concepts from network analysis in sociology that model how the configuration of actors in a network influences their ability to coordinate and act. Where there are structural "holes" preventing the direct exchange of information or resources, strategically positioned actors, or brokers, can perform a useful function for unconnected actors and derive power from their role. Embedded autonomous elites, who act as brokers in this scenario, can activate latent vertical and horizontal network ties for protest if they are challenged by the regime.

Chapters 2 through 4 detail the processes that gave rise to subversive clientelism and interelite networks in Kyrgyzstan, and but not in Uzbekistan. Chapter 2 draws on fieldwork to illustrate common approaches taken by ordinary people in both countries to cope with the shock of the Soviet collapse. Facing a decline in the provision of public goods, they availed themselves of informal networks in their communities, which aided in solving local collective action problems. These networks also provided the "pull" that would draw community members into mobilization to remedy local political or economic grievances.

At the same time, Uzbekistan and Kyrgyzstan implemented contradictory policies that had important consequences at the elite level. As chapter 3 explains, the new regimes' initial approaches to economic reform and the civic sphere gave rise to different elite configurations. In Kyrgyzstan, privatization with few informal barriers to wealth creation facilitated the emergence of a new class of autonomous elites. Uzbekistan, on the other hand, carried out limited privatization and put up significant formal and informal barriers to independent commerce. Kyrgyzstan's political orientation also permitted autonomous elites to coordinate and coalesce without the state's mediation, whereas Uzbekistan's policies impeded association.

The convergence of these two factors—the popular desire for public goods and different elite configurations—led to the creation of vertical ties linking nonstate elites with communities in Kyrgyzstan, but not in Uzbekistan. Chapter

---

17. I use the inelegant "medium-term" to distinguish the scope of my explanation from the *longue durée*. The medium term corresponds to what Ekiert and Hanson call "institutional time": "regularized patterns of social action enforced by institutional characteristics of particular regimes." Grzegorz Ekiert and Stephen Hanson, eds., *Capitalism and Democracy in Central and Eastern Europe: Assessing the Legacy of Communist Rule* (New York: Cambridge, 2003), 20.

4 introduces the concept of subversive clientelism and examines how elites in Kyrgyzstan went about winning the allegiance of people in their communities. I use qualitative and quantitative evidence to show how elites used a "portfolio" strategy of making both material and symbolic investments to cultivate a social support base.

Chapters 5 and 6 demonstrate how the processes described in earlier chapters can result in mobilization. The first is a detailed case study of an unprecedented mass protest that took place in rural Kyrgyzstan (Aksy) in 2002. The second is an analysis of the "Tulip Revolution," a mass mobilization that took place in Kyrgyzstan in March 2005. Consistent with the theoretical framework from chapter 1, neither incidence of mobilization was spontaneous or "bottom-up." The participation of poor villagers and the discipline and sophisticated organization they exhibited appeared to reflect an inspired effort by otherwise marginalized actors to resist regime transgressions, yet closer inspection reveals the essential role played by elites. Both cases reveal that mobilization occurred when elites who were challenged by the regime decided to organize protests. The first demonstrators, closest to the elite, then recruited laterally within their communities.

The top-down origins of the protests provide part of the explanation of how clientelist mobilization can expand more broadly. The Aksy protests were in many ways a diminutive version of the Tulip Revolution, occurring in twelve villages within a single *raion* (district), as opposed to the regime-changing events that saw demonstrations in six of the country's seven oblasts plus the capital three years later. This variation in the scale of mobilization can be explained by the *number of elites challenged*. In both cases, mobilization occurred after the regime threatened the position of embedded elites. Yet only one elite was challenged in the Aksy mobilization, whereas numerous elites were provoked simultaneously when the regime (reputedly) rigged elections to defeat independent and opposition parliamentary candidates.

I did not select these two cases according to the standard procedure in political science based on quantitative methodology: selecting based on variation in the explanatory variables without regard for the dependent variable (although I do use this procedure in a later chapter).[18] On the contrary, I selected them because they represent the largest instances of mobilization in Kyrgyzstan since independence in terms of both numbers and scope.[19] As such, they constitute

---

18. Gary King, Robert O. Keohane, and Sidney Verba, *Designing Social Inquiry: Scientific Inference in Qualitative Research* (Princeton: Princeton University Press, 1994), 140.

19. There were numerous small protests in the years leading up to 2005. In 2004, for example, Kyrgyzstan registered protests, pickets, and marches against corruption, Chinese bazaar merchants,

deviant cases, which "demonstrate a surprising value" on the dependent variable, given the outcomes the independent variables are expected to produce.[20] The purpose is to "probe for new—but as yet unspecified—explanations" in the hopes that "causal processes within the deviant case will illustrate some causal factor that is applicable to other (deviant) cases."[21]

To check observable implications of the theory on the individual and community levels of analysis, I compare different units *within* each case. I look at villages and electoral districts with high, medium, and low levels of participation and analyze how subversive clientelism and cross-regional elite networks help explain the variation.

In chapter 7, I analyze cases from different geographic and historical contexts in order to ascertain the potential range of phenomena that the theory helps to explain. Keeping the logic of the theory intact but altering explanatory variables yields different predictions about the scale and dynamics of mobilization. For a case of low economic and political openness, I return to the counterfactual case, Uzbekistan, and focus on a sizeable mobilization in the city of Andijan that nonetheless remained localized. To illustrate mobilization processes in a relatively permissive economic environment but one with limited political opportunities, I analyze rural China. I then examine episodes of rebellion from early modern France and England, and early nineteenth-century Mexico, where background characteristics and scale varied by time and place. Table 0.2 summarizes these comparisons and shows the parts of the theory they illustrate.

In the conclusion, I explore some of the theory's implications for the political economy of political opposition, hybrid regimes, and grassroots political change. I argue that the study of political change and social movements in nondemocratic

---

progressive health textbooks, the high price of gasoline, and power outages; and for fair elections, higher pensions, and lower energy prices. Each was localized and involved one hundred or fewer participants. Although not all protest incidents show up in the press, it is unlikely that any protests that were significantly larger would go unreported. See Radio Free Europe/Radio Liberty (RFE/RL); BBC Monitoring, Central Asia; Institute of War and Peace Reporting (IWPR), iwpr.net; and Russian-language sites: Ludwig Gibelgauss, "V stolitse Kyrgyzii proshel miting oppozitsii," *Nemetskaia Volna*, June 14, 2004; Alla Piatibratova, "Kyrgyzy vystupili protiv torgovtsev iz Kitaia [Kyrgyz went against traders from China]," kyrgyzby.narod.ru, April 12, 2004; "News Roundup September 26–October 2," bio.fizteh.ru; kyrgyzby.narod.ru, August 26, 2004.

20. Jason Seawright and John Gerring, "Case Selection Techniques in Case Study Research: A Menu of Qualitative and Quantitative Options," *Political Research Quarterly* 61 (2008): 302. See also Arend Lijphart, "Comparative Politics and the Comparative Method," *American Political Science Review* 65, no. 3 (1971): 682–693; Ali Kazancigil, "The Deviant Case in Comparative Analysis: High Stateness in a Muslim Society; The Case of Turkey," in *Comparing Nations: Concepts, Strategies, Substance,* ed. Ali Kazancigil and Mattei Dogan (Oxford: Oxford University Press, 1994).

21. Seawright and Gerring, "Case Selection Techniques," 302.

**Table 0.2**  Cases for comparison

| CHAPTER | CASE | CLIENTELISM | CHALLENGE TO MULTIPLE NETWORKED ELITES | PREDICTED GREATEST SCALE OF MOBILIZATION |
|---|---|---|---|---|
| 5 | Kyrgyzstan: Aksy | Yes | No | Regional |
| 6 | Kyrgyzstan: Tulip | Yes | Yes | National |
| 7 | Uzbekistan: Andijan | No | No | Localized |
| 7 | Rural China | Some | No | Localized/regional |
| 7 | Early modern Europe | Yes | Yes | Regional/national |
| 7 | Nineteenth-century Mexico | Yes | Some | Regional |

societies can benefit by placing greater weight on *economic opportunities,* which can explain the dispersion of resources and the empowerment of potential oppositions. I conclude with a discussion of (non-)democratization following popular uprisings in light of the book's findings.

Because a major part of the action portrayed in this book takes place at the individual and local levels, much of the data comes from personal observations and interviews. I conducted fourteen months of fieldwork in Kyrgyzstan and Uzbekistan between 2003 and 2006, which allowed me to reconstruct events as they were experienced by the main actors in their dual role as villagers and protest participants. I lived in several regions of both countries and conducted 140 interviews to document community institutions and subversive clientelist networks. Separately, I interviewed 129 protest organizers, activists, observers, ordinary participants, and nonparticipants in Kyrgyzstan in order to piece together the process of mobilization and account for variations in rates of participation.

I also collaborated in drafting an original survey in 2005 of one thousand respondents in each Uzbekistan and Kyrgyzstan. These quantitative data complement the qualitative component of my research to give a sense of community and vertical networks in the two countries as experienced at the individual level. The results are integrated into chapters 2 and 4. Details on fieldwork and survey methodology can be found in the methodological appendix.

In the following chapters, I will show how Kyrgyzstan's post-Soviet development laid the foundation for mobilization long before it happened—and how policy choices led to the creation of new elites and produced a redistribution of resources that those elites could later deploy against the regime. The most important lesson to draw from the cases examined in this book is that Kyrgyzstan is not unique. The processes that led to mass mobilization in Central

Asia can also be found in other parts of the world where governments are not responsive to their citizens and fail to restrain themselves from predation. This book identifies some of the informal strategies that aspiring economic and political actors in such systems employ to protect their interests, and shows how their responses to a challenge from the regime can result—inadvertently—in its overthrow.

# INSTITUTIONAL UNCERTAINTY AND ELITE-LED MOBILIZATION

In a world where most people live under nondemocratic rule and lack political and civic freedoms,[1] protest is, according to Sidney Tarrow, "the main and often the only recourse that ordinary people possess against better-equipped opponents or powerful states."[2] In recent years, the world has witnessed dramatic mass demonstrations, from Eastern Europe to Indonesia to Iran, as aggrieved people risk life and limb to express their dissatisfaction with authoritarian regimes. Sometimes they have succeeded in their objectives, sometimes not, yet the use of protest persists in the face of repression as the most brazen weapon of the weak.[3]

But protest is not a tool of the weak alone. The benefits of a show of collective public outrage—generating sympathy for a cause, delegitimizing rival actors, building new coalitions for political action—can be harnessed by strong actors as well as by weak ones. Historically, governments have used their vast means to coerce and cajole people to participate in mass collective endeavors, where protest serves a counterintuitive purpose—the display of (purported) popular

---

1. Freedom House estimates that 54% of the world's population lives in countries that are not free or partly free. "Freedom in the World 2009 Population Statistics," http://www.freedomhouse.org/template.cfm?page=479.

2. Sidney Tarrow, *Power in Movement: Social Movements, Collective Action and Politics* (Cambridge: Cambridge University Press, 1994), 3. Tarrow defines protest as "disruptive collective action aimed at institutions, elites, authorities, or other groups on behalf of the goals or the actions of those they claim to represent": Sidney Tarrow, *Democracy and Disorder: Protest and Politics in Italy 1965–1975* (Oxford: Clarendon Press, 1989), 8.

3. James C. Scott, *Weapons of the Weak* (New Haven: Yale University Press, 1985).

*support for* a regime. The Soviet Union and China, for example, mobilized thousands of their citizens for mass spectacles to produce the impression of legitimacy and public enthusiasm for state policies. The Chinese government buses activists to foreign embassies to create displays of nationalist fervor at times of international confrontation.[4] Corrupt leaders can strategically redirect blame from themselves by triggering emotional outbursts aimed at an external scapegoat.[5] The fact that "grassroots" citizen activity can be directed by powerful actors for their own benefit expands the scope for analysis of protest, especially in nondemocratic settings. The story of how otherwise apolitical citizens come to be involved in historically critical events, sometimes on a grand scale, may thus be more intricate than a simple narrative based on "people power."

In this chapter I investigate the origins of protest that is mobilized by powerful actors who are *not* part the regime. Protest occurs as a by-product of the insecurity inherent in political systems with inconsistent rule of law, and is carried out by actors who have cultivated a clientele from among the poor. The interests of those who launch protests will not necessarily coincide with those of the rank and file, yet ordinary people may have rational reasons for lending their support. The result may appear to be a straightforward expression of people's dissatisfaction with the target of protest, but its roots lie in the logic of *elite* self-preservation in uncertain institutional environments.

## Informal Strategies of Insurance

Since the third wave of democracy came to an end, many states have slid backward to become members of the dubious club of authoritarian and hybrid regimes. In these countries, the legal system is often politicized and courts are unable or unwilling to protect property rights and individual liberties. Regimes strive to preserve their power through various informal means. They work to engender distrust among the populace, starve potential sources of opposition of resources, monitor and harass perceived troublemakers, intimidate and control the media, keep workers dependent on the state, and stifle autonomous organizations. Rulers need not dominate all aspects of life; by keeping civil society weak and fomenting mistrust, they can weaken people's ability to carry out collective action.[6]

---

4. Jessica Weiss, "Powerful Patriots: Nationalism, Diplomacy, and the Strategic Logic of Anti-Foreign Protest" (PhD diss., University of California, San Diego, 2008).

5. Anne Applebaum, "Teddy Bear Tyranny," *Washington Post,* December 4, 2007; Jytte Klausen, *The Cartoons That Shook the World* (New Haven: Yale University Press, 2009).

6. See Quintan Wiktorowicz, "Civil Society as Social Control: State Power in Jordan," *Comparative Politics* 33, no. 1 (2000): 43–61; Andreas Schedler, "The Menu of Manipulation," *Journal of*

In such systems, the survival of a regime often depends on its ability to hold together its coalition and prevent actors outside the coalition from coalescing and gaining strength. Civic organizations can play a role in bringing down authoritarian regimes, but they rarely do so alone. In many cases, the final blow has come from the loss of support of critical elite actors, such as businessmen, independent members of the legislature, and informal leaders in society.[7] These actors, which I identify as independent elites, are potential kingmakers. I define *elites* as "those who wield power and influence on the basis of their active control of a disproportionate share of society's resources."[8] They are *independent* or *autonomous* if they are not formally part of the executive or ruling party—which I use interchangeably with "regime"—and their assets are under their discretionary control.[9] Independent elites occupy a tenuous niche in the social and political hierarchy. By definition, they are more likely to share demographic, material, and attitudinal characteristics with state rulers than with the poor, and they have an interest in maintaining or increasing their wealth and privileged status in society. Yet regimes have their own interests and may fear independent elites as a rival source of power. Independent elites in turn may see regimes, which control the instruments of coercion, as a threat to their liberty and property, and seek strategies of self-protection.[10]

*lenged: The Rise of Semi-Authoritarianism* (Washington, D.C.: Carnegie Endowment, 2003).

7. Leigh Payne, *Brazilian Industrialists and Democratic Change* (Baltimore: Johns Hopkins University Press, 1994); Elisabeth Jean Wood, *Forging Democracy from Below* (New York: Cambridge University Press, 2000); Eva-Lotta E. Hedman, *In the Name of Civil Society: From Free Election Movements to People Power in the Philippines* (Honolulu: University of Hawaii Press, 2006); John Higley and Michael Burton, *Elite Foundations of Liberal Democracy* (Lanham, Md.: Rowman and Littlefield, 2006).

8. Eva Etzioni-Halevy, *The Elite Connection: Problems and Potential of Western Democracy* (Cambridge: Polity Press, 1993), 29. This definition has three advantages over others for the purposes of this book. First, it contains no requirement that elites possess formal political authority, since official posts in former Soviet space do not necessarily yield political power while many informal roles do; second, it allows for change in elite status by the acquisition or loss of resources; third, it allows us to identify elites ex ante by objective and measurable characteristics and not by their behavior (e.g., organizing collective action), which prevents tautological reasoning. One of the following four criteria is usually sufficient to attain elite status in Central Asia: significant wealth; high state office (e.g., minister, deputy minister); position in parliament (where selection is independent of the executive, such as in Kyrgyzstan); or close family connections to a member of any of the first three categories.

9. Defectors from a regime coalition can also be considered independent and elite if, after defecting, they retain significant assets that are under their discretionary control.

10. Independent elites in this scenario share the predicament of the middle class (as explained in works by Carles Boix and Daron Acemoglu and James Robinson), which acts as a buffer between the rich (seen as coterminous with the ruling class) and the poor. The middle class is reflexively aligned with the rich in fearing expropriation by revolution or redistributive voting by the poor. It concedes to full democracy (i.e., aligns itself with the poor) only when the wealth of the poor is sufficiently

What kinds of strategies are available to independent elites in such uncertain institutional environments? One school of thought centers on the creation of formal institutions that countervail the state. Based on a stylized history of the process of democratization in Europe, it asserts that capitalists sought to have their property rights protected through formal legal guarantees and institutions such as parliaments and an independent judiciary, which bind the state to credibly commit against predation.[11] The inexorable logic of formal institutional development stemming from economic uncertainty has been thought to apply in the recent past as well, as property owners in countries transitioning from state socialism were expected to lobby governments to have their property rights protected.[12]

However, the assumption that insecure elites act to further the rule of law, while perhaps an accurate description of institutional development in Europe—albeit over an extended time period—leads to flawed analysis in most contemporary cases. The creation of rule of law is a collective action problem. Businessmen in uncertain institutional environments are likely to be better off seeking private rents than lobbying on behalf of other capitalists.[13] In addition, in nondemocratic states, the open advocacy of group interests attracts unwanted attention from the regime and exposes elites to the possibility of repression or expropriation. Their (justified) distrust of the system would counsel them to keep a low profile and search for other, less risky avenues. Although there are normative reasons to emphasize formal institutional development—the rule of law is a critical component of a functioning democracy—it is more realistic, in systems where formal rules are often little more than a façade, to direct our attention to *informal* strategies of self-protection.

In uncertain institutional environments, independent elites are prone to take measures outside the formal political system in order to minimize dependence

---

close to the middle class so that the cost of repression exceeds the costs of universal suffrage (Boix, 52), or when a "relatively large and affluent middle class" ensures that redistribution under full democracy would not significantly harm the rich (Acemoglu and Robinson, 258). A sufficiently poor middle class will ally with the poor in favoring a revolt against the rich if they perceive a reasonable probability of succeeding (Acemoglu and Robinson, 266; Boix, 49). See Carles Boix, *Democracy and Redistribution* (New York: Cambridge University Press, 2003); Daron Acemoglu and James A. Robinson, *Economic Origins of Dictatorship and Democracy* (New York: Cambridge, 2005).

11. Douglass North and Barry Weingast, "Constitutions and Commitment: The Evolution of Institutions Governing Public Choice in Seventeenth-Century England," *Journal of Economic History* 49, no. 4 (1989): 803–32; Hilton Root, "Tying the King's Hands," *Rationality and Society* 1 (October 1989): 240–58.

12. Advocates for economic reform in Russia argued that the beneficiaries of privatization would become the future champions of formal property rights. See Anders Åslund, *How Russia Became a Market Economy* (Washington, D.C.: Brookings Institution, 2005); Maxim Boycko, Andrei Shleifer, and Robert W. Vishny, *Privatizing Russia* (Cambridge: MIT Press, 1995).

13. Konstantin Sonin, "Why the Rich May Favor Poor Protection of Property Rights," *Journal of Comparative Economics* 31, no. 4 (2003): 715–31; Leonid Polishchuk and Alexei Savvateev, "Spontaneous (Non)Emergence of Property Rights," *Economics of Transition* 12, no. 1 (2004): 103–27.

on unreliable institutions and avoid exposure to predatory officials. Formal institutions are the predominant object of study in political science because they are easily observable, measurable, and normatively appropriate, whereas informal interactions are hard to observe and quantify, and can be an object of disapproval. As Kellee Tsai (2007) writes, "formal institutions implicitly represent the baseline from which we evaluate the desirability of various outcomes."[14] Yet in noninstitutionalized democracies, not least among them countries transitioning from state socialism, informal politics frequently substitutes for, if not supplants, the formal political system. Political scientists have only recently begun paying serious attention to informal politics in nondemocratic states.[15]

There are several insurance strategies that can be used by independent elite contenders that do not take place within formal political institutions. One is to exercise leverage by maintaining the option of exit. By credibly threatening to move their capital out of the country and reduce the state's tax base, industrialists can protect their assets from arbitrary expropriation. As some have argued, exit is more feasible with mobile assets such as financial capital than with immobile assets such as land or extractable resources.[16] Landed elites have the least mobile assets and therefore lack the exit option, giving them little choice but to throw in their lot with authoritarian rulers.[17]

A second option available to autonomous elites in uncertain institutional en-

maintaining control over popular unrest, or sharing a portion of their profits with their patron.[18] Late developing countries have also witnessed alliances between regimes and capital, in which the latter's dependence on the former

---

14. Kellee Tsai, *Capitalism without Democracy* (Ithaca: Cornell University Press, 2007), 38.

15. See, for example, Alena V. Ledeneva, *How Russia Really Works* (Ithaca: Cornell University Press, 2006); Gretchen Helmke and Steven Levitsky, *Informal Institutions and Democracy* (Baltimore: Johns Hopkins University Press, 2006).

16. Albert O. Hirschman, "Exit, Voice, and the State," *World Politics* 31, no. 1 (1978): 90–107; Ronald Rogowski, "Democracy, Capital, Skill, and Country Size: Effects of Asset Mobility and Regime Monopoly on the Odds of Democratic Rule," in *The Origins of Liberty: Political and Economic Liberalization in the Modern World*, ed. Paul W. Drake and Mathew D. McCubbins (Princeton: Princeton University Press, 1998).

17. Boix, *Democracy and Redistribution*; Carles Boix, "Economic Roots of Civil Wars and Revolutions in the Contemporary World," *World Politics* 60, no. 3 (April 2008): 390–437. The landed elite may also benefit from a collusive alliance with the state to repress labor. See Barrington Moore, *Social Origins of Dictatorship and Democracy* (Boston: Beacon Press, 1966); Dietrich Rueschemeyer, Evelyne Huber Stephens, and John D. Stephens, *Capitalist Development and Democracy* (Chicago: University of Chicago Press, 1992); Wood, *Forging Democracy*.

18. Stephen Haber, Armando Razo, and Noel Maurer, *The Politics of Property Rights: Political Instability, Credible Commitments, and Economic Growth in Mexico, 1876–1929* (New York: Cambridge

helps to allay pressures to democratize.[19] Where elites benefit from rent-seeking under the regime, the advantages of remaining in the country outweigh the hazards of arbitrary expropriation. However, such arrangements do not guarantee protection against expropriation. Officials may be unable to credibly commit to protect independent elites, for example, if their short time horizons increase the benefits of predation.[20] Even if officials can commit to exercising restraint, they themselves may fall out of favor or be unexpectedly replaced due to personalistic and arbitrary appointment practices. An additional drawback to seeking state patronage is that it increases dependence and limits the political freedom of ambitious elites, who may be compelled to support prevailing policies even if they work against their interests.[21]

A third way for independent elites to defend or advance their interests without unnecessarily exposing themselves to predatory officials or capricious policy making is to coalesce into informal networks based on common economic or political interests. Networks facilitate collective action in the case of a common threat and may be tolerated by the regime if they do not appear overtly political. Associations are generally better able to act collectively if they are formalized (e.g., provide membership lists, collect dues) because they can effectively monitor and sanction their members, develop corporate identities, and perhaps grow into political parties.[22] On the other hand, formal organizations are more likely to attract the suspicion of the regime, which may fear the potential of an independent party or economic interest group. In response, it can shut down the organization or, more subtly, create burdensome procedures for registration or monitor the organization's activities, thus sowing mistrust and weakening its influence. In nondemocratic societies, associations for collective action are therefore likely to remain informal and small, trading greater effectiveness for survival.

Weighing the costs and benefits of the above strategies reveals that none is fool-proof, nor is any clearly superior to the others. Depending on factors such

---

University Press, 2003); Beatriz Magaloni, *Voting for Autocracy: Hegemonic Party Survival and Its Demise in Mexico* (New York: Cambridge University Press, 2006).

19. David Waldner, *State Building and Late Development* (Ithaca: Cornell University Press, 1999); Eva Bellin, *Stalled Democracy* (Ithaca: Cornell University Press, 2002).

20. Mancur Olson, "Dictatorship, Democracy, and Development," *American Political Science Review* 87, no. 3 (1993): 567–76; Barry R. Weingast, "The Political Foundations of Democracy and the Rule of Law," *American Political Science Review* 91, no. 2 (1997): 245–63; Robert Bates, Avner Greif, and Smita Singh, "Organizing Violence," *Journal of Conflict Resolution* 46, no. 5 (2002): 599–628.

21. Bellin, *Stalled Democracy*; Scott Greenwood, "Bad for Business? Entrepreneurs and Democracy in the Arab World," *Comparative Political Studies* 41 (2008): 837–60.

22. Michael Hechter, *Principles of Group Solidarity* (Berkeley: University of California Press, 1987).

as the repressiveness of the regime, the capacity of the state, the state's control of the economy, and the elite's acceptance of risk, one or more of these strategies may be seen as worth pursuing, yet they all carry disadvantages.

One additional strategy that has not gained attention in the work on hybrid and authoritarian regimes is *subversive clientelism:* the development of the capacity to mobilize citizens through clientelist ties. Although the creation of cross-class alliances is somewhat costly and requires medium- to long-term commitment, it has some advantages over other strategies and avoids some of the risks they entail. In particular, it takes seriously the array of instruments that hybrid and authoritarian regimes can wield to stay in power, while also considering their weaknesses. It is likely to occur only under certain conditions.

The theory I propose posits how independent elites can tap into the latent power and unexpressed grievances of society to serve their own interests in conditions of institutional uncertainty. It depicts a three-way interaction involving the regime, independent elites, and impoverished communities. Independent elites may choose to ally with (or be co-opted by) the regime to ensure the maintenance of their privileges and property. Or they may harness the power of the masses to mobilize against the regime. The actions of independent elites in such systems have implications for the well-being of the citizenry and, in extraordinary cases, for the survivability of the regime. The elaboration of the theory

as occurred in Kyrgyzstan.

## Mobilization through Clientelist Ties

### Communities as Sites for Collective Action

The basis of clientelist mobilization, like for clientelism itself, lies in communities. The community—a collectivity sharing many-sided and direct relations and proximity of residence[23]—has special characteristics that makes it amenable to collective action. Early students of peasant rebellion began from the premise that villages were inherently solidary. Village cohesion was based on custom, tradition,

---

23. Adapted from Michael Taylor, "Rationality and Revolutionary Collective Action," in *Rationality and Revolution,* ed. Michael Taylor (New York: Cambridge University Press, 1988), 68. Note that this definition differs from popular usages of the term that describe people sharing a common identity or ethos, but who may not know each other, such as "scholarly community" or "Jewish community."

and shared norms.[24] Later theorists of rural life gave the moral economy of the peasant a rational underpinning, arguing that selective incentives were necessary to secure cooperation in collective action.[25] Both schools agreed that communities were the principal vehicle for rebellion in undeveloped rural societies. There are several reasons why an emphasis on communities to the exclusion of other collectivities is warranted even in many contemporary settings.

First, the face-to-face ties that underlie everyday community life are critical in making available the information necessary to monitor the behavior of members and facilitate cooperation, whereas "imagined communities" based on ideas of shared identities or values—although they may be a source of attachment and affection—do not produce the same amount of cohesion.[26] In particular, the latter type of collectivity lacks the ability to effectively monitor, shame, sanction, and motivate its members.[27]

Second, in many low-income societies, geographically based networks are the primary venue in which people regularly interact. Community members face similar challenges, such as dealing with food production, climate, limited public services, security, and competition for scarce resources, and often develop informal mechanisms for solving these problems collectively.[28] Interaction also produces affection; while there is no guarantee that familiarity based on proximity will develop into sentimental attachments—it can also breed contempt—the relationships built around dealing with shared challenges can easily trump more abstract common identities such as real or imagined ethnic, kin, or religious ties.[29]

Third, unlike formal civic associations, the informal nature of social life in communities provides shelter from the state. Communities can endure as

---

24. James C. Scott, *The Moral Economy of the Peasant: Rebellion and Subsistence in Southeast Asia* (New Haven: Yale University, 1976); Jeffery M. Paige, *Agrarian Revolution: Social Movements and Export Agriculture in the Underdeveloped World* (New York: Simon and Schuster, 1978); Eric R. Wolf, *Peasant Wars of the Twentieth Century* (Norman: University of Oklahoma Press, 1999).

25. Samuel L. Popkin, *The Rational Peasant* (Berkeley: University of California Press, 1979).

26. Benedict Anderson, *Imagined Communities: Reflections on the Origin and Spread of Nationalism* (London: Verso, 1983).

27. Hechter, *Principles;* Margaret Levi, *Consent, Dissent, and Patriotism* (New York: Cambridge University Press, 1997), 25.

28. Leslie Anderson, *The Political Ecology of the Modern Peasant* (Baltimore: Johns Hopkins University Press, 1994); Jeffrey P. Carpenter, Amrita G. Daniere, and Lois M. Takahashi, "Cooperation, Trust, and Social Capital in Southeast Asian Urban Slums," *Journal of Economic Behavior & Organization* 55, no. 4 (2004): 533–51.

29. On the contact hypothesis, see "Intergroup Contact Theory," *Annual Review of Psychology* 49 (1998): 65–85; Rupert Brown, *Group Processes: Dynamics within and between Groups* (Oxford: Blackwell, 2000). On contempt within communities, see Edward C. Banfield, *The Moral Basis of a Backward Society* (Glencoe, Ill.: Free Press, 1958); Charlotte Viall Wiser and William Henricks Wiser, *Behind Mud Walls, 1930–1960* (Berkeley: University of California Press, 1963); Oscar Lewis, *Life in a Mexican Village: Tepoztlán Restudied* (Urbana: University of Illinois Press, 1963).

repositories of social capital because they are not inherently political and therefore do not pose an overt threat to authority, even where nondemocratic regimes work to weaken civil society and eliminate potential rival sources of power.[30] Regimes that try to preempt resistance by keeping tabs on all social activity are doomed to fail because disaffection is easily concealed in private spaces.[31] Where there is little space for civil society, the boundary between social and political activity in daily life can become blurred and opposition can emerge from mundane interactions.[32]

Finally, communities often contain built-in mechanisms of survival, such as informal social insurance schemes, that make them resilient in difficult times. Understanding that because of events outside of people's control, one may be self-sufficient today and needy tomorrow, people invest in an implicit shared risk system based on reciprocity and mutual obligation.[33] Those who stand to benefit from this system in the long run have an incentive to contribute to the collective and adhere to community norms—or face social sanction, denial of assistance in difficult times, or, in the worse case, exclusion.[34] Counterintuitively then, uncertainty and hardship, rather than weakening communities, can trigger self-reinforcing coping mechanisms that conspire to make community networks *more* cohesive and capable of collective action.

for everyday scarcities, it serves only to redistribute wealth within a network rather than to infuse new resources from outside it.[35] A second way for communities to improve their fortunes is to seek out partnerships with actors or

30. Aleksander Smolar, "From Opposition to Atomization," *Journal of Democracy* 7, no. 1 (1996): 24–38; Hank Flap and Beate Volker, "Communist Societies, the Velvet Revolution, and Weak Ties: The Case of East Germany," in *Social Capital and the Transition to Democracy*, ed. Eric Uslaner and Gabriel Badescu (New York: Routledge, 2003).

31. On the "niche society" in the German Democratic Republic, see Steven Pfaff, *Exit-Voice Dynamics and the Collapse of East Germany: The Crisis of Leninism and the Revolution of 1989* (Durham: Duke University Press, 2006), chapter 3, 61–80.

32. Scott, *Weapons of the Weak;* Diane Singerman, *Avenues of Participation: Family, Politics, and Networks in Urban Quarters of Cairo* (Princeton: Princeton University Press, 1995).

33. See Scott, *Moral Economy;* Anderson, *Political Ecology.*

34. Michael Taylor, *Anarchy and Cooperation* (New York: Wiley, 1976); Hechter, *Principles*, 50; Russell Hardin, *One for All* (Princeton: Princeton University Press, 1999), 102.

35. Social network theorists argue that people reap greater benefits by acquiring resources from actors in heterogeneous networks. See Mark Granovetter, "The Strength of Weak Ties," *American Journal of Sociology* 78, no. 6 (1973): 1360–80; Nan Lin, *Social Capital* (New York: Cambridge University Press, 2001), 60–69.

organizations that possess resources they do not have. The demand for public goods—often unmet by the state—enables outside actors to fill the void and, perhaps inadvertently, erode the state's infrastructural power.[36]

Public goods are resources that redound to the benefit of society but are unlikely to be provided by private individuals because others cannot easily be excluded from enjoying their benefits.[37] Competent states resolve the problem of underprovision by collecting taxes from their citizens and using the revenues to deliver desired goods and services. Yet many states do not act in the best interests of their citizens. A state that restrains itself from predation, protects its citizens, provides for their welfare, treats them equitably, and judges them impartially is so uncommon that perhaps it has never existed.[38]

Public goods deficits can occur for a variety of reasons. Sometimes a state lacks the capacity or is unable to afford the delivery of services that people demand. A government may choose to provide minimal public goods, instead diverting state revenues to the private bank accounts of officials or their families. Or, it may distribute them unevenly, rewarding supporters or co-ethnics while neglecting opponents and rival groups.[39]

When a state does not provide sufficient public goods to meet its citizens' needs, other actors can emerge to meet that demand, with major implications for state-society relations. In Western democracies, nonstate organizations often work with local governments to provide charity or services to complement public provision.[40] In other instances, where the state is weak, private actors have emerged to fill the void. In order for a private benefactor or nonstate organization to offer services to the public with any regularity, it must have a source of

---

36. Infrastructural power is "the capacity of the state to actually penetrate civil society and to implement logistically political decisions throughout the realm." Michael Mann, *States, War, and Capitalism* (Oxford: Blackwell, 1988), 5.

37. Paul Samuelson, "The Pure Theory of Public Expenditure," *Review of Economics and Statistics* 36, no. 4 (1954): 387–89. In the context of theories of government, the term refers to goods that modern states are normatively expected to provide to their citizens, including intangibles such as national defense and property rights, and material goods such as roads and schools. See also Lily Tsai, *Accountability without Democracy* (New York: Cambridge University Press, 2007), 5.

38. Lant Pritchett and Michael Woolcock, "Solutions When the Solution Is the Problem: Arraying the Disarray in Development," *World Development* 32, no. 2 (2004): 191–212. See also Barry Weingast, "Constitutions as Governance Structures: The Political Foundations of Secure Markets," *Journal of Institutional & Theoretical Economics* 149, no. 1 (1993): 286–311.

39. Bruce Bueno de Mesquita, Alastair Smith, Randolph M. Siverson, and James D. Morrow, *The Logic of Political Survival* (Cambridge: MIT Press, 2003); Nicolas Van de Walle, "Meet the New Boss, Same as the Old Boss? The Evolution of Political Clientelism in Africa," in *Patrons, Clients, and Policies: Patterns of Democratic Accountability and Political Competition,* ed. Herbert Kitschelt and Steven I. Wilkinson (New York: Cambridge University Press, 2007), 50–67.

40. Peter B. Evans, ed., *State-Society Synergy: Government and Social Capital in Development* (Berkeley: University of California Press, 1997).

revenue independent of the state it seeks to supplant. The ability of a nonstate actor to freely access and control resources depends on the degree of state control over the economy.

There are a variety of economic models that encompass different degrees of state control. At one extreme, the state manages the economy and puts up myriad informal barriers to generating independent wealth.[41] Only those who control the levers of power—or are explicitly favored by the regime—will be able to amass significant wealth because they alone can divert state funds to themselves or their families, acquire licenses to trade, dispense subsidies, manipulate exchange rates, and exploit the legal system to stifle competition.[42] By the same token, those who lack the ability to penetrate or control a part of the state will have limited opportunities to earn and invest. In such a system, power and wealth are fused, and the path to both runs through the state.

By contrast, in other systems, the state does not dominate economic activity or impose overweening regulations on commerce, whether because it is too weak or because it voluntarily restrains itself. In this case, it is possible to accumulate wealth without the approval of the regime, enabling a wider array of actors to aspire to greater levels of influence. Individuals who are not part of the regime can generate revenues through private business, buy and sell property, and use their wealth as they see fit. If there is an independent legislature, its members can use their institutional prerogatives

political stasis that obtains in state-controlled economies, in more permissive systems a fluid dynamic can develop between regime and nonregime (autonomous) elites, as each employs a set of strategies to improve their respective positions. For example, government officials can use a state's coercive apparatus—the police, intelligence services, and prosecutor—to expropriate property from private businessmen, harass political rivals whose assets make them a (perceived) threat, and enact regulations to burden successful

---

41. Although state-controlled economies have become less common since the decline of socialism and the rise of neoliberalism in much of the world, they are still present in parts of the former Soviet Union, the Middle East, and Africa. See Kelly M. McMann, *Economic Autonomy and Democracy: Hybrid Regimes in Russia and Kyrgyzstan* (Cambridge: University Press, 2006); M. Steven Fish and Omar Choudry, "Democratization and Economic Liberalization in the Postcommunist World," *Comparative Political Studies* 40, no. 3 (2007): 254–282; Ian Bremmer, "The Return to State Capitalism," *Survival* 50, no. 3 (2008): 55–64.

42. For examples of strategies of economic manipulation in postcolonial Africa, see Robert Bates, *Markets and States in Tropical Africa: The Political Basis of Agricultural Policies* (Berkeley: University of California Press, 1981).

entrepreneurs or put a veneer of legality on naked power grabs.[43] In turn, autonomous elites recognize that their control over assets and access is insecure, and they have an incentive to insure themselves and their property against a predatory regime.

In such a situation, elites may consider the options mentioned earlier: threatening to exit or seeking protection from above (ties to patrons in the executive) or horizontally (forming interest-based organizations of peers). A fourth and more reliable way for elites to strengthen their position is to seek protection *from below* by creating a social support base. Instead of placing their assets in foreign bank accounts and lightening their load to ensure an easy exit, they tie themselves down by embedding themselves more deeply in society. Rather than appeal to higher authorities working within the system, they invest resources to earn the support of people who are essentially excluded from the system, in order to defend against abuses of that system. Although elites may engage in some combination of insurance strategies, engaging in *subversive clientelism* may be the last line of defense.

## Subversive Clientelism

Clientelism involves asymmetrical, vertical exchanges of targeted benefits for support.[44] Depending on the demand from society and the resources available to an aspiring patron, he can work to establish a clientelist base by making a combination of material and symbolic "investments."[45] On the material side, he may donate some of his wealth as charity, either by direct transfers to individuals or through targeted donations to fix infrastructure or fund construction projects. He need not give away a major part of his assets, nor make significant improvements in the stock of collective goods.[46] Instead, he should strive to get

43. Jonathan Wheatley, *Georgia from National Awakening to Rose Revolution* (London: Ashgate Press, 2005), 106.

44. I provide a more detailed definition in chapter 4. My use of the term clientelism is broader than that of Stokes ("the proffering of material goods in return for electoral support") in that the patron need not necessarily interested (only) in electoral support; and can win support through means besides the provision of material goods. Additionally, it differs from Kitschelt and Wilkinson ("a particular mode of 'exchange' between electoral constituencies as principals and politicians as agents in democratic systems") in that it need not take place in a democratic context. Susan C. Stokes, "Political Clientelism," in *Handbook of Comparative Politics,* ed. Carles Boix and Susan C. Stokes (Oxford: Oxford University Press, 2007), 605. Kitschelt and Wilkinson, *Patrons, Clients, and Policies,* 7.

45. Throughout the text, I use the pronoun "he" when referring to elites, since the vast majority of those to whom this theory applies are, in fact, men.

46. Because most goods described here are targeted at particular communities rather than at the whole polity, it is more accurate to describe them as collective goods or local club goods (benefits provided to small groups of citizens) than as "public." Herbert Kitschelt and Steven I. Wilkinson,

as much public exposure as possible—more "bang for his buck." Projects should be centrally located, visited by many people, and socially useful. To maximize the return on his investment, he should also work to advertise his contribution, for example by honoring himself through public monuments and plaques, and alerting the media to cover his laudable deeds.

Material goods are not the only resource that can be spent to develop political support. Another effective but less costly type of investment that complements financial contributions is the symbolic display of solidarity with the community. An elite can build support by engaging in public demonstrations of respect for local traditions and concern for the welfare of the community's members. This may entail frequenting venues where ordinary people interact and accrue social capital, such as community centers or religious sites. An elite who has left his native village for the capital can win plaudits by visiting frequently, especially on holidays, and organizing and financing festivities. He might attend—or send a representative to—major life-cycle events in the community such as weddings and funerals, where he might hand out small symbolic gifts.

An aspiring patron may also offer to use his political clout to assist local people in dealing with the bureaucracy or acquiring scarce goods. He might expedite the acquisition of bureaucratic documents, secure jobs for co-villagers, or influence the authorities to release (or reduce the fines imposed on) local development organizations to invest in local infrastructure. By claiming credit for such windfalls, an elite who lacks personal wealth can cultivate a reputation as benefactor.

Through all of these activities, and with the help of his immediate beneficiaries in advertising them, the elite can earn substantial prestige and come to be seen as indispensable to the community's well-being.[47] People will perceive the community's welfare as inextricably bound up with the elite's continued success

---

"Citizen-Politician Linkages: An Introduction," in Kitschelt and Wilkinson, *Patrons, Clients, and Policies,* 23.

47. Prestige is "the esteem, respect, or approval that is granted by an individual or collectivity for performances or qualities they consider above the average." William Josiah Goode, *The Celebration of Heroes: Prestige as a Social Control System* (Berkeley: University of California Press, 1978), 7. On the strategic exchange of resources for prestige, see ibid., 272–73. On the evolutionary basis of conferring prestige on perceived altruists, see Joseph Henrich and Francisco J. Gil-White, "The Evolution of Prestige: Freely Conferred Deference as a Mechanism for Enhancing the Benefits of Cultural Transmission," *Evolution and Human Behavior* 22 (2001): 165–96; Mark Van Vugt and Charlie L. Hardy, "Nice Guys Finish First: The Competitive Altruism Hypothesis," *Personality and Social Psychology Bulletin* 32, no. 10 (2006): 1402–13.

and prosperity, while downplaying his faults and hypocrisies such as a lavish lifestyle, unethical or criminal behavior, or residence outside of the community. Not everyone will be an apologist for the elite. In fact, some may grumble—or openly allege—that the elite's ostensibly altruistic actions are a cynical ploy for personal enrichment or self-advancement.[48] But universal approval is neither attainable nor essential.

The result is an implicit bargain between some elites and selected communities that has major ramifications for citizen allegiance and compliance. By maintaining a revenue base apart from the state, autonomous elites are able to disburse some of their personal fortunes as charity, performing a vital function— the provision of welfare—that the state is unable or unwilling to perform. Elites' symbolic investments add a moral dimension to the relationship, increasing the likelihood that the beneficiaries of elite largesse will view the transaction as legitimate. As nonstate actors usurp the functional role and legitimacy of the state stemming from the state's failure to provide for its citizens, clientelism can easily take on a political cast—and may even become *subversive*.

Autonomous elites, in the course of their clientelist activities, can also strengthen a community's financial and social capital, enhancing their ability to mobilize society. Dependence on the state for employment or welfare limits the capacity of individuals to engage in opposition politics.[49] Elite charity, insofar as it offers a lifeline to people with few assets or provides an alternative channel of support from that of the state, can free ordinary people from complying with state directives and enable them to take risks. Those most closely associated with the elite can acquire prestige, mobility, and resources of their own by "riding his coattails." However, they are not completely unhindered, having effectively replaced one master with another.

Elites can also strengthen the collective potential of communities by acting as a focal point or broker, by facilitating interaction among individuals who would otherwise have limited contact. Possessing greater mobility and more diverse social connections than ordinary citizens, elites can link together people who inhabit different social niches or reside in different communities.[50] Networks

---

48. On disapproval and dispraise, see Goode, *Celebration of Heroes,* chapter 12.

49. McMann, *Economic Autonomy.*

50. "Brokerage is the linking of two or more currently unconnected social sites by a unit that mediates their relations with each other and/or with yet another site." Doug McAdam, Sidney Tarrow, and Charles Tilly, *Dynamics of Contention* (New York: Cambridge University Press, 2001), 142. See also Granovetter, "Strength of Weak Ties"; Roger V. Gould, "Power and Social Structure in Community Elites," *Social Forces* 68, no. 2 (1989); John F. Padgett and Christopher Ansell, "Robust Action and the Rise of the Medici, 1400–1434," *American Journal of Sociology* 98, (1993): 1259–1319; Ronald S. Burt, *Structural Holes: The Social Structure of Competition* (Cambridge: Harvard University Press, 1995); Mario Diani, "'Leaders' or Brokers? Positions and Influence in Social Movement Networks," in

that are mediated by autonomous elites acquire the potential to articulate griev-ances by gaining shelter from the state, but they also fail to evince the cross-cutting ties considered favorable for democracy, since they are—again—captive to the elite.[51]

To summarize, if an elite has made sufficient investments—symbolic and material—in cultivating a base, he can count on a loyal network of activists and a reliable voting bloc if running for office or, if necessary, as a resource to be mobilized as a last line of defense against a predatory state.

## Reaching Out

One more factor must be considered to understand how clientelist mobiliza-tion can threaten a regime—relationships among elites. A social support base gives independent elites the means to defend themselves, but they are still at a disadvantage vis-à-vis the state if they act alone. They can level the playing field if they are able to act collectively with other elites, which is more likely to occur in the presence of existing networks. Horizontal networks of autonomous elites are most likely to develop when a regime permits a modicum of free association. Where policies (or weak state capacity) allow nonstate elites to interact with-out being monitored or sanctioned, they can share information and develop ties

the national level, a parliament can play a mediating role for local power brokers analogous to the function of communal gatherings at the village level. Through frequent face-to-face interaction, members of parliament (MPs) can monitor one another's compliance and, over time, build the trust necessary to sustain more intensive cooperation.[52] A parliament is also a forum for the expression of diverse preferences, as its members represent constituents in different regions. Through these long-distance contacts, MPs can acquire useful information that

*Social Movements and Networks: Relational Approaches to Collective Action*, ed. Mario Diani and Doug McAdam (New York: Oxford University Press, 2003), 105–122; Ronald S. Burt, *Brokerage and Closure: An Introduction to Social Capital* (Oxford: Oxford University Press, 2005).

51. Hierarchical and clientelistic networks tend to reinforce autocracy rather than undergird democracy. See Robert Putnam, *Making Democracy Work* (Princeton: Princeton University Press, 1993); Amaney Jamal, *Barriers to Democracy: The Other Side of Social Capital in Palestine and the Arab World* (Princeton: Princeton University Press, 2007).

52. William Brustein and Margaret Levi, "The Geography of Rebellion: Rulers, Rebels, and Re-gions, 1500–1700," *Theory and Society* 16, no. 4 (1987): 487; Margaret Levi, *Of Rule and Revenue* (Berkeley: University of California Press, 1988), 63.

would otherwise be difficult to obtain.[53] Below the national level, regional or city councils may have similar effects, but because they do not bridge great distances, they tend to strengthen existing networks rather than contribute to the formation of new ones.

The manner in which elites are selected, especially in postcolonial societies, can shape the character and durability of elite networks. Where colonial powers selected agents from particular social strata or educated them in segregated environments, indigenous elites would develop distinct attitudes and identities that separated them from the masses. Another basis for elite cohesion is a formative event such as a war, revolution, or other crisis that brings together like-minded but unacquainted people and creates new networks—sometimes whole "generations"—based on shared experiences. These networks may endure as a political force and become the foundation of a new regime or social movement.[54]

A last source of network formation is an exogenous change that weakens existing authorities or otherwise changes the cost-benefit calculations of challengers to compete for power or resources. A natural disaster or economic crisis can weaken a regime's cohesion or harm its legitimacy.[55] Opportunistic actors have an incentive to respond to the increased vulnerability of those in power or the sudden availability of resources by joining forces to increase their chances of success. A regime's failure to use repression may likewise lower the expected costs of group formation or expansion.[56] This process can become self-reinforcing, as

---

53. Brustein and Levi, "Geography of Rebellion," 478.

54. For example, Bolsheviks who fought together in the Russian civil war developed informal personal networks that they maintained in building the new Soviet state. The Arab-Israeli wars, the U.S. civil rights movement, and the 1956 Hungarian uprising all contributed to the formation of new networks and collective identities that later coalesced into major political or social forces. Gerald Easter, *Reconstructing the State: Personal Networks and Elite Identity in Soviet Russia* (New York: Cambridge University Press, 2000), 47; Volker Perthes, "Politics and Elite Change in the Arab World," in *Arab Elites: Negotiating the Politics of Change*, ed. Volker Perthes (Boulder, Colo.: Lynne Rienner, 2004), 1–32; Bill Martin, "Continuity and Discontinuity in the Politics of the Sixties Generation: A Reassessment," *Sociological Forum* 9, no. 3 (1994): 403–30; Doug McAdam, *Freedom Summer* (Oxford: Oxford University Press, 1988); Szonja and Ivan Szelenyi and Imre Kovach, "The Making of the Hungarian Postcommunist Elite: Circulation in Politics, Reproduction in the Economy," *Theory and Society* 24, no. 5 (1995): 697–722.

55. Stephan Haggard and Robert R. Kaufman, *The Political Economy of Democratic Transitions* (Princeton: Princeton University Press, 1995).

56. Charles D. Brockett, "The Structure of Political Opportunities and Peasant Mobilization in Central America," *Comparative Politics* 23, no. 3 (1991): 253–74; Sidney Tarrow, "State and Opportunities: The Political Structuring of Social Movements," in *Comparative Perspectives on Social Movements*, ed. Doug McAdam, John D. McCarthy, Mayer D. Zald (New York: Cambridge University Press, 1996).

emboldened challengers encourage state elites to defect, which further erodes the state and swells the ranks of the opposition.[57]

## The Mass Mobilization Infrastructure

The two strategies that autonomous elites adopt in uncertain institutional environments—creating a social support base and developing ties with other autonomous elites—combine to create a set of relationships that in some ways mimics, but also presents a challenge to, the state. I call this set of interlocking vertical and horizontal networks the *mass mobilization infrastructure.*

As depicted in figure 1.1, these two types of networks are fused into a single interconnected structure. The state hovers over the diagram because it is detached from both communities (depicted as small ovals) and autonomous elites (depicted as nodes). Embedded, autonomous elites play the critical role of holding the structure together, as they maintain ties to communities and to one another, represented by vertical lines and horizontal arcs, respectively. Embedded elites are responsible for activating its various parts to bring about mass mobilization.

This model, as a conceptual tool, naturally represents some simplifications of reality. First, communities are rarely as isolated from each other or detached from the state as they are depicted here. Second, rather than being identical as

elite, when in fact nothing prevents several (or no) elites from competing in the same community.

The model's simplifications make it amenable to a wide variety of applications, where the identity of the actors and the nature of the ties between them may change, but the structural relationships remain the same. For example, similar models have be used to represent the ties between patrons and clients in preindustrial societies,[58] cores and peripheries in empires,[59] rulers and local notables in

---

57. Sidney Tarrow, *Power in Movement* (New York: Cambridge, 1994), chapter 9.

58. Scott, "Patron-Client Politics"; Shmuel Noah Eisenstadt and Luis Roniger, "Patron-Client Relations as a Model of Structuring Social Exchange," *Comparative Studies in Society and History* 22, no. 1 (1980): 42–77.

59. See David A. Lake, "Anarchy, Hierarchy, and the Variety of International Relations, *International Organization* 50, no. 1 1996): 1–34; Valerie Bunce, *Subversive Institutions* (New York: Cambridge University Press, 1999); Daniel Nexon and Thomas Wright, "What's at Stake in the American Empire Debate," *American Political Science Review* 101, no. 2 (2007): 253–71; Alexander Motyl, *Revolutions, Nations, Empires: Conceptual Limits and Theoretical Possibilities* (New York: Columbia University Press, 1999); Alexander Cooley, *Logics of Hierarchy: The Organization of Empires, States, and Military Occupations* (Ithaca: Cornell University Press, 2005).

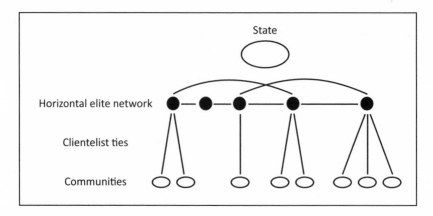

**FIGURE 1.1.**   The mass mobilization infrastructure

the process of state formation,[60] networks of civil society organizations,[61] agents and principals in firms and bureaucracies,[62] and, of course, mobilization.[63]

Despite the wide range of applications, the dynamics governing interaction within the structure should be roughly similar in diverse cases. For example, communities (ovals) maintain internal cohesion but find it difficult to act collectively with other units without an intermediary or broker. Autonomous elites (nodes) act as brokers and maintain an information and resource advantage over

60. Sharon Kettering, *Patrons, Brokers, and Clients in Seventeenth-Century France* (Oxford: Oxford University Press, 1986); Sharon Kettering, "The Historical Development of Political Clientelism," *Journal of Interdisciplinary History* 18, no. 3 (1988): 419–47; Karen Barkey, "Rebellious Alliances: The State and Peasant Unrest in Early Seventeenth-Century France and the Ottoman Empire," *American Sociological Review* 56, no. 6 (1991): 699–715; Peter S. Bearman, *Relations into Rhetorics* (New Brunswick, N.J.: Rutgers University Press, 1993); Roger V. Gould, "Patron-Client Ties, State Centralization, and the Whiskey Rebellion," *American Journal of Sociology* 102, no. 2 (1996): 400–429; Wayne te Brake, *Shaping History: Ordinary People in European Politics, 1500–1700* (Berkeley: University of California Press, 1998).

61. Theda Skocpol, "How Americans Became Civic," in *Civic Engagement and American Democracy,* ed. Theda Skocpol and Morris P. Fiorina (Washington, D.C.: Brookings Institution, 1999), 27–80; Jim Igoe, "Scaling Up Civil Society: Donor Money, NGOs, and the Pastoralist Land Rights Movement in Tanzania," *Development and Change* 34, no. 5 (2003): 863–85.

62. Oliver E. Williamson, *Markets and Hierarchies* (New York: Free Press, 1975); John Winsor Pratt and Richard Zeckhauser, *Principals and Agents: The Structure of Business* (Cambridge: Harvard Business School Press, 1985); Gary J. Miller, *Managerial Dilemmas: The Political Economy of Hierarchy* (New York: Cambridge University Press, 1992).

63. Popkin, *Rational Peasant;* Craig Jackson Calhoun, "The Radicalism of Tradition and the Question of Class Struggle," in *Rationality and Revolution,* ed. Taylor, 129–175; Michael Taylor, "Rationality and Revolutionary Collective Action," in Taylor, *Rationality and Revolution,* 63–97; Will Moore, "Rational Rebels: Overcoming the Free-Rider Problem," *Political Research Quarterly* 48, no. 2 (1995): 417–54; Kurt Schock, *Unarmed Insurrections: People Power Movements in Nondemocracies* (Minneapolis: University of Minnesota Press, 2005).

communities.[64] Since elites are linked to each other, they can confederate to connect social sites to which they have access and increase the scale of collective action. Nodes that are not directly connected must rely on another broker to link them together, giving that broker disproportionate influence. But control by the nodes only goes so far. If they are co-opted by an "umbrella" network that spans multiple nodes, then the lower units will automatically be absorbed into the superstructure.[65]

Finally, the structure can be modified to model different relationships, while retaining the same dynamics, in the process of mobilization. For example, where units other than communities, such as trade unions or churches, are a viable structure for collective action, they can substitute for communities in the diagram and scale up through a vehicle other than autonomous elites. The structure can also be adapted to model transnational mobilization, where organizations in different states mobilize on a national scale but are linked internationally through actors with cross-national ties to create a single movement.

## Triggering Mobilization: A Challenge from Above

The trigger that brings about mass mobilization is set off when the regime challenges embedded elites. Both elites and their communities have an interest in maintaining

..., ... ... political posts that provide access to resources, or demotion. Elements within the regime may target an elite because they seek to appropriate his assets for private gain, because they fear he poses a political threat, or out of personal or ideological motivations.

If the system does not provide a means to resolve the conflict through formal institutional channels, an elite who has been challenged can respond in several ways. He can quietly submit, especially if the state threatens to retaliate against him for his noncompliance by harming him or his family. If he has influential contacts, he can "pull strings" to eliminate the threat or employ various means

64. Karen Barkey, *Bandits and Bureaucrats: The Ottoman Route to State Centralization* (Ithaca: Cornell University Press, 1994); Motyl, *Revolutions;* Mario Diani, "Networks and Social Movements: A Research Program," in *Social Movements and Networks,* ed. Diani and McAdam, 310; Cooley, *Logics of Hierarchy,* 46; Daniel H. Nexon, *The Struggle for Power in Early Modern Europe: Religious Conflict, Dynastic Empires, and International Change* (Princeton: Princeton University Press, 2009).

65. McAdam et al., *Dynamics,* 116; Theda Skocpol, *States and Social Revolutions* (New York: Cambridge University Press, 1979), chap. 7; Charles Tilly, *European Revolutions, 1492–1992* (Oxford: Blackwell, 1993), 129.

that are commonly used to regulate power in nondemocratic systems, such as backroom deals, bribery, and blackmail.[66]

However, individual elites are usually at a disadvantage relative to the regime. States concentrate power that can be mobilized efficiently. In the course of securing the compliance of the citizenry, states maintain the latent threat of coercion to enforce their directives.[67] Nonstate elites have fewer material resources than the state that they can use to protect or advance their interests and (usually) lack a credible threat of coercion.

Elites who have cemented a social support base possess an additional option in their choice set. Because of their local comparative advantage in "human capital," sending their supporters into the streets may be an effective response. As social movement theory recognizes, mass protest can be a powerful weapon. It disrupts the usual course of politics, undermines the appearance of stability, and publicly challenges the legitimacy of those in power. It is likely to be especially damaging in an authoritarian political system, where the regime promotes myths of social harmony, yet does not provide institutional channels to raise claims against it.

Because there is a risk in arousing a regime's wrath, elites will only mobilize if they calculate that the costs of submission are greater than the costs of challenging the regime. This is why, absent a threatening precipitating event, elites are unlikely to mobilize their supporters. Psychologically, it is easier to justify taking risks to defend what one is about to lose (or regain what one has lost) rather than to press one's advantage.[68]

Structural conditions are also likely to restrict the circumstances in which elites will bring about mobilization. According to William Brustein and Margaret Levi, writing of early modern Europe, "It is only where the region possessed sufficient economic and political resources to make success [in avoiding taxation] likely but not certain that rebellion became a good strategy for achieving the ends sought."[69] This logic applies more broadly: elites must occupy a middle position between power and powerlessness to initiate mobilization. They are *able* to mobilize people if they have invested in a social support base, but they are *likely* to do so only if they lack other means. That is, if they are too constrained economically or politically, they cannot acquire the resources necessary to secure a

66. On blackmail, see Keith A. Darden, "Blackmail as a Tool of State Domination: Ukraine under Kuchma," *East European Constitutional Review* 10, nos. 2–3 (2001): 67–71.

67. Levi, *Rule and Revenue,* 50.

68. Amos Tversky and Daniel Kahneman, "The Framing of Decisions and the Psychology of Choice," *Science* 211 (1981): 453–58; Payne, *Brazilian Industrialists,* 12–13; Daniel Masters, "Support and Nonsupport for Nationalist Rebellion: A Prospect Theory Approach," *Political Psychology* 25, no. 5 (2004): 703–26.

69. Brustein and Levi, "Geography of Rebellion," 482. Emphasis on *where* removed.

base and will have difficulty mobilizing people. If they are extremely well off or possess some leverage over state officials, they can resolve the crisis in less disruptive and less costly ways, such as by negotiating a side payment or making a credible threat.[70]

## Local Dynamics

Once challenged, an embedded elite can begin the process of turning the community's latent mobilization potential into a reality. Those with the most direct ties to the threatened elite, such as friends, relatives, employees, and colleagues, are also his greatest beneficiaries and the most likely to expend time and energy in organizing resistance. As this initial core of activists uses the elite's resources to recruit people, mobilization can spread laterally through a community.

A second group of people is likely to join the mobilization through social ties emanating from the initial group of activists. Some, who have benefited personally or perceive that the elite's well-being advances their own welfare, may agree to participate spontaneously upon hearing of his troubles. Others who are more distant from the elite may join after being solicited by other community members. The three most influential appeals that induce an individual to join a mobilization are those from family or close associates, to whom loyalty is likely

that started the process—an individual may evince no interest in the elite or his problems, but will join out of the imperative of honoring his social obligations and maintaining his reputation.

Depending on the elite's reputation, the initial mass of activists, and the intensity of their recruitment efforts, the equilibrium participation level within a community can range from a small number of committed activists to all able-bodied members. In general, the more people who participate, the more additional community members can be expected to join, a dynamic halted only by the boundaries of people's social networks. This mechanism, called "critical mass" or "tipping," activates two distinct logics, both of which work to induce participation: (1) when repression is a possibility, the chances that any individual participant will be harmed decreases as the size of the crowd increases, and (2) as more people join, the shirking of every remaining nonparticipant

---

70. An elite with a social base may be emboldened to take greater political risks than an elite without one, inadvertently making a challenge more likely. Thus, the elite's initial fear of predation can become self-fulfilling.

becomes more conspicuous, thus increasing the social costs of refusing to become involved.[71]

## Large-Scale Dynamics

Given the parameters of the mass mobilization infrastructure, the ultimate scale of mobilization will be determined by how many elites decide to bring about mobilization in their communities. This in turn depends on the number of elites that are simultaneously challenged, the extent of their ties to other elites, and their perceptions of the political opportunity structure. When an individual elite is challenged, other elites may be reluctant to come to his aid if they themselves are not threatened. If the regime challenges several elites at once, it is possible that each elite will calculate that mobilizing—even individually—is the best strategy. However, imperiled elites face a dilemma: they fear attracting targeted repression and will therefore be reluctant to act alone; the perceived damage caused to the elite must be severe to justify acting without assurances. The existence of elite networks as a device to coordinate collective action can lower the threshold of the severity of the triggering event necessary to provoke mobilization.[72]

Thus, the probability that any single elite will put himself at risk will be higher if elites are linked through preexisting networks. This is the case because, first, before the decision to mobilize, networked elites can rapidly exchange information about their intentions, perceptions of others' intentions, and expectations of the regime's response. Second, as a result of past experience and the establishment of some degree of interelite trust, networked elites are more likely than socially isolated elites to have confidence that they will not be acting alone. Finally, within a single locale, elite networks allow for the rapid pooling of material and human resources to increase the size of protests. Especially where the number of protesters that elites can muster—or the resources available for them to mobilize—is small, combining assets can dramatically increase mobilization size and scale.

---

71. The first logic is that of assurance games, in which individuals seek to participate, but wait until crowds grow large enough to ensure their safety. In the second variant, the presumption may be to *not* participate, but in small groups individuals are compelled to join out of social obligation and fear of sanctions. See Pamela Oliver, Gerald Marwell, and Ruy Texeira, "A Theory of the Critical Mass I: Interdependence, Group Heterogeneity, and the Production of Collective Action," *American Journal of Sociology* 91, no. 3 (1983): 522–56; Rasma Karklins and Roger Petersen, "Decision Calculus of Protesters and Regimes: Eastern Europe 1989," *Journal of Politics* 55, no. 3 (1993): 588–64; Roger V. Gould, "Collective Action and Network Structure," *American Sociological Review* 58, no. 2 (1993): 182–96.

72. Payne, *Brazilian Industrialists;* Barry R. Weingast, "The Political Foundations of Democracy and the Rule of Law," *American Political Science Review* 91, no. 2 (1997): 245–63.

Perceptions of the relative power of the regime vis-à-vis the opposition may also play a role in the decision to mobilize. Once mobilization has begun in one region, regardless of previous ties, elites' cost-benefit calculations may change in favor of mobilizing their own bases. The logic of assurance games plays a role, as the likelihood of receiving the brunt of retribution from the coercive apparatus decreases as more regions mobilize.[73] Another factor affecting the decision is elites' ability to "sense which way the wind is blowing" and the desire to be on the winning side. Just as states tend to bandwagon with the anticipated victor in a war, elites are inclined to change sides if they perceive that they will benefit by doing so.[74]

If elites decide to ally with their like-minded compatriots by mobilizing their own resources, the whole will be greater than the sum of its parts. Separate outbreaks can be combined into a single movement with a unified command structure and tactics, and a coherent set of demands. Elites in this scenario act as brokers, joining together otherwise isolated communities. This new mobilization structure consists of individual communities undergoing their own internal mobilization processes and linked together through networks of elites. Such a movement poses a greater threat to a regime than isolated protests making separate claims, or an equivalent number of protesters gathered at a single site.[75] Participants from different communities will not know each other and may be acting

This chapter analyzed clientelist mobilization in the context of the dynamics of nondemocratic regimes. In a system that allows political and economic opportunities but which has a weak rule of law, new entrepreneurs and political aspirants outside the regime have an incentive to secure informal means to protect themselves. These elites can take advantage of gaps in the state's provision of public goods by investing in communities through charity and symbolic appeals. They also have an incentive to identify and develop relationships with elites who share common interests. By doing so, autonomous elites may acquire a useful weapon of defense against a predatory regime.

---

73. Regimes may want to set an example by cracking down on early challengers to deter further mobilization by others. See Daniel S. Treisman, *After the Deluge: Regional Crises and Political Consolidation in Russia* (Ann Arbor: University of Michigan Press, 1999); Barbara F. Walter, "Building Reputation: Why Governments Fight Some Separatists but Not Others," *American Journal of Political Science* 50, no. 2 (2006): 313–30.

74. See Randall Schweller, "Bandwagoning for Profit: Bringing the Revisionist State Back In," *International Security* 19, no. 1 (1994): 72–107.

75. Weingast, "Political Foundations"; Nexon makes a similar point (*Struggle for Power,* 111).

When elites have cultivated a support base, they can bring about clientelist mobilization to defend themselves against a challenge from above. They use their financial and social resources to recruit supporters to protest, while coordinating with sympathetic or opportunistic elites who can trigger mobilization in other regions. Thus, mass mobilization can come about as the product of medium-term investments in self-protection, a precipitating crisis, and the strategic use of informal networks within communities. The regime may have sown the seeds of its destruction, but it will not realize this until it is too late.

# 2

# THE VIEW FROM BELOW

## Communities as Sites for Collective Action

Over decades of research on social movements, scholars have repeatedly noted the crucial role played in collective action by preexisting social networks, which facilitate action by disseminating information, enabling recruitment, generating

alysts of the antiregime collective action described in this book, communities were the social basis of protest. Yet networks come in many shapes and sizes. Why would communities, rather than some other type of social aggregate, be the foundation for antiregime collective action?

When the Soviet Union collapsed, ordinary people were compelled to find ways to cope with hardships brought on by impoverishment and the decline of public services. The most immediate solution, described in this chapter, was to deepen their reliance on their preexisting and most proximate networks, usually extended family and neighbors, a move that required large investments of time,

---

1. See Roger V. Gould, *Insurgent Identities: Class, Community, and Protest in Paris from 1848 to the Commune* (Chicago: University of Chicago, 1995); Jeff Goodwin, James M. Jasper, and Francesca Polletta, "Why Emotions Matter," in *Passionate Politics*, ed. Goodwin, Jasper, and Polletta (Chicago: University of Chicago Press, 2001); Roger D. Petersen, *Resistance and Rebellion* (New York: Cambridge University Press, 2001); Elisabeth Jean Wood, *Insurgent Collective Action and Civil War in El Salvador* (New York: Cambridge University Press, 2003), Florence Passy, "Social Networks Matter, but How?" in *Social Movements and Networks*, ed. Mario Diani and Doug McAdam (New York: Oxford University Press, 2003), 21–48.

energy, and compliance with local norms. For those who invested, the return was the capacity to solve pressing collective action problems, which also turned out to be fungible for mobilization. The second, complementary adaptation, which will be elaborated on in chapter 4, was to enter into clientelistic relationships with independent elites.

Both of these strategies, which were undertaken to relieve economic hardship, had political implications because they created the possibility that politically ambitious elites would ally themselves with networks of poor but mutually supportive citizens. Considering the perspectives of ordinary people in their social context can help explain the reasons elites invested in communities as social support bases. Mass and elite responses to their respective conditions of insecurity are thus jointly necessary to explain mobilization through clientelist ties.

In this chapter, I show that community-based social networks were crucial in solving collective action problems in the first decade and a half of independence in Central Asia. The findings also lay the groundwork for understanding why people are receptive to assistance from elites and why communities are an efficient and effective vehicle for rapidly mobilizing people for protest. I first discuss how postindependence shocks contributed to impoverishment and decreased public goods provision in Uzbekistan and Kyrgyzstan. Using ethnographic material, I describe how people coped by relying on networks within their communities. I then explain how these network ties influenced people's behavior, through habit, affection, and calculation, to induce them to participate in collective action.

The evidence in this chapter comes from fieldwork I conducted in Kyrgyzstan and Uzbekistan in 2003–04.[2] In order to make the findings generalizable beyond a specific locale, I selected field sites based on economic and demographic variation. In Kyrgyzstan, I worked in the city of Osh, which consists of a rough split between ethnic Kyrgyz and Uzbeks and possesses substantial trade and manufacturing; and the district of Aksy, which is ethnically Kyrgyz, rural, and poor. In Uzbekistan, I selected Namangan in the densely populated and fertile Fergana Valley; Karshi and its rural outskirts, which are arid and sparsely populated; and the capital, Tashkent. The relevant characteristics of these sites are displayed in table 2.1 and figure 2.1 shows their geographic locations. Details on methods of selecting respondents and interviewing can be found in the methodological appendix.

## A Shock to the System

When the Soviet Union collapsed, many institutions that connected people in different parts of the vast multinational state were destroyed. Central Asia, the

---

2. To avoid excessive footnoting, I did not cite the interviews that lay behind most examples and vignettes in this chapter.

bribes rather than preventing crime, and courts were known to act on behalf of the powerful but rarely protected individual rights.[8]

The impact of state withdrawal and economic decline on ordinary people varied somewhat between Uzbekistan and Kyrgyzstan, but the extent of their respective troubles tended to balance out. By most measures, the decline in public spending in Uzbekistan was not as sharp as in Kyrgyzstan. However, this fact is offset by the level of impoverishment, which was somewhat less severe in Kyrgyzstan than in Uzbekistan, due in part to the greater opportunities for cross-border petty (shuttle) trading and small business development in Kyrgyzstan's more liberal economy.[9] Figures indicating several aspects of economic decline and reduced state expenditure are shown in table 2.2.

Within both countries, local-level commonalities emanating from similar circumstances generally outweighed their differences, with one exception. In the capitals, Tashkent and Bishkek, the concentration of resources, international ties, and greater public investment shielded most residents from the most damaging effects of decline. In both countries, the standard of living in cities was higher than in rural areas. However, the difference between the respective capitals and the rest of the country was even greater than that between urban and rural areas.[10]

## It Takes a Village

Communities come about in part as an accident of geography, yet they also provide the social structure for individuals to coalesce into enduring networks based on trust and reciprocity, enabling people to solve collective problems.[11]

---

8. The Corruption Perceptions Index supports the notion that economic decline was also caused by poor governance and not attributable to structural factors alone. In the most recent (2009) survey, Kyrgyzstan placed 162nd and Uzbekistan 174th out of 180 countries in corruption perceptions. This is worse than Russia, ranked 146th, and Tajikistan, ranked 158th. http://www.transparency.org/policy_research/surveys_indices/cpi/2009/cpi_2009_table.

9. Evidence from my 2005 survey confirms the latter differential. Respondents were asked, "Which of the following best describes the level of well-being of your household?" and given the following choices: (1) It is difficult for us to afford even basic goods and food, (2) We can afford food, but it is difficult for us to pay for clothes and utilities, (3) We can afford food, clothing, and utilities, but we cannot afford such things as a new television or refrigerator, (4) We can afford food, clothing, utilities, and such things as a television or refrigerator, (5) We can buy everything we need. The mean was 2.71 for respondents in Kyrgyzstan and 2.44 for respondents in Uzbekistan. In both countries, the average respondent was able to afford basic necessities but struggled to purchase anything more, yet Kyrgyzstanis were somewhat better off.

10. The urban-rural split is 2.61–2.55, while the difference between the capital and the rest is 2.76–2.55.

11. It is important to note that communities cannot "act" as such. Instead, they provide the structure for individuals to act collectively through networks.

**Table 2.2**  Declining economic indicators in Kyrgyzstan and Uzbekistan during the transition period

|  | SOVIET SUBSIDIES (% GDP, 1990) | POVERTY RATE, 1989[a] | POVERTY RATE, 2003[b] | CORRUPTION PERCEPTIONS, RANKING (2009)[c] | EDUCATION EXPENDITURE, 1996 (1991 BASE, 100) | HEALTH CARE EXPENDITURE, 1996 (1990 BASE, 100) | PURCHASING POWER (1=LOWEST, 5=HIGHEST)[d] |
|---|---|---|---|---|---|---|---|
| Kyrgyzstan | 13 | 33 | 70 | 162 | 38 | 36 | 2.71 |
| Uzbekistan | 20 | 44 | 47 | 174 | 67 | 72 | 2.44 |

*Sources:* Umirserik Kasenov, "Post-Soviet Modernization in Central Asia: Realities and Prospects," in Boris Rumer and Stanislav Zhukov, *Central Asia: The Challenges of Independence* (Armonk, N.Y.: M.E. Sharpe, 1998), 64; Richard Pomfret and Kathryn Anderson, "Economic Development Strategies in Central Asia since 1991," *Asian Studies Review* 25, no. 2 (2001): 187; "Growth, Poverty and Inequality: Eastern and the Former Soviet Union" (Washington, D.C.: World Bank, 2005); http://www.transparency.org; Jane Falkingham, "Welfare in Transition: Trends in Poverty and Well-Being in Central Asia" (London: Center for Analysis of Social Exclusion, London School of Economics, 1999), 6–7; Scott Radnitz, Jonathan Wheatley, and Christoph Zuercher, *Survey on Social Capital in Central Asia* (survey, 2005).

[a] Based on household monthly income of seventy-five rubles.
[b] Based on $2.15 (PPP)/day.
[c] Out of 180 countries.
[d] Self-reported.

These networks can be used for material exchange, including rotating credit associations; to disseminate information about community events and projects; and to coordinate collective action to make demands on the state or other actors. Many of these networks originated in the Soviet era, when people relied on personal contacts to cope with shortages and gain access to scarce goods.[12] Yet rather than dissolve in favor of impersonal market-based relations after independence, informal networks remained critical in everyday life.

One important role communities continue to play is facilitating the exchange of essential goods and services among the poor. This type of exchange is usually ad hoc and intermittent, but given repeated interaction it can develop into enduring institutions through reciprocity. An informal institution with historical roots called a *hashar* (in Uzbek) or *ashar* (in Kyrgyz) involves voluntary assistance with physical labor.[13] Numerous informants from my fieldwork reported having participated in *hashars,* many of which substituted for lapsed state functions or

---

12. Alena V. Ledeneva, *Russia's Economy of Favours* (New York: Cambridge University Press, 1998); Marc Morjé Howard, *The Weakness of Civil Society in Post-Communist Europe* (New York: Cambridge University Press, 2003).

13. On informal institutions, see Douglass C. North, *Institutions, Institutional Change and Economic Performance* (Cambridge: Cambridge University Press, 1990), 3–10; Elinor Ostrom, *Governing the Commons: The Evolution of Institutions for Collective Action* (New York: Cambridge University Press, 1990).

allowed people to economize. Examples included cleaning out a canal used for drainage and sometimes drinking water, renovating and cleaning a hospital, refurbishing a mosque, laying asphalt for a new road, and assisting in a number of construction projects. When a person voluntarily donates his or her time to such an effort, the contribution is not forgotten; the helper can call upon the initiator of the *hashar* to return the favor at a future time.

Some exchange networks are institutionalized into rotating credit associations, which have roots in the pre-Soviet period and were reinvigorated in the post-Soviet era. The most burdensome expenses for ordinary Central Asians are weddings, for which people spend years saving and often go into debt. Making *plov* (a national dish of rice, meat, and carrots) for a typical-sized wedding of one thousand guests can cost the groom's parents up to $3,000. To soften the impact, community members chip in to buy a supply of communal plates and cooking implements that the event's organizers can use for free. Some communities have systems of rotating credit that require contributions from all members. In one neighborhood outside of Namangan, the community leader's assistants (*aktivisty*) would go door-to-door to gather money for holiday celebrations and collect 2–3,000 *som* ($2–$3) from every household.[14] Leftover money was deposited in a fund for use by needy members in extraordinary circumstances, such as weddings or medical treatment, from which they could borrow without interest. At the time I visited, the fund contained $200.

Similar funds circulate among subsets of community members on their own initiative, through a *gap*, an informal group of (usually male) cohorts that meets regularly.[15] In a town outside of Osh, an informal group of twenty-five men living on the same street met on Sundays at the bazaar. Each member would contribute 25–35 som ($.70-$.90) to a fund used for cooking *plov* for the group's meetings and for financing small communal projects. In one instance, after a girl had been hit by a speeding car, the group paid to place a speed bump in the street.

The collection of money could also occur on an ad hoc basis, as active citizens would press their neighbors to make voluntary donations to finance important

---

14. A community leader (*domashnyi komitet* in Russian, *mahalla raisi* or *yuz boshi* in Uzbek) is a salaried position at the lowest level of government in Uzbekistan and Kyrgyzstan, analogous to the chair of the village soviet or neighborhood committee in Soviet times. Community leaders are local and are usually well known and respected by their neighbors. However, it has been argued, especially in Uzbekistan, that one of their roles is to monitor and control local political activity. See Eric W. Sievers, "Uzbekistan's Mahalla: From Soviet to Absolutist Residential Community Associations," *Journal of International and Comparative Law at Chicago-Kent* 2 (2002): 91–158; Neema Noori, "Delegating Coercion: Linking Decentralization to State Formation in Uzbekistan" (PhD diss., Columbia University, 2005).

15. I attended several *gaps*, which usually consist of groups of middle-aged men consuming large quantities of plov, imbibing vodka, and gossiping about work and their families. In recent years, educated and wealthier women have also begun organizing their own *gaps*.

local projects. One frequent source of frustration was the decay of physical infrastructure, which many local governments lacked the wherewithal to repair. One community leader in Osh explained that when the transformer in his neighborhood blew out, he called the city to have it replaced, but the agency did not have a new one to spare. After two days of going door-to-door, he and his neighbors collected enough money to buy a transformer and pay workers to install it.

A related function of community networks is to enable and enhance the spread of information. In Aksy, where newspapers can arrive up to a month late, residents spread information about current events by word of mouth, often through taxi drivers who make trips to Kerben, the district capital. People then disseminate the news at informal gatherings. In Namangan and Karshi, pension-age men and women would sit in the street outside their houses, observe passers-by, and note violations of local norms. Men could then share this information informally with others at mosques and with women at teahouses, increasing the chances that the violator would find out that the community was aware of his or her transgression.

Mosques not only had a spiritual function but also acted as focal points for the dissemination of information and coordination of collective action within and between communities. Mosques traditionally acted as the center of historical Uzbek neighborhoods, called *mahallas*. Mosque networks are used to rapidly disseminate information between isolated villages or disconnected *mahallas*. When a resident dies, the head of the mosque—the imam—sends a letter to mosques in other communities to inform them of the funeral. Imams then pass the information on to worshippers. Community leaders also use mosques as forums to discuss problems and make important announcements. Even if only 10 percent of the men in the community attend regularly—though many more come to Friday prayers—leaders can reach a larger audience as the (exclusively male) worshippers inform their wives. NGO employees involved in community-driven development consider the mosque a convenient venue to inform people about meetings and encourage participation in community projects.[16] Candidates for parliament or city council also find it expedient to speak at mosques during their campaigns. Yet mosques are heavily regulated and closely monitored by the state, making them less practical for disseminating information that undermines government policy.

Last, community networks served as means for aggregating complaints and coordinating collective demands to address to local authorities. In one

---

16. On community driven development, see "The Context for Community Driven Development in Central Asia: Local Institutions and Social Capital in Kyrgyz Republic, Tajikistan and Uzbekistan" (Washington, D.C.: World Bank, 2002).

neighborhood in Osh, when the city shut off power in midwinter because of accumulated debts, forty elders gathered and demanded that the power station restore electricity. After being told that delinquents first had to pay their bills, the men spent the next three days gathering money from residents to settle their accounts. In several cases in Osh and Karshi, residents lobbied district authorities to remove community leaders who were lazy, corrupt, or alcoholics. In other places I visited, small groups had protested to local authorities against home demolitions to make way for government buildings, the intermittent availability of heating gas, and indiscriminant arrests of suspected members of banned Islamic organizations.

# Maintaining Status and the Status Quo

Because of the important functions fulfilled within the community, people have an incentive to remain a "member in good standing" in the eyes of their neighbors. Yet people I interviewed expended far more than the minimum time and energy required to maintain this status. Community-oriented behavior was, for most, so ingrained that they rarely paused to question their actions.[17] Their reflexive behaviors included demonstrably adhering to local norms of behavior and propriety; accruing "face time" with other community members by attending public events; participating in time-intensive projects; and living a transparent lifestyle.

## Involvement and Investment

One way people maintained status in the community was by demonstrating adherence to local norms, even if they were burdensome to uphold or at odds with one's convictions. The lengths to which some people would go to conform are best illustrated by Eldar, the head of my host family in one location in southern Kyrgyzstan. Eldar was one of the wealthiest men in the town. Besides working as the director of the local UN development program office and owning a new Volga (a high-priced Russian car), he also possessed a marble sauna and the only indoor toilet in town. Eldar's affluence stemmed from the influence of his family lineage in the region. His father had been the first secretary of the Communist Party district committee (*raikom*) during the Soviet period, his mother the supervisor of all education and youth organizations in the district (*zavraion*), and his uncle the *akim* (post-Soviet successor to *raikom* first secretary). While I was

---

17. See Leslie Anderson, *The Political Ecology of the Modern Peasant* (Baltimore: Johns Hopkins University Press, 1994), 8–9.

staying with Eldar's family, three laborers would arrive each day to work in his garden, an unusual sight in a country where people do not typically hire gardeners. Eldar's mother explained that her son had decided to plant potatoes because other people in the neighborhood tended private gardens and prepared food for their guests using home-grown products. Eldar was ashamed at his inability to offer his guests the fruits of his labor. He therefore decided to create his own garden (though not by his own labor), and had purchased two cows that were being looked after by hired hands.

This story is revealing about two realities of village life. First, community perceptions matter even to those least dependent on it. Far from suffering financially, Eldar was planning to buy a laptop and move to Bishkek to work for a high-paying organization. He had little to lose materially if the community were to minimize interaction with him. Yet he tried to fit in. Why? Perhaps he feared other consequences of being seen as a nonconformist. Eldar's children attended schools in Kerben and his wife shopped at the same market as everyone else. Some people I spoke with privately derided Eldar and his patrician roots, an opinion Eldar must have sensed. His feeble attempt at conformity was likely driven by a desire to reduce these perceptions of elitism.

At the same time, this episode demonstrates that even people who fail to conform thoroughly to community norms will still be tolerated and included in community institutions. Because Eldar was unwilling to get his own hands dirty, it is unlikely that he would have succeeded in convincing his neighbors that he was genuinely like them. Yet despite whatever contempt they may have had for him privately, his neighbors did not show it publicly. Eldar still attended community events and people could interact with him without fear of being tainted by the association. For all intents and purposes, Eldar and his family were bona fide members of the community. This example is typical of a tendency I observed throughout the sites I visited: residents went out of their way to conform, yet were rarely ostracized for failing to do so.

Like Eldar, other informants were cognizant of community expectations and often struggled to comply with them—or avoid being caught violating them. In the center of Osh, young unmarried couples tend to walk several paces apart in order to disguise their courtship, the revelation of which would create a scandal at home, since dating as such is prohibited in many neighborhoods. In communities where abstention from alcohol was the norm, men made sure to drink only in places where they did not expect to be seen by their neighbors. In such religious communities, people made exaggerated shows of their piety through dress and behavior. In the opposite case, where religiosity was suspect, such as in the national capitals, devout men did not grow beards or exhibit excessive religiosity for fear of attracting the scorn of their neighbors. Failure to adhere to local norms could in principle be sanctioned by the community. Community leaders and elders told me that shaming was an effective way of inducing desired behavior. They used the device effectively to prod parents to discipline their children, wealthy residents to give money, alcoholics to quit drinking, girls to dress "modestly," and young men to attend mosque.

Developing a reputation as a good citizen is not only a matter of being seen as morally upright; it also requires attendance at community functions.[18] Weddings, circumcisions, and funerals—the most important life-cycle events—present challenges and opportunities to both hosts and guests. Hosts endeavor to throw a lavish party, which can elevate their reputation by demonstrating that they respect tradition and care enough to redistribute a significant part of their wealth (and borrowed money) to the community. Neighbors are expected to attend simply by virtue of their proximity and regardless of the quality of their relationship with the hosts. Neighbors who habitually fail to show up and have no good excuse attract notice. In the extreme, respondents said, jilted neighbors might refuse to attend the wedding of a frequent no-show, although nobody could recall such retribution actually taking place.[19] My host in Namangan, upon receiving a wedding invitation in late August—matrimonial high season in Uzbekistan—complained that he was exhausted from attending innumerable weddings, but planned to attend anyway out of obligation.

Another expectation of community members is to contribute their time and energy to neighborhood-wide tasks. One example is a Soviet-era practice called the *subbotnik,* in which people "volunteer" their labor for public works, such as building canals and harvesting crops.[20] Today, the most common type of *subbotnik,* which is still initiated by the state, involves neighborhood beautification. Respondents expressed a range of attitudes about participating in *subbotniki,* from outright enthusiasm to seeing the institution as "a sign of totalitarian government." Yet, as with other tasks, concerned about developing a reputation for shirking, they would volunteer their time—but not too much. As a rule, people would expend only as much energy as was expended by people living close enough to observe them.[21]

---

18. Thus, Woody Allen's famous aphorism that "80 percent of success is showing up" is an apt description of Central Asian social life.

19. A caveat to this is the possibility of boycotting a person's wedding as retribution for graver offenses.

20. See Theodore H. Friedgut, *Political Participation in the USSR* (Princeton: University Press, 1979), 284.

21. Gould offers a similar logic explaining how social norms induce participation. Roger V. Gould, "Collective Action and Network Structure," *American Sociological Review* 58, no. 2 (1993): 184.

A final, but no less important, means of maintaining status in the community is to act transparently in one's personal and family life. The norm of transparency ensures that members of the community have access to information about everybody else and can monitor their behavior. It permits invasions of privacy to a degree that would be considered scandalous in most Western societies.[22] The traditional basis for these intrusions was the need to maintain solidarity in the face of outside threats. A contemporary rationale is to ensure stability and prevent crime and other untoward behavior, such as membership in Hizb ut-Tahrir, a banned Islamic organization. People who violate the norm, by refusing to share personal information or by leading reclusive lives, automatically incur the suspicion of their neighbors. The norm of transparency helps to maintain other norms, as common knowledge about one's neighbors makes it easier to verify their compliance.[23]

Why do people comply so readily with burdensome demands? Is it out of genuine affection for the people in one's network, rational self-interested behavior, or ingrained habits of participation? Most likely, all these motivations are present, but they are difficult to disentangle because they all produce the same effect—solidifying informal community networks as a crucial aspect of people's lives and guaranteeing the inclusion of social considerations in decisions about how much time, money, and energy to contribute to a cause.[24]

## Blaming and Shaming

The consistent and occasionally arduous efforts that people make to maintain status are in many cases unnecessary, since it is exceedingly rare for an individual to be excluded from community benefits. To achieve such dubious renown requires being not only unpleasant but also profligate. In eight years, Ganijon, a community leader from Osh, expelled two people from his *mahalla*. One was a prostitute and the other "quarreled, drank too much, and did not participate." Even in these cases, the decision was not taken lightly—the latter offender had been warned by elders three times before being asked to leave. "By law," Ganijon said, "we can't kick people out, but sometimes we have to break the law to maintain traditions." If an offender violates state laws but has not offended community norms, he need not be punished. Such cases are increasingly common.

---

22. See Brad Knickerbocker, "America Wrestles with Privacy vs. Security," *Christian Science Monitor* (July 22, 2005).

23. Michael Hechter, *Principles of Group Solidarity* (Berkeley: University of California Press, 1987), 59.

24. James G. March and Johan P. Olsen, *Rediscovering Institutions: The Organizational Basis of Politics* (New York: Simon and Schuster, 1989).

Most community leaders I interviewed said they preferred to handle potential criminal matters, such as young men who joined groups like Hizb ut-Tahrir, within the community, by pressuring parents to persuade their child to quit the organization.

Can someone be ostracized simply for not attending community events or participating in group tasks? People face moderate sanctions in some circumstances according to a norm of reciprocity: they do not support those who do not patronize others.[25] In a community in Karshi, my assistant, Bekzod, identified one family in which a father and two sons—all police officers—were renowned for their excessive complaining. They were the only family in the neighborhood that people did not inform about weddings, but they usually attended anyway. When one of those sons got married, Bekzod attended because he was a friend of the groom, but Bekzod's parents—and most neighbors—boycotted. It is rarer to be punished for shirking *subbotniki* or holiday celebrations. Those who abstain are excused if they offer acceptable justifications, such as working or taking care of family. Community leaders, who try to ensure that work was divided equitably, take various approaches in dealing with shirkers. Some delegate the task by encouraging hard-working citizens to reprimand them. Other community leaders have a more direct approach: "Warn him, gather *aksakals* [elders; literally "whitebeards"], try to persuade him, then give him twice as much work as others." Shaming is thus a preferred strategy to exclusion.

In this chapter I have described the negative effects of post-Soviet shocks on everyday life in Kyrgyzstan and Uzbekistan and the ways that ordinary people responded. I showed how informal community institutions are used to solve everyday problems stemming from the loss of a steady income and the decay of state functions. Communities can mitigate hardships by providing a structure for everyday material exchange, rotating credit, information sharing, and coordination of collective action. In order to ensure continued access to these benefits, community members attempt to maintain their standing by visibly adhering to community norms, attending neighborhood functions, contributing their labor to collective projects, and leading transparent lives. When the same people repeatedly interact in multiple situations and venues—weddings, *subbotniki*, mosques—they develop prosocial habits and subsets of the community might coalesce into durable networks. Although these networks do not eliminate everyday problems, they are nonetheless an important form of social insurance and a basis for organizing collective action.

---

25. Jon Elster calls this the norm of fairness: *The Cement of Society* (New York: Cambridge University Press, 1989), 123.

In addition to performing mundane activities such as keeping the neighborhood clean and collecting money, networks are also occasionally mobilized to articulate grievances and present demands to government officials. As the examples above showed, such protests typically involve tens of people organized to voice a local, (usually) material grievance. Citizen demands to the authorities are most often dealt with in a conciliatory fashion. As in other nondemocratic states, local governments in Kyrgyzstan and Uzbekistan are willing to tolerate such dissent because it brings important problems to their attention and does not threaten their power. Localized contention therefore usually lacks political implications.

The next two chapters will complete the logical sequence that began in this chapter, showing how communities are drawn into a system in which they can be mobilized for protests of political significance. It is only when elites with political ambitions or the capacity to challenge the regime make communities part of their arsenal of defense that ordinary people, through their everyday social networks, may become involved in extraordinary events. Thus, chapter 3 lays out the political and economic conditions under which a regime must contend with independent elites; and chapter 4 explains how those elites embed themselves in communities, thus linking the upper and lower strata of society and, in some circumstances, transforming social interaction into political contention.

3

# THE VIEW FROM ABOVE
## State Influences on Elite Opportunities

Whereas communities are the social basis for mobilization, it is elites who act as the initiators, by allying themselves with communities as a form of self-protection. One precondition for this practice, subversive clientelism, is the presence of independent elites, which did not emerge in large numbers in most Central Asian countries. The region's regimes evinced a high degree of continuity with the old elite and ran some of the more autocratic states in the world. It was only where reforms created the possibility of prosperity outside the regime that independent elites could emerge.

The contrasting political development of post-Soviet Kyrgyzstan and Uzbekistan, neighboring countries with similar cultures and historical legacies, illustrates that pluralism was possible in Central Asia. Although seventy years of Soviet rule gave rise to similar political and economic configurations in all republics, crucial decisions made by the Uzbek and Kyrgyz governments at the beginning of the independence period created different opportunity structures over the ensuing fifteen years for new elites to arise, form independent power centers, coalesce, and engage in subversive clientelism. This divergence had major implications for regime stability and change. In Kyrgyzstan, many independent elites appealed to impoverished communities to create social support bases and collaborated with other elites on the basis of common interests. In Uzbekistan, the state maintained a monopoly of political and economic power, precluding the formation of clientelist ties or elite networks outside the state.

In the first part of this chapter I contrast the postindependence economic policies of the consolidating regimes in Uzbekistan and Kyrgyzstan, in which the former concentrated resources centrally and presided over a state-controlled economy, whereas the latter privatized much of its economy and created economic opportunities for individuals outside the regime. Second, I discuss the political and civic components of the institutional setting. I argue that Uzbekistan's preemption of civil society and top-down control precluded the formation of elite networks, whereas Kyrgyzstan's more liberal policies created an environment in which they could identify common interests and coalesce.

As a result of these policy differences, the balance of power between the state and society in the two countries had diverged by the late 1990s. Specifically, in Uzbekistan, as in the Soviet Union, the state was the sole bastion of power. In Kyrgyzstan, by contrast, autonomous elites held substantial economic resources and were able to form alliances based on common interests. After several years of pursuing liberalizing reforms, the Akaev regime reversed course and cracked down on actual and potential economic and political challenges. However, Kyrgyzstan's favorable opportunity structure had dispersed power to the extent that it was too late to "put the genie back in the bottle." In the last section, I describe how specific elite opposition networks developed in Kyrgyzstan throughout the 1990s and 2000s. These networks would later prove crucial in organizing the mass mobilization that toppled the regime.

The diagram in figure 3.1, adapted from the general model depicted in figure 1.1, shows the differences between Kyrgyzstan and Uzbekistan in terms of elite autonomy from the state and elite network formation, a result of processes described in this and the previous chapter. The withdrawal of the state on the grassroots level, which occurred in both countries, is represented by the absence of ties between the state and communities in both countries. The second level of this diagram—the horizontal row of nodes—represents elites, who gained autonomy from the state in Kyrgyzstan, but were part of the state in Uzbekistan. The horizontal arcs indicate the possibility of linkages between elites in Kyrgyzstan and the absence of such ties, except through the state, in Uzbekistan. The final and most consequential difference between the two diagrams is the vertical ties between elites and communities in Kyrgyzstan and their absence in Uzbekistan.

# Economic Opportunities in Uzbekistan and Kyrgyzstan

The independence of the fifteen Soviet republics, although presenting new challenges for their citizens, also opened up new opportunities for a select few. Initially, the greatest beneficiaries were not the hardest working or most enterprising

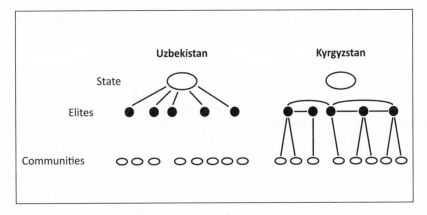

**FIGURE 3.1.**  Mobilization structures of Uzbekistan and Kyrgyzstan

people, but rather those endowed with control over important resources at the time of independence or those closely associated with the new regimes.[1] Over time, as the institutional context changed, new opportunities might become available to people who occupied different positions or possessed a different mix of skills. Variations in institutional incentives would determine, for example, whether enterprise managers would devote their energies toward asset stripping or productive business. The evolving configuration of economic opportunities would also have political ramifications, determining whether new elites could emerge who were not dependent on the state, and whether those elites would support or oppose the regime.

Whereas some republics of the Soviet Union advocated for secession as the state's coercive power weakened in the late 1980s, the republican leaderships in Central Asia worked to remain part of the union. Central Asia's political elite owed its privileged status, including the exclusive right to distribute resources in its republic, to its patrons in Moscow and faced little nationalist opposition at home. Only when the state collapsed and resources ceased flowing from the center did Central Asian elites accept national independence.[2] State-owned

---

1. There is a voluminous literature documenting the flawed post-Soviet privatization process. On the enrichment of a small, well-placed cohort, see Chrystia Freeland, *Sale of the Century: The Inside Story of the Second Russian Revolution* (New York: Little, Brown, 2000); Stefan Hedlund, "Property without Rights: Dimensions of Russian Privatisation," *Europe-Asia Studies* 53, no. 2 (2001): 213–37; Andrew Scott Barnes, *Owning Russia: The Struggle over Factories, Farms, and Power* (Ithaca: Cornell University Press, 2006).

2. For a psychologically based theory on why the Central Asian republics opposed secession, see Henry E. Hale, *The Foundations of Ethnic Politics: Separatism of States and Nations in Eurasia and the World* (New York: Cambridge University Press, 2008).

enterprises were automatically transferred to newly sovereign states, whose leaders would pursue a broad range of approaches to privatization, from Kyrgyzstan's enthusiastic acceptance of neoliberal reforms to Turkmenistan's maintenance of state control over the economy.[3]

The economic outcome with the greatest significance for subsequent political development in Central Asia is *actual privatization with limited informal barriers to independent wealth generation.* That is to say, privatization on paper is not sufficient to guarantee a true redistribution of assets. For example, a regime can partially privatize a firm to maintain a controlling stake or create front companies to ensure state control, in both cases giving the mistaken impression of private ownership. It can ensure that the beneficiaries of privatization are the relatives or close associates of its inner circle, so that management decisions are driven by political considerations and revenues remain in friendly hands. Finally, even if assets are legitimately privatized, a state can still stifle private business activity through a number of administrative and legal maneuvers, including exchange rate controls, excessive or selective regulation, taxes and tariffs, subsidies for state enterprises, and restrictions on trade. As a result, official statistics produced by the region's governments and quoted by international financial institutions do not necessarily reflect the extent of actual private sector activity. To gain an accurate assessment of the relative weight of the state and private economic actors, it is necessary to investigate the political context in which "privatization" takes place and capital is allocated.[4]

In Uzbekistan, the regime's appropriation of state assets coupled with Soviet-style centralized economic policies secured power for the ruling oligarchy and constrained actors who were not included in the regime coalition. To defend its monopoly on resources and preempt potential opposition, the regime enacted draconian restrictions on independent commerce and political freedom, and maintained hierarchical control over regional and local decision making through personnel replacements and administrative laws.[5]

In Kyrgyzstan, early economic reforms and flirtation with democratic pluralism created a more favorable environment for the private accumulation of capital

3. Richard Pomfret, *The Central Asian Economies since Independence* (Princeton: Princeton University Press, 2006), 1–24.

4. Kathryn H. Anderson and Richard W. T. Pomfret, *Consequences of Creating a Market Economy: Evidence from Household Surveys in Central Asia* (Cheltenham, U.K.: Edward Elgar, 2003), 146; Pauline Jones Luong, "Political Obstacles to Economic Reform in Uzbekistan, Kyrgyzstan, and Tajikistan: Strategies to Move Ahead," paper presented at the Lucerne Conference of the CIS-7 Initiative, January 20–22, 2003, 9.

5. Alisher Ilkhamov, "The Limits of Centralization: Regional Challenges in Uzbekistan," in *The Transformation of Central Asia,* ed. Pauline Jones Luong (Ithaca: Cornell University Press, 2004), 163.

and network formation among elites. Kyrgyzstan's economic environment was characterized by actual privatization that transferred significant assets outside the state's hands, along with sufficient latitude for independent commerce to proceed without significant state intervention.

Although it is impossible to know for certain why Uzbekistan and Kyrgyzstan adopted differing policies, two explanations suggest themselves. First, the two countries varied in economic potential, as reflected in natural resources and manufacturing capacity. Uzbekistan was the world's fifth largest producer of cotton and had large endowments of natural gas, coal, gold, and uranium.[6] It also had a sizeable industrial sector (for Central Asia) that included the production of military equipment and civilian aircraft. Kyrgyzstan, a mountainous country with little arable land, had been developed to specialize in animal husbandry and produced few manufactured goods. The republics' structural inheritances shaped the economic opportunities and challenges they would face as independent states. Uzbekistan could continue to earn significant revenue from the export of natural resources and manufactured goods, whereas Kyrgyzstan was heavily reliant on international assistance in order to survive.[7]

A second factor accounting for differences in economic policy is leadership. Islam Karimov became president of Uzbekistan after rising through the ranks of the state and Party hierarchy, culminating in his appointment to first secretary of the Uzbek Republic's Communist Party, which predisposed him to Soviet-style economic policies and governing strategies.[8] Askar Akaev, by contrast, came from outside the nomenklatura system and championed liberal ideas. A distinguished physicist, he was selected as a nonthreatening compromise candidate to replace a discredited Party insider. Akaev immediately signaled a break with the past by fashioning himself a democrat and courting Western investment. The convergence of economic inheritance and the predilections of their leaders set the course for the two countries' post-Soviet development.[9]

---

6. "The Curse of Cotton: Central Asia's Destructive Monoculture," International Crisis Group (ICG), May 28, 2005.

7. See Gregory Gleason, "Political Reform Strategies: Early Starters, Late Starters, and Non-Starters," in *In the Tracks of Tamerlane*, ed. Daniel L. Burghart and Theresa Sabonis-Helf (Washington, D.C.: National Defense University, 2004), 43–64.

8. Neil Melvin, "Authoritarian Pathways in Central Asia," in *Democracy and Pluralism in Muslim Eurasia*, ed. Yaacov Ro'i (New York: Frank Cass, 2004), 136.

9. These are not meant to be exhaustive explanations. Keith Darden has argued that post-Soviet economic policies were a result of elite economic ideas that were not a function of any prior variables. Keith Darden, *Economic Liberalism and Its Rivals: The Formation of International Institutions among the Post-Soviet States* (New York: Cambridge University Press, 2009).

## The Fusion of Wealth and Power in Uzbekistan

Islam Karimov became the leader of Soviet Uzbekistan as a compromise choice between rival factions.[10] During the September 1991 coup against Gorbachev and later, as Uzbekistan was thrust reluctantly into independence, Karimov shrewdly maneuvered to strengthen the executive's power over regional actors and nascent civic associations. He presided over the formation of a ruling coalition dominated by loosely knit factions representing Tashkent and Samarkand, the forebears of which had alternated in power over the Soviet Union's duration.[11] The Tashkent elite, which had historically predominated in technical and economic jobs, secured control of ministries dealing with trade and finance.[12] The Samarkand faction, which had run the republic from 1959 to 1983, took control of lucrative raw materials, including the ministries of gold, oil and gas, and agriculture, which handled the extraction and export of cotton.[13] Control over the "power ministries," comprising the SNB (Sluzhba Natsional'noi Bezopasnosti, or National Security Services) and the Ministry of Internal Affairs (which includes the police), was split between the Tashkent and Samarkand contingents, respectively.[14]

The new regime rewarded its supporters—the "winning coalition"—with lucrative economic opportunities.[15] Possession of insider status—being a high-ranking official or in that official's inner circle—was the most reliable determinant of wealth.[16] Conversely, the elite's hold on power was contingent on its control over the economy. As in the Soviet era, regime security rested on a system in which the population was kept politically docile as a result of its being dependent on state employment or tied to the land.[17] Substantial economic reforms

---

10. Previously Karimov, an orphan from the Samarkand region, had been known as a technocratic economist. He was considered politically neutral and lacked a clientele of his own.

11. Donald S. Carlisle, "Power and Politics in Soviet Uzbekistan," in *Soviet Central Asia*, ed. William Fierman (Boulder, Colo.: Westview Press, 1991), 93–130; Melvin, "Authoritarian Pathways," 129. The Samarkand group includes Bukhara and Jizzakh; the Tashkent group includes the Fergana Valley.

12. The former granted import and export licenses and the latter distributed international loans. Ilkhamov, "Limits of Centralization," 179.

13. Kathleen Collins, *Clan Politics and Regime Transition in Central Asia* (New York: Cambridge University Press, 2006), 262–64.

14. Ibid., 274–75. Usman Haknazarov, "MVD and SNB: Voorujyonnie Sily Raznykh Klanov" [Ministry of Internal Affairs and National Security Service: The Armed Forces of Different Clans], www.centrasia.ru, January 7, 2003.

15. Bruce Bueno de Mesquita, Alastair Smith, Randolph M. Siverson, and James D. Morrow, *The Logic of Political Survival* (Cambridge: MIT Press, 2003), 51–55.

16. The International Crisis Group reports that "this elite is largely self-perpetuating and does not let independent figures into its midst." "The Failure of Reform in Uzbekistan: Ways Forward for the International Community," International Crisis Group, March 11, 2004, 24.

17. Jones Luong, "Political Obstacles," 21; ICG, "Curse of Cotton," 12.

threatened to undermine the means through which ruling elites maintained political control. Consequently, despite encouragement by the International Monetary Fund, Uzbekistan was reluctant to carry out significant economic reforms.

Karimov instead took Uzbekistan on a "gradual" path of economic transition, taking incremental, but ultimately limited, steps. Uzbekistan privatized all housing and 90 percent of small enterprises by 1995—at least on paper—while retaining large and strategic enterprises in state hands.[18] The state also maintained control over extractable resources such as gold, oil, gas, and uranium, while seeking foreign investment to obtain needed capital in favored industries.[19] Official figures on privatization are misleading: a large number of businesses were classified as privatized when they were in fact only converted into joint stock companies, in which the government retained ownership of most or all of the company's shares.[20] Such enterprises were effectively run by government officials.[21]

The state made even fewer concessions in the countryside, retaining agriculture in state hands and continuing to issue production quotas for cotton. Agriculture employed 44 percent of the population, and cotton comprised the largest part of Uzbekistan's exports.[22] Superficial "reforms" turned collective and state farms into "cooperatives," which replicated the Soviet farm system: the state appointed farm management, decreed what could be grown, set prices for agricultural output, and compelled the sale of crops to state-controlled associations, which then resold them on the world market for a profit.[23] Without the right to lease their land or decide what to grow, farmers were compelled to accept salaries set by the state—$6 per month—but were often paid in oil or flour.[24] They

---

18. "Republic of Uzbekistan: Recent Economic Developments," IMF Staff Country Report 00/36, March 2000, 14.

19. Gleason, "Political Reform Strategies," 30.

20. European Bank for Reconstruction and Development statistics show that, as of 1999, 45% of Uzbekistan's GDP came from the private sector. Although this is among the lowest proportions among "transitional" economies—Kyrgyzstan's was 65%—experts consider even that figure too high. For example, the Economist Intelligence Unit (EIU) estimated the figure at less than 25% of GDP. See *Transition Report 1999: Ten Years of Transition* (London: European Bank of Reconstruction and Development, 1999), 24; "Country Report: Uzbekistan," EIU, first quarter 2000, 19. A more comprehensive measure of the institutional setting for private economic activity can be seen in the Index of Economic Freedom, which in 2005 ranked Uzbekistan 147th in the world, while Kyrgyzstan's ranking is 97. See http://www.heritage.org/Index/.

21. ICG, "Failure of Reform," 19.

22. CIA World Factbook, estimate from 1995, https://www.cia.gov/library/publications/the-world-factbook/geos/uz.html#Econ; ICG, "Curse of Cotton," 3.

23. Pomfret, *Central Asian Economies,* 33; ICG, "Curse of Cotton," 4; Alisher Ilkhamov, "Shirkats, Dekhqon Farmers and Others: Farm Restructuring in Uzbekistan," *Central Asian Survey* 17, no. 4 (1998): 539–60.

24. ICG, "Curse of Cotton," 5.

also inherited the debts that their farm incurred from the purchase of agricultural inputs, and were obliged to continue working for the farm until they paid them off. Many farmers smuggled cotton across the border to Kyrgyzstan where it would attract higher prices, or illegally grew unsanctioned but profitable fruits and vegetables to sell on the black market, as they had done in Soviet times.[25]

For "outsiders," who were neither part of the ruling elite nor associates of those who were, petty trade and small businesses represented the only opportunities to earn a living outside the state sector. A common source of livelihood, especially for those unable to raise capital or penetrate local monopolies, was shuttle trading, which involved buying consumer goods from Russia or China and reselling them in Uzbekistan's bazaars. Selling at the bazaar entailed high transaction costs, including purchasing a business license, renting space, and paying off police and health and safety inspectors. Traders also had to compete with stores selling higher-quality products, usually run by associates or relatives of local authorities who were guaranteed to have lower overhead.[26]

A small number of brave and enterprising individuals with business acumen and an understanding of the informal rules of the political economy could raise some initial capital from family members, open a small business, and hope to turn a profit. Yet they suffered from the regime's informal barriers to productive commerce if they were not protected by a "roof" (*krysha*) within the state.[27] One means of strangling the independent accumulation of capital was the regulation of access to foreign currency. The Central Bank of Uzbekistan restricted the amount of cash in circulation and did not allow convertibility of Uzbek som until 2003—and even then only a limited amount—which prevented international investors from converting their profits into currency usable outside Uzbekistan.[28] Banks worked in service of the state and awarded loans based on personal and political, rather than economic, criteria.[29]

Two laws further squeezed independent traders. The first, passed in 2003, prohibited the unlicensed trading of consumer goods in bazaars. It limited trade

---

25. Ilkhamov, "Limits of Centralization," 168. On the cultivation of illicit private plots in the Soviet era, see Sergei P. Poliakov, *Everyday Islam: Religion and Tradition in Rural Central Asia* (Armonk, N.Y.: M. E. Sharpe, 1993).

26. ICG, "Failure of Reform," 16–17.

27. See ibid., 17. On the *krysha* in post-Soviet states, see Vladimir Shlapentokh and Christopher Vanderpool, introduction to Vladimir Shlapentokh, Christopher K. Vanderpool, Boris Zusmanovich Doktorov, *The New Elite in Post-Communist Eastern Europe* (College Station: Texas A&M University Press, 1999), 3–23.

28. Mark Baker, "Uzbekistan: Som Restrictions Reluctantly Relaxed, but How Real Is the Commitment?" Radio Free Europe/Radio Liberty (RFE/RL), October 20, 2003.

29. *Strategy for Uzbekistan* (London: European Bank of Reconstruction and Development, 2005), 7.

to merchants who could lease closed cubicles, which were auctioned off start-ing at $3,000 per year. Karimov claimed the purpose was to "civilize" commerce in Uzbekistan, but the upshot was to restrict trading activity to only those with significant capital, which excluded petty traders and merchants without govern-ment connections.[30] Second, a 2004 law prohibited shuttle traders from selling goods through intermediaries and required them to purchase cash registers and place all their earnings in bank accounts, or risk losing their licenses.[31] This law, which many found it difficult to comply with, drove legitimate business under-ground and increased the market share of government insiders.

When independent entrepreneurs surmounted these barriers and managed to run a profitable business, they were often harassed, threatened, or arrested. Visits from the prosecutor and tax authorities would become more frequent, neces-sitating the payment of large bribes to avoid additional harassment.[32] Legal chal-lenges based on dubious evidence and short-term incarceration were used by authorities to intimidate business owners and justify expropriation, sometimes out of simple greed. Reports of seizures of businesses by local officials, with the collaboration of politicized courts, indicated concerted efforts by the authori-ties to minimize the accumulation of capital outside the state's control.[33] These informal predatory practices ensured that the institutional context for business would remain untenable. The regime succeeded in preventing outsiders from rivaling insiders in wealth or influence.

The upshot of Uzbekistan's economic policies by the mid-1990s was to have effectively precluded the formation of an independent business class. The wealthiest Uzbeks were government officials who controlled the country's most lucrative assets—mainly natural resources—and maintained direct ties to inter-national investors and buyers. Only state-run enterprises and businesses run by regime members or their allies could count on the official protection and privi-leges necessary to turn a profit. It was nearly impossible for ordinary Uzbeks to become wealthy autonomously from the state. Further reinforcing the fusion of power and wealth, the incentives for regime members to remain in the ruling coalition were overwhelming because opportunities for enrichment ran through the state. Elites who were bold enough to defect from the regime were not only

---

30. ICG, "Failure of Reform," 16.

31. Matlyuba Azamatova and Hamdam Sulaimonov, "Uzbekistan: Furious Traders Riot," Insti-tute of War and Peace Reporting (IWPR), November 2, 2004.

32. "Country Report: Uzbekistan," Economist Intelligence Unit (EIU), September 2001, 14; Jones Luong, "Political Obstacles," 15.

33. ICG, "Failure of Reform," 20–21; Lawrence I. Markowitz, "Sources of State Weakness and Collapse: Regionalism, Strongmen, and Patronage in Tajikistan and Uzbekistan," (PhD diss., Uni-versity of Wisconsin, 2004); "Uzbekistan," in 2005 National Trade Estimate Report on Foreign Trade Barriers (Washington, D.C.: U.S. Trade Representative), 485.

guaranteed to lose their access to resources but might also be robbed of their assets and deprived of their freedom, since independent wealthy elites were seen as inherently threatening to the status quo.

## Opportunities and Opportunism in Kyrgyzstan's Transition

As in Uzbekistan, elites in Kyrgyzstan rallied around their newly chosen president, Askar Akaev, as the date of independence approached. Yet unlike Uzbekistan, Akaev did not attempt to centralize power to the extent that Karimov did. Arriving from an academic milieu and presiding over a feeble economy, Akaev governed cautiously, ceding power to regional elites and adopting reforms that could win him friends (and funds) from abroad.[34] Although his governing approach won Kyrgyzstan a designation as "Central Asia's island of democracy" and succeeded in minimizing state control over the economy, his reforms disproportionately benefited a small number of well-positioned and resourceful actors rather than society at large.[35] Nonetheless, the dispersion of state resources was significant and would later have important ramifications.

Akaev's reforms created an environment in which actors outside the ruling apparatus could operate profitable businesses and retain their revenues. Akaev first introduced a new currency, restructured banks, and privatized housing and small enterprises.[36] His government privatized 85 percent of the country's forty-seven hundred enterprises by 1994.[37] Using a system similar to Russia's, it distributed vouchers to all Kyrgyz citizens, entitling them to purchase shares of newly privatized companies.[38] Already by 1995, the private sector was estimated to be producing 40 percent of the GDP.[39]

Second, the government privatized land. Kyrgyzstan has little arable land even though a large portion of the population is dependent on agriculture. Experts advised that dismantling collective farms and distributing land plots to collective farm employees would increase efficiency and allow farmers to compete in

---

34. Pauline Jones Luong, *Institutional Change and Political Continuity in Post-Soviet Central Asia* (New York: Cambridge University Press, 2002), 106–20.

35. John Anderson, *Kyrgyzstan: Central Asia's Island of Democracy?* (Amsterdam: Harwood, 1999).

36. Richard Pomfret, "Aid and Ideas: The Impact of Western Economic Support on the Muslim Successor States," in Ro'i, *Democracy and Pluralism,* 85.

37. Anderson and Pomfret, *Consequences,* 145.

38. Richard Pomfret, *The Economies of Central Asia* (Princeton: Princeton University Press, 1995), 113–14.

39. Oleh Havrylyshyn and Donal McGettigan, "Privatization in Transition Countries: A Sampling of the Literature," IMF Working Paper, 99/6, 1999, 7.

a market economy.[40] In addition, privatization in the agricultural sector would weaken the government's control over the countryside and empower people by vesting them with rights to use or transfer their land.[41] The two phases of land reform, in 1992 and 1995, successfully loosened the state's control over the countryside, but had unanticipated consequences. Rather than empowering ordinary farmers by giving them land title and increasing productivity, the reforms ended up benefiting collective farm directors, who exploited their personal connections and knowledge of the system to secure control over privatized land or sell off the farm's assets.[42]

Third, Akaev opened the country to foreign trade. By passing laws protecting property rights for foreign investors and allowing unrestricted currency convertibility and repatriation of capital, Akaev succeeded in gaining membership for Kyrgyzstan in the World Trade Organization in 1995.[43] Revenue from the Kumtor goldmine—a joint venture with a Canadian company—was reported to account for 40 percent of Kyrgyzstan's industrial output and up to 16 percent of GDP.[44] Foreign investment also benefited well-connected actors, who were best positioned to solicit foreign investors and prevent others from sharing in the profits.

Akaev's "liberal" tendencies did not prevent corruption within the state. Akaev's first cabinet was heavily represented by people from his or his wife's native regions in the northern part of the country, while largely excluding southerners.[45] As in Uzbekistan, members of the regime (including the president's family) used their leverage to appropriate control over the most powerful bureaucracies and took advantage of a corrupt privatization process. A commission created after Akaev's ouster in 2005 compiled a list of forty-two businesses reputedly owned or partially controlled by Akaev's family, including a cement factory,

40. *Kyrgyzstan: The Transition to a Market Economy* (Washington, D.C.: World Bank, 1993), 123.

41. Anders Åslund, *Building Capitalism: The Transformation of the Former Soviet Bloc* (New York: Cambridge University Press, 2002).

42. Peter C. Bloch and Kathryn Rasmussen, "Land Reform in Kyrgyzstan," in *Land Reform in the Former Soviet Union and Eastern Europe*, ed. Stephen K. Wegren (New York: Routledge, 1998), 125; Peter C. Bloch, "Land Privatization and Land Market Development: The 'Unsuccessful' Cases of Kyrgyzstan and Uzbekistan," in *Building Market Institutions in Post-communist Agriculture: Land, Credit, and Assistance*, ed. David A. J. Macey, William Pyle, Stephen K. Wegren (Lanham, Md.: Lexington Books, 2004), 19. For a comprehensive analysis of the pathological results of similar land reforms in Ukraine, see Jessica Allina-Pisano, *The Post-Soviet Potemkin Village* (New York: Cambridge University Press, 2008).

43. Gregory Gleason, *Markets and Politics in Central Asia* (New York: Routledge, 2003), 74.

44. Anderson and Pomfret, *Consequences*, 32.

45. Vladimir Khanin, "Political Clans and Political Conflicts in Contemporary Kyrgyzstan," in Ro'i, *Democracy and Pluralism*, 219.

the Kumtor gold mine, Kyrgyzstan's largest cellular phone company, and the fuel supplier to an American air base.[46] Akaev's brother-in-law was reputed to own the largest bazaar in Bishkek.[47]

A high-placed job in the Kyrgyz government was a means to access lucrative resources. With no legacy of transparency or accountability, it was not long before personalistic politics became rampant and the state became a major source of rent-seeking. A market developed in which individuals could buy government jobs in the hopes of making a "return" on their "investment" before being replaced.[48] Ambitious bureaucrats could expect to become rich after a stint in a high office. Kurmanbek Bakiev, who followed Akaev as president of Kyrgyzstan, had held high-level positions in the USSR, including factory manager and chairman of the *gorkom* (city Party committee) in Jalalabad, and later worked for the State Property Committee. After leaving the government and placing his earnings in real estate and business ventures, Bakiev was reputed to be one of the one hundred richest people in Kyrgyzstan.[49]

A comparison of the political economies of Uzbekistan and Kyrgyzstan reveals that while both systems lent themselves to corruption, some important differences stand out. Whereas Uzbekistan's economic policies redounded to the benefit of the regime, reforms in Kyrgyzstan ensured that hardworking people could gain control of important physical assets on their own initiative, and not due to their regime connections alone. Kyrgyzstan would best be characterized then as a "crony capitalist" system—in which state officials meddled in the economy to benefit themselves and their close associates, but did not attempt to dominate all economic activity[50]—while the Uzbek state actively allocated resources and refused to relinquish control over economic assets. As the next section demonstrates, private economic activity in Kyrgyzstan's functioning but flawed market economy provided myriad avenues to prosperity and allowed the rich to maintain political autonomy. It should be kept in mind, however, that these independent beneficiaries of the system were not necessarily "democrats."

---

46. Daniel Kimmage, "Kyrgyzstan: Follow the Money—The Akaev Investigation," RFE/RL, May 4, 2005; Valerii Kodachigov and Dina Karat, "Imenem kontrrevolutsii syn Askara Akaeva pytaetsia vernut' sobstvennost'" [In the name of counterrevolution, Askar Akaev's son tries to return his property], *Kommersant*, May 24, 2005.

47. "Ramazan Dyryldaev, Chairman of the Kyrgyz Committee for Human Rights," Kyrgyzstan Daily Digest, RFE/RL, June 7, 2001. Regine A. Spector, "Securing Property in Contemporary Kyrgyzstan," *Post-Soviet Affairs* 24, no. 2 (2008): 160.

48. See "Kyrgyzstan at Ten: Trouble in the 'Island of Democracy,'" International Crisis Group, August 28, 2001, 5; Jones Luong, "Political Obstacles," 17.

49. Akyl Stamov, "Politicheskaia likhoradka v Kyrgyzstane" [Political turmoil in Kyrgyzstan], www.gazeta.kg, June 21, 2005; Akyl Stamov, "Fergana: 100 samykh bogatykh liudei Kyrgyzstana 2004 goda" [Fergana: The 100 richest people in Kyrgyzstan], www.akipress.kg.

50. David C. Kang, *Crony Capitalism: Corruption and Development in South Korea and the Philippines* (New York: Cambridge University Press, 2002).

## Autonomous Elites in Kyrgyzstan

As a result of Kyrgyzstan's permissive economic policies and the failure to concentrate resources within a small winning coalition, there was a wide dispersion of wealth. Entrepreneurs imported goods from China and sold them at bazaars, or revived inefficient factories and sought international investment. In Bishkek, businessmen opened Internet cafes and chic bars for the small but growing middle class. Ethnic Uzbeks, constituting about 15 percent of the population and concentrated in the south, traded across the border with Uzbekistan. The privatization of collective farms left large and profitable pieces of countryside in the possession of former farm directors-turned-businessmen and newly empowered local officials acting independently of the central state.[51]

Independent elites in Kyrgyzstan did not have unanimous preferences vis-à-vis the regime. Depending on how they perceived their interests, they could adopt one of three stances—support the regime unconditionally, remain neutral or conditionally supportive, or oppose it outright—and often moved between the categories. The first group included Soviet-era officials who naturally gravitated toward power, ethnic minority elites (mostly Russians and Uzbeks) who were attracted to Akaev's multinational orientation, and wealthy Bishkek businessmen.[52] In exchange for their support, these actors enjoyed informal assurances of protection from harassment, to the extent that the center could control officials in the regions. At election time, this group would contribute resources to support the president and proregime parliamentary candidates.

A second group, often fluctuating in size, was passively supportive of the regime as long as it did not meddle in their personal or business affairs. Consisting of most of the intelligentsia, ordinary businessmen, and the nascent middle class, it valued economic growth and political stability above all else.[53] However, these fence-sitters could turn on Akaev if they saw him as responsible for economic problems or instability, rather than as a guarantor of their interests.

Initially, the third category—the political opposition—was composed of few elites but many former members of the liberal intelligentsia of the USSR.

51. Bloch and Rasmussen, "Land Reform."

52. Eugene Huskey, "Kyrgyzstan: The Fate of Political Liberalization," in *Conflict, Cleavage, and Change in Central Asia and the Caucasus*, ed. Karen Dawisha and Bruce Parrott (New York: Cambridge University Press, 1997), 266; Rafis Abazov, "Politicheskie preobrazovaniia v Kygyzstane i evoliutsiia prezidentskoi sistemy" [Political transformation in Kyrgyzstan and the evolution of the presidential system], *Central Asia and the Caucasus* 1, no. 2 (1999).

53. "Political Transition in Kyrgyzstan," International Crisis Group, August 11, 2004, 4. On conditional regime support among business communities in Latin America and East Asia, see Leigh Payne, *Brazilian Industrialists and Democratic Change* (Baltimore: Johns Hopkins University Press, 1994); Stephan Haggard and Robert R. Kaufman, *The Political Economy of Democratic Transitions* (Princeton: Princeton University Press, 1995).

The earliest members of this group included lawyers, journalists, academics, and members of the nascent NGO community. Some became *pravozashchitniki* (literally, rights defenders), activists trained by western NGOs to inform people about their rights and pressure the state to act in accordance with the law, and were a thorn in Akaev's side. Only in the late 1990s did the opposition grow to include officials who broke with Akaev over personal or ideological issues, and disaffected businessmen who no longer saw Akaev as a guarantor of stability. Some influential former officials with preexisting constituencies (mostly from rural areas) established political parties; others tried to oppose the president from parliament.

By the early 2000s, slow economic growth and perceptions of increasing corruption led to a decline in support for Akaev. As the resources available to Akaev to hold together his coalition were depleted in the face of large external debts, while the privileges awarded to members of his family expanded, the incentives for remaining loyal to the regime declined, and some officials who were once loyal to Akaev defected.[54] Of this group, some joined the opposition, hoping to return to power some day, while others quietly hedged their bets and sought out new allies in the event the regime fell.

Two prominent officials who defected to the opposition, Kurmanbek Bakiev and Felix Kulov, demonstrate the erosion of Akaev's power.[55] Bakiev was a life-long member of the nomenklatura and Akaev's prime minister until 2002. After being dismissed following the shooting of protestors in Aksy (see chapter 5), Bakiev appealed to his rural base near Jalalabad to win a parliamentary seat. Over the next two years he would emerge as the leader of an emergent opposition, leading to his selection as the head of a coalition of opposition parties in September 2004, in anticipation of the 2005 elections.[56]

Kulov was also a member of the nomenklatura and served in a number of influential positions in postindependence Kyrgyzstan, including as Akaev's vice president, the minister of national security, and mayor of Bishkek. When a close relationship with Akaev turned sour over personal and policy differences, Kulov resigned as mayor of Bishkek and established an opposition party.[57] Kulov announced his intention to challenge Akaev for the presidency in 2000 and, as a well-known and popular politician, presented a serious threat. Akaev first used

54. Collins, *Clan Politics,* 247.

55. After Akaev's ouster in 2005, Bakiev and Kulov became president and vice-president, respectively.

56. "New Political Bloc Formed In Kyrgyzstan," RFE/RL, September 23, 2004.

57. Some claimed that Kulov and his associates attempted a coup against Akaev in 1999. After the arrests of many of the accused plotters, Kulov resigned as mayor of Bishkek in protest. See Collins, *Clan Politics,* 246.

informal legal procedures to hinder his candidacy but, when that failed, had Kulov arrested and jailed for "abuse of power."[58]

Independent businessmen joined the opposition in the late 1990s and early 2000s out of disaffection with Akaev, the perception that his regime had weakened, or simple hubris. Typical of this type was Jenishbek Nazaraliev, a wealthy psychiatrist and member of the Bishkek business elite. He used his comparative advantage—money—to bankroll opposition activities in Bishkek prior to the 2005 elections.[59] In southern Kyrgyzstan, the new opposition was typified by Bayaman Erkinbaev, a former sportsman with reputed ties to organized crime. Having secured a prosperous existence from his ownership of part of Kara-su bazaar (the largest in the country), a cotton-processing factory, and several entertainment complexes, Erkinbaev began financing opposition activities and won a seat in parliament in 2000. He later hoped to become a major figure in a post-Akaev regime.[60]

## Political Influences on Elite Interaction

Besides economic opportunities, the institutional context for nonstate elites is determined by ability to coordinate and organize around common interests. Juan Linz and Alfred Stepan identify the arenas of democratization to include economic, political and civil society. Whereas economic society "provides the material base for…pluralism and autonomy,"[61] the strength of civil society influences the possibilities for successful collective action. A robust civil society enables "self-organizing groups, movements, and individuals" to "articulate values, create associations and solidarities, and advance their interests."[62]

58. See Naryn Idinov and Bruce Pannier, "Kyrgyzstan: Bishkek Mayor Resigns as Investigation Begins," RFE/RL, April 28, 1999; Dmitri Klimentov, "Nastoiaschii polkovnik Feliks Kulov" [The real colonel Felix Kulov], *Iezhenedel'nik Ekspress,* June 1, 2000.

59. Nazaraliev was a rare case of an extremely wealthy businessman who had not taken in part in political activities prior to 2005. He opened his first private clinic treating drug addiction in 1991, spent the next fourteen years publishing and earning patents, and did not even run for a seat in parliament. "Kyrgyz Doctor Became 'Man of the Year' at American Institute," Organization of Asia-Pacific News Agencies, Foreign Broadcast Information Service, January 8, 2003.

60. Spector, "Securing Property," 169; "The Unsung Role of Kung-fu in the Kyrgyz Revolution," Agence-France Presse, March 28, 2005.

61. Juan J. Linz and Alfred Stepan, *Problems of Democratic Transition and Consolidation: Southern Europe, South America, and Post-Communist Europe* (Baltimore: Johns Hopkins University Press, 1996), 14.

62. Ibid., 7. See also Marc Morjé Howard, *The Weakness of Civil Society in Post-Communist Europe* (New York: Cambridge University Press, 2003), 32–38.

Whereas neither Uzbekistan nor Kyrgyzstan—nor most other post-Soviet states—can be said to have developed strong civil societies, differences in the two regimes' approaches to independent civic activity resulted in distinct institutional contexts for nonstate elites. Whereas the Uzbek government's low levels of toleration for political parties, civic groups, independent media, and religious expression made it difficult for citizens to establish enduring ties with like-minded people outside the community, Kyrgyzstan's early flirtation with democratic reform provided space for autonomous elites to seek out common interests, coalesce, and collectively act.

## Obstructed Avenues in Uzbekistan

From the time Karimov took power in Uzbekistan, he strictly limited the development of pluralism in the political realm by suppressing potential challenges to his regime. He accomplished this by using coercion, shuffling regional cadres around, and creating an extensive system of monitoring and surveillance. His consolidation of power after winning the newly established presidency in 1991 entailed eliminating organized opposition of all kinds. The two most popular opposition parties, which had developed in the later years of the Gorbachev era, Erk and Birlik, were banned in 1993; Birlik's leader and Karimov's first rival for the presidency fled the country. At the same time as it neutralized the opposition, the regime created several pro-government parties, the largest being the People's Democratic Party, successor to the Communist Party, which Karimov chaired until 1996.[63] After 1994, with few exceptions, only pro-government parties were allowed to compete in elections or hold sanctioned meetings.[64] Karimov also ensured that parliament would be weak and pliable; its members were handpicked by the president and it met three or four times a year for several days to "confirm laws and other decisions drafted by the executive branch rather than to initiate legislation."[65]

Centralized control over regional and local governments imposed another barrier to collective action. The president retained the Soviet system of appointing regional governors (*hokims*), while strengthening the power of the executive vis-à-vis hokims by limiting their responsibilities and eliminating their power to

---

63. "Uzbekistan at Ten: Repression and Instability," International Crisis Group, August 21, 2001, 9–10. Other pro-government parties, all with indistinguishably pro-Karimov platforms, included Adolat (Justice), Millii Tiklanish (National Rebirth), and Fidokorlar (Self-Sacrifice).

64. "Country Profile: Uzbekistan," EIU, 1999–2000, 7.

65. "Uzbekistan: Country Reports on Human Rights Practices—2001," U.S. Department of State, Bureau of Democracy, Human Rights, and Labor, March 4, 2002.

appoint lower-level officials.[66] Further, to minimize the possibility of capture by local interests, Karimov appointed new hokims to oblasts where they had never served and created an agency to monitor their activities.[67] Hokims that failed to meet targets for cotton production, tolerated too much independent economic or political activity, or were considered too predatory were removed.[68] Subnational officials thus had strong incentives to keep a tight grip on political and social activity in their regions, lest they be dismissed and harshly denounced.[69] Noncompliance with or lax implementation of presidential directives could be costly, dangerous, and a bad career move.

On the local level, Uzbekistan preempted opposition through a broad network of police and informers that monitored society.[70] The 1993 Law on Community Self-Government made the *mahalla* into an arm of the state. "Neighborhood guardians" (*posbons*) in the employ of the state were placed in every *mahalla* and charged with maintaining order, gathering information on residents, and passing information to police.[71] Mosques, used as a venue for political association and collective action in other parts of the world, came under the thumb of the state in Uzbekistan.[72] After a proliferation of new mosques opened in 1990–92, many financed by the Gulf states, the state began to crack down. It obligated mosques to register with the Ministry of Justice and required imams to pass loyalty tests and deliver sermons written by the state.[73] Worshipping at unregistered mosques was made a criminal offense and many religious believers were imprisoned without trials in massive sweeps aimed at curtailing suspected Islamic extremism.[74]

Other measures taken by the regime impeded the development of civil society in Uzbekistan. The regime stifled the independent media by shutting down newspapers and threatening journalists who did not write favorably of the regime's

---

66. Jones Luong, *Institutional Change*, 123.

67. Ibid., 123–25; Ilkhamov, "Limits of Centralization," 163.

68. ICG, "Uzbekistan at Ten," 18.

69. For example, the dismissed hokim of Samarkand was accused in 2004 of "unworthy tendencies, criminal activities, abuses of power, violations of justice and, worst of all, clannishness, regionalism, and serious errors in the training, selection, and assignment of staff." Daniel Kimmage, "Week at a Glance," RFE/RL 4(29), July 27, 2004.

70. ICG, "Uzbekistan at Ten," 2; Bobomurod Abdullaev, "Uzbekistan: Police Surveillance Fears," IWPR, June 7, 2002.

71. "From House to House: Abuses by *Mahalla* Committees," Human Rights Watch, September 2003, 11; Eric W. Sievers, *The Post-Soviet Decline of Central Asia* (New York: Routledge Curzon, 2003), 114.

72. See Quintan Wiktorowicz, introduction to *Islamic Activism: A Social Movement Theory Approach*, ed. Quintan Wiktorowicz (Bloomington: Indiana University Press, 2004).

73. Adeeb Khalid, *Islam after Communism* (Berkeley: University of California Press, 2007), 171.

74. Abdumannob Polat, "Can Uzbekistan Build Democracy and Civil Society?" in *Civil Society in Central Asia*, ed. M. Holt Ruffin and Daniel Clarke Waugh (Seattle: University of Washington Press, 1999), 144.

policies.[75] Consistent with Karimov's belief that civil society should be developed by the state,[76] he limited NGOs to nonpolitical activity and subjected them to excessive monitoring and regulation.[77] International organizations were allowed to operate, though subject to an arbitrary registration process and harassment, until 2005, when they were shut down completely.[78] In order to channel collective action, the regime created a state-led organization for youth, which by 2006 had 4.7 million members, to succeed the Union of Communist Youth. Universities and workplaces mobilized students and state employees, as the Soviet Union did, to participate in spectacles, public works, and elections.[79]

As a result of these policies, potential opposition forces and even groups intent on carrying on innocuous civic activities faced immense obstacles. Ordinary people already faced structural and financial barriers that limited social activity to existing communities. Political restrictions conspired to raise the costs of extra-community civic activity—especially that which might be perceived as political—to unacceptable levels.

## Conditions for Coalescing in Kyrgyzstan

In contrast to Uzbekistan, Kyrgyzstan reduced the power of the state compared to 1991, laying the foundation for genuine pluralism. Whereas Uzbekistan retained the infrastructure of the Communist Party in the form of the president's People's Democratic Party, in Kyrgyzstan regional elites appropriated Party assets and used them to increase their leverage vis-à-vis the central state.[80] Also, while Karimov aggressively targeted regional leaders and replaced them with more pliant ones, Akaev purposely devolved power to *akims* for the sake of economic efficiency.[81]

Eager to prove his democratic credentials to the international community, Akaev encouraged the formation of political parties and presided over relatively

75. "Country Report on Human Rights Practices, 2004: Uzbekistan," U.S. Department State, Bureau of Democracy, Human Rights, and Labor, February 28, 2005. For a list of prohibited topics to write on, see Daniil Kislov and Andrei Kudriashov, "News, Views and the Internet," *Index on Censorship* 43, no. 1 (2005).

76. Islam Karimov, *Uzbekistan on the Threshold of the Twenty-First Century* (New York: St. Martin's Press, 1998), 99.

77. Polat, "Can Uzbekistan Build?" 149.

78. "Uzbek Government Exerting Pressure on Local NGOs to Close 'Voluntarily,'" www.eurasia net.org, October 4, 2005.

79. Eric McGlinchey, "Regeneration or Degeneration? Youth Mobilization and the Future of Uzbek Politics," paper presented at the 38th National Convention of the American Association for the Advancement of Slavic Studies, November 16–19, 2006, Washington, D.C.

80. Jones Luong, *Institutional Change*, 112.

81. Melvin, "Authoritarian Pathways," 129; Jones Luong, *Institutional Change*, 115.

free and fair elections. New parties, with orientations ranging from communist to nationalist to social-democratic, came into and out of existence throughout the 1990s.[82] These parties did not serve the function that they do in Western democracies, aggregating the interests of society and translating those preferences into public policy. Instead, parties were vehicles for ambitious elites to gain or retain a seat in parliament. They were regionally concentrated and weakly rooted in society, and had little organizational capacity.[83] Thus, only one-third of the members of the 1995 parliament were elected as members of a party, while the rest were independents.[84]

Parliament was nonetheless an important venue for elites to gain access to resources, identify common interests, and coalesce. Unlike Karimov, Akaev initially favored the creation of an independent parliament that would act as a check on presidential power. From the outset, parliament displayed independence and opposed the president on a number of initiatives, including land reform, privatization, budgets, and attempts to increase the power of the presidency.[85] Yet personality played a greater role than ideology in Kyrgyzstan's political system and parliamentary elections primarily revolved around local, and especially rural, interests and issues. Although they sometimes faced informal obstacles to winning, regime outsiders—even adversaries—could win a seat, which bestowed prestige, access to state resources, and the ability to assist their home constituency.[86] Wealthy elites could use their fortunes to invest in a parliamentary bid and gain immunity from prosecution. The national-level institution brought together local elites who would otherwise have had little contact and enabled them to share information and identify common interests. To the extent that blocs coalesced within parliament, they were defined primarily in terms of support for, or opposition to, the president.[87]

---

82. Leonid Levitin, "Liberalization in Kyrgyzstan," in Ro'i, *Democracy and Pluralism;* "Kyrgyzstan's Political Crisis: An Exit Strategy," International Crisis Group, August 20, 2002, 14. For explanations of similarly weak parties in Russia, see Michael McFaul, "Explaining Party Formation and Nonformation in Russia: Actors, Institutions, and Chance," *Comparative Political Studies* 34, no. 10 (2001): 1159–87; Henry Hale, *Why Not Parties in Russia?* (New York: Cambridge University Press, 2006).

83. Gregory Koldys, "Constraining Democratic Development: Institutions and Party System Formation in Kyrgyzstan," *Demokratizatsiya* 5, no. 3 (1997): 351–75.

84. Huskey, "Kyrgyzstan," 263.

85. ICG, "Kyrgyzstan at Ten," 8; Anderson, *Kyrgyzstan,* 50, 53–54.

86. Huskey, "Kyrgyzstan," 260. One example of projects that benefited regions selectively was the establishment of free economic zones (FEZ), which provide tax breaks to foreign investors. FEZs were created only in some districts in Issyk Kul, Chui, and Talas oblasts in the north, which benefited economically as a result. Collins, *Clan Politics,* 244.

87. See Mira Karybaeva, "Development of a Multiparty System in Central Asia," *Central Asia and the Caucasus* 2, no. 32 (2005).

Kyrgyzstan's relatively free political society was complemented by a civil society, which, by Central Asian standards, was modestly thriving. Various associations sprang up in the 1990s, providing forums for business and political elites to establish ties and exchange information.[88] NGOs sprouted by the hundreds, totaling 430 in the cities of Osh and Naryn alone in 1997.[89] Kyrgyzstan's liberal political orientation allowed an independent media to flourish, and a number of independent newspapers and journals were established, including ones that were critical of the president and his policies.[90]

Much of this progress was tempered by Soviet legacies and the incentive structure of Western democratic assistance. The legacy of state control over meeting facilities and the dependence of activists on state salaries limited their effectiveness in checking state power.[91] The desire of NGO activists to please Western funding organizations militated against long-term strategizing and limited their efforts to meet the needs of society and increase their membership.[92] Nonetheless, although NGOs failed to live up to the ideals of their proponents, they performed a vital social and political function, as platforms for opposition activists and venues where diverse actors could meet to discuss political matters.

The harassment of independent groups and preemptive monitoring of individuals was less pervasive in Kyrgyzstan than in Uzbekistan. Kyrgyzstan could not afford the extensive coercive apparatus of Uzbekistan and was not as concerned about threats to its security. Whereas Uzbekistan never allowed Hizb ut-Tahrir, an international Islamist party, to operate on its soil, Kyrgyzstan declared it illegal only in 2003 and at the urging of Uzbekistan.[93] The state permitted a wider scope of religious activity than Uzbekistan, allowing unregistered communities to worship with impunity, while also keeping a watchful eye on religious activity.[94] Parliamentary independence also translated into greater concern about executive power to monitor society. The discovery in January 2004 that the security services had bugged the offices of several opposition deputies in parliament

88. John Anderson, "Creating a Framework for Civil Society in Kyrgyzstan," *Europe-Asia Studies* 52, no. 1 (2000): 82.

89. Kelly M. McMann, "The Civic Realm in Kyrgyzstan," in Jones Luong, *Transformation*, 220.

90. Such publications included *Delo Nomer, Ekonomika, Banki, Biznes,* and *Obshchestvennyi Reiting.*

91. Kelly McMann, *Economic Autonomy and Democracy* (New York: Cambridge University Press, 2006).

92. Pauline Jones Luong and Erika Weinthal, "The NGO Paradox: Democratic Goals and Non-democratic Outcomes in Kazakhstan," *Europe-Asia Studies* 51, no. 7 (1999): 1267–84.

93. Alexey Sukhov, "Kyrgyz Ban on Radical Islamic Group Lacks Legal Foundation—Ombudsman," eurasianet.org, October 8, 2003. On Uzbekistan's surveillance state, see "From House to House: Abuses by Mahalla Committees," Human Rights Watch, September 22, 2003.

94. Antoine Blua, "Kyrgyzstan: Survey Reports Positive Findings on Religious Freedom," eurasianet. org, January 11, 2004.

created a scandal and led to a parliamentary investigation, at which members of the ultra-secretive SNB were forced to testify.[95]

Kyrgyzstan's relative freedom began to change in the mid-1990s, when Akaev attempted to retract some of his earlier reforms.[96] From the start, Kyrgyzstan lagged in establishing an independent judiciary; Akaev had packed the courts with loyal judges. Following the lead of his Central Asian neighbors, in 1998 Akaev secured a ruling from the constitutional court allowing him to run for a third five-year presidential term in 2000. He also clamped down on the media, closing down a critical newspaper, suing another, and jailing several prominent journalists on libel charges.[97] Civic organizations were constrained by laws that required registration with the Justice Ministry and limited public meetings.[98] Opposition political activists were harassed, beaten up, or jailed. These repressive moves coincided with greater awareness by the population of corruption in the Akaev "family," which engendered ill will among both elites and masses. By 2004, his increasingly authoritarian actions had convinced many that he would yet again engineer a constitutional change to prolong his rule.[99] Yet, Akaev's survival strategies never reached the level of repressiveness of his counterpart in Uzbekistan. Even after Akaev's authoritarian turn, the high degree of pluralism that resulted from his earlier reforms was impossible to suppress.

## Elite Opposition Networks in Kyrgyzstan

Kyrgyzstan's favorable political opportunity structure allowed elites to develop interest-based networks and associations to an extent that was impossible in Uzbekistan. Elite networks tend to form when there are institutions facilitating interaction, and in response to major political events and perceptions of regime weakness. In Kyrgyzstan, networks uniting individuals possessing organizational resources, ties to local communities, and political savvy would turn out to be critical in the 2005 mass mobilization. Some of the relationships that turned

---

95. Of course, it is possible the outrage was a defense of parliamentary prerogatives rather than being based on principle. Leila Saralaeva, "Kyrgyzstan's Not-so-secret Service," IWPR, May 28, 2004.

96. Explanations for Akaev's backsliding include the erosion of formal institutions by informal, rent-seeking networks; infusions of foreign aid, strengthening the executive; and the example of Akaev's more autocratic neighbors. See Regine A. Spector, "The Transformation of Askar Akaev, President of Kyrgyzstan," Berkeley Program in Soviet and Post-Soviet Studies Working Paper Series, 2004; Collins, *Clan Politics;* Eric McGlinchey, "Paying for Patronage: Regime Change in Post-Soviet Central Asia," (PhD diss., Princeton University, 2003); Jeffrey S. Kopstein and David A. Reilly, "Geographic Diffusion and the Transformation of the Postcommunist World," *World Politics* 53, no. 1 (2000): 1–37.

97. Anderson, *Kyrgyzstan,* 55–58.

98. Anderson, "Creating a Framework," 84–85.

99. Nazgul Baktybekova, "Resignation and Extension Campaigns Face Off in Kyrgyzstan," *Central Asia-Caucasus Analyst,* February 9, 2005.

out politically significant developed in parliament. Parties, though not deeply rooted, had an important coordinating role, facilitating the interaction of oppositional and independent elites. In Bishkek, NGO-sponsored events (e.g., conferences, round tables) that took place throughout the 1990s brought journalists, lawyers, opposition activists, businessmen, and members of parliament (MPs) into contact. These networks were later expanded and strengthened by events that discredited the regime and emboldened the opposition.

Opposition alliances began forming in the mid-1990s and consolidated in 2002. In 1995, while Akaev was still popular, the first opposition developed among southern elites who believed they had been short-changed. It revolved around the personalities of two parliamentarians, Omurbek Tekebaev, a former schoolteacher, and his friend from a nearby village, Dooronbek Sadyrbaev, a film director. Later open oppositionists included Almaz Atambaev, a wealthy Bishkek businessman, and Usen Sydykov, a deputy chairman of the Council of Ministers (and a southerner), who broke with Akaev.[100]

The run-up to the 2000 presidential elections provided a new impetus to coalesce against Akaev, who had by this time lost much of his initial popularity. Felix Kulov, having split with Akaev, planned to join with Tekebaev to challenge Akaev for the presidency, until Akaev had Kulov jailed. MPs and other disaffected elites began searching for allies, leading to the formation of several new opposition parties.

In 2002, the mass protests in Aksy, which are described in chapter 5, provided a focal point that cemented alliances between new and old oppositionists and pushed fence-sitters into the opposition camp. The main instigator was Azimbek Beknazarov, a new MP whose arrest had sparked the mobilization. His supporters included MPs Adahan Madumarov (who was close to Tekebaev and Sadyrbaev), Bektur Asanov, and Duishenkul Chotonov, deputy chairman of a party comprising several other elites called Ata-Meken ("fatherland"), all of whom took part in the demonstrations and marches. Their participation in the events helped to cement a network of like-minded opposition politicians.

Proximity and family connections facilitated the formation of networks of elites who had otherwise diverse backgrounds. For example, a tacit alliance between three unlikely bedfellows came into being between 2003 and 2004. Roza Otunbaeva was a former foreign minister and Akaev loyalist before splitting over personal differences. Bayaman Erkinbaev was a famous wrestler, reputed drug smuggler, and owner of large amounts of valuable property. Anvar Artykov was an ethnic Uzbek (unlike the other two, who were ethnic Kyrgyz) son of a kolkhoz

---

100. Author's interviews with Kyrgyz journalists, political activists, 2004–05.

director who became a member of parliament in 1995. Artykov turned to the opposition over his objection on moral grounds to the proliferation of casinos in the country. Artykov and Erkinbaev reputedly ran a joint venture together in Bishkek. Artykov and Otunbaeva began a working relationship in 2002 and formed a party called later Ata-Jurt ("fatherland").[101] Erkinbaev facilitated ties between this group and the other opposition network because he was Chotonov's brother-in-law, while Otunbaeva would later act as a broker to urban opposition elites with ties to Western organizations. In March 2005, this alliance played a critical role in Kyrgyzstan's so-called Tulip Revolution, bringing together actors who would lead and finance demonstrations in Osh and coordinate the opposition in Bishkek.

A similar coincidence of interests based on proximity and family ties developed outside of regional capital of Jalalabad. Jusupbek Jeenbekov, a parliamentary candidate in 2005, was the brother of a deceased popular opposition journalist, through whom he established ties with Tekebaev and Sadyrbaev.[102] He was also closely aligned with Tagaibek Jarkynbaev, the head of the local branch of the Communist Party from the village next to Jeenbekov's; and Jalalabad natives Asanov (of Aksy renown) and Jusupbek Bakiev, which also gave him indirect access to Jusupbek's older brother and former prime minister, Kurmanbek Bakiev. This alliance was important within Jalalabad Oblast, but it also helped establish a link to Bishkek. Similarly intricate informal alliances stemming from a variety of affiliations were typical throughout Kyrgyzstan.

Uzbekistan's twin strategies of limiting economic activity outside of the state and restricting autonomous associations had a chilling effect on entrepreneurship and politics. Significant wealth could be generated only by having access to state resources, which was regulated by the regime. To retain one's wealth it was necessary to remain loyal to the regime. Outsiders who accumulated too much wealth or dared to challenge the status quo were had their businesses harassed or confiscated. Furthermore, the political space necessary for elites to resist these encroachments by acting collectively was severely limited by measures that ensured that elite-level interaction was mediated by the state. On the whole, therefore, the potential for elites to develop independent power centers and form autonomous organizations was limited. Despite deteriorating economic conditions, in 2005 the regime was still largely capable of preempting challenges from rivals, who had been intimidated into submission or were in hiding.

---

101. Interview, Izzatulla, director, human rights NGO and election observer, Osh, July 1, 2006.

102. Interviews, Asylbek Tekebaev (Omurbek's brother), June 25, 2006; Sovetali Nazaraliev, head of Sadyrbaev's campaign committee, June 25, 2006.

Despite the Akaev regime's occasional use of coercion against opponents, the opportunities for independent economic and political activity were favorable throughout most of the 1990s. Although regime members appropriated a large share of state resources, the relatively unfettered economic environment meant that commerce could be conducted by those outside of the regime, and an independent business class could develop. The regime later attempted to clamp down on the opposition and prevent pro-Akaev and neutral elites from defecting, but the balance of power had shifted. Informal alliances of business and political elites, which would later challenge the regime, were already in formation. These two divergent paths taken after independence would become politically consequential, as Kyrgyzstan's independent elites strengthened their power outside of the state by tapping into community networks, while Uzbekistan ensured that the balance of power between state and society would continue to heavily favor the former.

# 4

# LINKAGES ACROSS CLASSES
## The Development of Subversive Clientelism

The previous two chapters have portrayed communities and elites as distinct and separate entities. The poor have, for the most part, been left to their own devices, while the former nomenklatura have availed themselves of rent-seeking opportunities, access to international markets, and, in Kyrgyzstan, privatization. However, in Kyrgyzstan, where a class of political and economic elites emerged that was separate from the regime, new linkages developed between the powerful and the powerless. These relationships stemmed from an awareness by insecure or ambitious elites that they could benefit in the long run by redistributing some of their wealth; and a desire on the part of the poor for assistance. The ties that developed altered the political dynamic in Kyrgyzstan by subverting people's allegiance to the state and creating a new structure for mobilization.

In this chapter I discuss the development and implications of subversive clientelism, using examples from fieldwork and evidence from a mass survey. I begin by describing how lax supervision of Central Asia in the late Soviet period contributed to the development of patronage networks devoted to capturing resources outside of the formal economy. These networks persisted, to some extent, throughout Central Asia's transition to independent statehood.

Next, I explain how autonomous elites in the independence period made investments in communities based on "portfolios" consisting of material assistance and symbolic appeals. This section draws on personal observation and in-depth interviews with elites and their close associates in three regions of Kyrgyzstan. The evidence supports the conclusion that such assistance is largely instrumental: elite charity is not targeted at the neediest citizens, tends to co-incide with electoral cycles, and often comes with an unspoken expectation of reciprocity.

The third section is an analysis of my 2005 survey of Kyrgyzstan and Uzbeki-stan, which provides quantitative data on the correlates of clientelist linkages, suggesting, among other things, that they are pervasive throughout Kyrgyzstan but limited in Uzbekistan. Finally, I include short biographies of some elite pa-trons and provide additional support for the chapter's argument with concrete examples of their actions.

## Patron-Client Networks in the Late Soviet Era

One precedent for hierarchical relationships premised on unequal control over resources was established in Central Asia during the late Soviet period. The cen-tralized Soviet economy subordinated regional officials to Moscow in a hub-and-spokes structure, and resources trickled down to society through state-owned enterprises and farms. Because goods were scarce, informal personal networks developed as an adaptive response to the ongoing shortages. There arose both horizontal networks of roughly equal (and equally poor) actors, and vertical net-works, in which supplicants would be expected to provide loyalty in exchange for obtaining needed goods or services acquired thanks to a distributor's privileged position, for example, in state procurement agencies, party organs, or collective farm management. An informal system of patron-client relations, both among politicians and between elites and nonelites, provided a vital lifeline to people without direct access to resources.[1]

In Soviet Central Asia, a region that scholars have characterized as a pseudo-colonial territory that was "under-administered" compared to other regions of the USSR, opportunities to subvert the formal economy were rife.[2] In the Brezh-nev era (1964–82), Moscow turned a blind eye to corruption, allowing republic-level officials to collude and divert state resources for personal use with impunity. The systematic underreporting of cotton production in Uzbekistan and its sale

---

1. See T. H. Rigby, "The Origins of the Stalinist Political System," *Soviet Studies* 33, no. 1 (1981): 3–28; Graeme Gill, *The Origins of the Stalinist Political System* (New York: Cambridge University Press, 1990); John P. Willerton, *Patronage and Politics in the USSR* (Cambridge: Cambridge Univer-sity Press, 1992).

2. Gregory Gleason, "Fealty and Loyalty: Informal Authority Structures in Soviet Asia," *Soviet Studies* 43, no. 4 (1991): 618; Olivier Roy, *The New Central Asia* (London: I. B. Tauris, 2000), 89; Kath-leen Collins, *Clan Politics and Regime Transition in Central Asia* (New York: Cambridge University Press, 2006), 132, 140.

on the black market generated substantial revenues for regional and local officials—a ruse that, when uncovered in 1983, led to massive purges of officials in
the republic.[3]

Corruption among subversive officials within Central Asian Communist
parties has been well documented, but it is less widely noted that these elites
diverted some of their unofficial revenues to the mass populace. Because Central
Asia had always lagged behind other regions developmentally, Moscow rarely
promoted indigenous Party elites to positions outside their native republics;
ambitious cadres could usually aspire only to leadership positions atop their native provinces—or, in the best case, the republic.[4] This ceiling provided Central
Asian elites with incentives to invest downward by cultivating ties with people
from the same region, rather than ingratiating themselves with upwardly mobile patrons who could carry them to prestigious posts throughout the USSR,
a strategy favored by the nomenklatura in most other republics.[5] Additionally,
within republics competition for resources along regional lines led leaders (ob-
koms) to reward followers within their regions at the expense of people in other
regions.[6]

As a result of these pressures, vertical redistribution took place within republics on several levels. For example, when rural elites were promoted to serve in
the oblast or republican capital, they would typically provide jobs or secure favors for co-villagers and co-regionalists who had moved to the city.[7] Venal Central Asian party officials would engage in "unauthorized but necessary public
construction" and "provid[e] goods and services that would otherwise be unavailable" to support people in their communities.[8] At a lower level, collective
farm directors could strengthen their legitimacy by maintaining an open home
where people in the village could stop by and avail themselves of a constant supply of expensive food.[9] Farm directors would also supply ordinary farmers with

3. Gregory Gleason, "Nationalism or Organised Crime–The Case of the Cotton Scandal in the
USSR," *Corruption and Reform* 5, no. 2 (1990): 87–108; Sergei P. Poliakov, *Everyday Islam: Religion
and Tradition in Rural Central Asia* (Armonk, N.Y.: M. E. Sharpe, 1992), chapter 7. See also James
Critchlow, "Prelude to 'Independence': How the Uzbek Party Apparatus Broke Moscow's Grip on
Elite Recruitment," in *Soviet Central Asia,* ed. William Fierman (Boulder, Colo.: Westview Press,
1991), 131.

4. Steven L. Burg, "Central Asian Elite Mobility and Political Change in the Soviet Union," *Central Asian Survey* 5, nos. 3–4 (1986): 77–89; Pauline Jones Luong, *Institutional Change and Political
Continuity in Post-Soviet Central Asia* (New York: Cambridge University Press, 2002), 70.

5. Willerton, *Patronage,* 225; Roy, *New Central Asia,* 97.

6. Jones Luong, *Institutional Change,* chapter 3.

7. Roy, *New Central Asia,* 99.

8. James Critchlow, *Nationalism in Uzbekistan* (Boulder, Colo.: Westview Press, 1991), 45.

9. The notable's unofficial obligations to his constituents included "defending the *kolkhoz* [col-
lective farm] in its dealings with the state apparatus, taking care of supplies, and redistributing part

subsidized inputs and allow them to maintain private plots for extra cash as "side payments" in exchange for compliance and political passivity.[10] In some cases, patronage networks grew into parallel power structures that rivaled the state itself. For example, in Namangan, Uzbekistan, the director of a cotton combine who presided over thirty thousand residents had created his own "small, sovereign state," replete with a police force and a prison system.[11]

When the Soviet Union dissolved in 1991, the hierarchy of governance that had administered the vast country for seventy years broke down. The extent to which the formal governance structure and informal networks from the old regime would persist varied across the successor states: in Kyrgyzstan Soviet-era patronage networks were severely weakened as the economy was privatized. Agriculture and industry fell into private hands, depriving the state of its monopoly on the distribution of resources as a means of political control. By contrast, Uzbekistan quickly recentralized the distribution of resources from Tashkent, keeping most large enterprises and collective farms in state hands, setting production quotas for cotton, and rewarding or punishing governmental officials for the economic performance of their regions. As a result, economic activity was subordinated to the political objectives of the regime.

In Kyrgyzstan, the confluence of several factors—the breakdown of old hierarchies, the state's inability to provide sufficient public services, economic liberalization, and partially competitive elections—resulted in a new institutional environment. Economic elites and those with political ambitions were free, for the first time, to innovate politically in response to developments from above and below. When the regime turned out to be less faithful to the rule of law than it had proclaimed, but strong political parties and civil society groups did not materialize to counteract the executive, independent elites took notice. Coupled with this was the growing demand of a frustrated populace for relief from their deteriorating standards of living. Together, these developments provided autonomous elites with the incentive to partially fill the void left by the state, a solution that simultaneously mitigated the deprivation felt by the masses and bolstered the position of the elites.

---

of his wealth in the form of ostentatious expenditure, which thereby reinforces his prestige." Olivier Roy, *The New Central Asia: The Creation of Nations* (New York: I. B. Tauris, 2000), 93.

10. Erika Weinthal, *State Making and Environmental Cooperation: Linking Domestic and International Politics in Central Asia* (Cambridge: MIT Press, 2002), 100.

11. Boris Rumer, *Soviet Central Asia: A Tragic Experiment* (Boston: Unwin Hyman, 1989), 151. Rumer portrays the official in question as a dictator and sadist—the prevailing Soviet view of subversive locals.

# Poverty, Portfolios, and *Plov*

Clientelism can help to consolidate or disperse power, depending on who is providing the goods.[12] Where it is a practice used by (usually ruling) parties to mobilize voters in semiauthoritarian systems or emerging democracies, clientelism tends to reinforce the regime's hold on power. For example, political machines can effectively produce favorable electoral outcomes by targeting state resources at critical constituencies.[13] Analogously, where clientelism is employed by weak or centralizing states, patron-client ties can act as the sinews that hold together an otherwise fragmented polity by providing critical links from the state to society, which can be beneficial for political consolidation.[14]

Scholars of new postcolonial states in the 1960s and 1970s, on the other hand, saw clientelism as a hindrance to state-building. Patron-client relations were viewed as a long-standing social institution that was difficult to eradicate. Local elites or "strongmen" maintained a base of support in society and enjoyed high levels of legitimacy, which gave rise to corruption, prevented the consolidation of power, and inhibited the formation of a national identity.[15]

However, these are not the only possible ways in which clientelism may affect the consolidation of power. Clientelism can also disperse power in a polity in which a regime has already consolidated power, but actors independent of the regime decide to engage in clientelism. Recognizing that providing ersatz public goods can

---

12. Clientelism is a practice that "involves asymmetric but mutually beneficial relationships of power and exchange, a nonuniversalistic quid pro quo between individuals or groups of unequal standing." Luis Roniger, "Political Clientelism, Democracy, and Market Economy," *Comparative Politics* 36, no. 3 (2004): 353.

13. Javier Auyero, *Poor People's Politics* (Durham: Duke University Press, 2000); Susan C. Stokes, "Perverse Accountability: A Formal Model of Machine Politics with Evidence from Argentina," *American Political Science Review* 99, no. 3 (2005): 315–25; Beatriz Magaloni, *Voting for Autocracy: Hegemonic Party Survival and Its Demise in Mexico* (New York: Cambridge University Press, 2006).

14. Sharon Kettering, *Patrons, Brokers, and Clients in Seventeenth-Century France* (Oxford: Oxford University Press, 1986); Guilain Denoeux, *Urban Unrest in the Middle East: A Comparative Study of Informal Networks in Egypt, Iran, and Lebanon* (Albany: State University of New York Press, 1993); Peter S. Bearman, *Relations into Rhetorics: Local Elite Social Structure in Norfolk, England, 1540–1640* (New Brunswick: Rutgers University Press, 1993); John F. Padgett and Christopher Ansell, "Robust Action and the Rise of the Medici, 1400–1434," *American Journal of Sociology* 98 (1993): 1259–1319; Anna Grzymala-Busse, "Beyond Clientelism: Incumbent State Capture and State Formation," *Comparative Political Studies* 41 (2008): 638–73.

15. James C. Scott, "Patron-Client Politics and Political Change in Southeast Asia," *American Political Science Review* 66, no. 1 (1972): 91–113; James C. Scott, *The Moral Economy of the Peasant: Rebellion and Subsistence in Southeast Asia* (New Haven: Yale University, 1976); René Lemarchand, "Political Clientelism and Ethnicity in Tropical Africa: Competing Solidarities in Nation-Building," *American Political Science Review* 66, no. 1 (1972): 68–90; Joel S. Migdal, *Strong Societies and Weak States* (Princeton: Princeton University Press, 1988).

win local support, aspiring patrons can embed themselves in society by using their private resources to complement or substitute for state functions. In doing so, they create new dependence relationships. Although allegiances are not necessarily zero-sum, insofar as independent actors take it upon themselves to deliver services that the state does not, the disposition of constituents may change in ways that favor their patron at the expense of the incumbent, giving the patron a latent source of power. To the extent that this form of clientelism undermines support for the regime and compliance with its directives, it can be considered *subversive*.[16]

Unlike in postcolonial societies, where local elites maintained a social base prior to attempts by state-builders to consolidate power, the aspirant who engages in subversive clientelism faces the burden of creating a clientele from scratch. Although the means he uses will vary depending on the society and the resources at his disposal, a useful starting point is to conceive of clientelist provision as an investment portfolio. According to Beatriz Magaloni, Alberto Diaz-Cayeros, and Federico Estevez, politicians attempt to maximize the amount of votes they receive, given a fixed level of investment, by providing the optimal combination of excludable private goods and nonexcludable public goods. On the one hand, delivering private goods is more conducive to exerting leverage over voters but requires an extensive organizational network to target and monitor likely supporters. On the other hand, public goods, although they reach more people simultaneously and do not require an organization to screen individuals, do not guarantee that recipients will behave as intended. They argue that effective candidates will provide a mix of both kinds of goods, depending on the electorate's income level, the extent of political competition, and the candidate's willingness to accept risk.[17]

This materialist approach to clientelism excludes an important nonmaterial component of vertical exchange that is not costly in monetary terms but can nonetheless be an effective means of solidifying relationships. Early anthropological research on postcolonial societies noted the affective and ritualistic, rather than purely instrumental, nature of patron-client relationships. James C. Scott and others argued that strong redistributive norms compelled those who were

---

16. Thus, the subversive aspect is a function of the *effect* of privately administered clientelism in shifting the allegiances of clients, and not a product of the type of goods provided, or even the intention of the patrons; the regime's loss of support may simply be a by-product of the patron's decision to redistribute resources for the purpose of winning elections or for self-protection, rather than because a patron seeks to undermine its authority.

17. Beatriz Magaloni, Alberto Diaz-Cayeros, and Federico Estevez, "Clientelism and Portfolio Diversification: A Model of Electoral Investment with Applications to Mexico," in *Patrons, Clients, and Policies: Patterns of Democratic Accountability and Political Competition*, ed. Herbert Kitschelt and Steven I. Wilkinson (New York: Cambridge University Press, 2007), 182–205.

better off to attend to the welfare of poorer members of a village.[18] Clients, in turn, viewed the patron's role as legitimate because of the "moral idea of reciprocity, of mutual rights and obligations, which gives them their social force."[19] In return for his largesse, the patron enjoyed psychic benefits including "growing prestige" and "a grateful clientele which helps validate [his] position in the community."[20]

Research from more contemporary settings has uncovered cases in which elite beneficence can win the support and affection of powerless or impoverished people even though it does not emanate from primordial sources of attachment. Lily Tsai, for example, argues that local government officials in China can obtain moral approval by delivering services that people in their villages desire.[21] Javier Auyero characterizes the urban poor in Argentina as grateful for useful services, such as medical care, that Peronist party brokers provide in exchange for attending rallies and voting for the party.[22] Similar forms of culturally embedded redistribution have been found to play a role in sub-Saharan African politics.[23]

In Central Asia in the 1990s, public dissatisfaction over deficits of public goods and widening inequality provided an opening for new actors to earn support from below on the basis not of traditional or primordial attachments, nor of a sense of obligation based on fear of losing benefits, but of genuine gratitude. Yet it was only in Kyrgyzstan that economic opportunities provided the means, while insecurity and ambition produced a motive, for elites to engage in clientelism.

## Clientelist Cocktails

To understand the task confronting aspiring patrons in Kyrgyzstan in their efforts to cultivate a social support base, it is useful to apply a variation of the rationalist portfolio model that not only considers a trade-off between the provision of private and collective[24] outlays, but also includes the possibility of nonmaterial

---

18. Scott, *Moral Economy*, 41.

19. Ibid., 169.

20. Ibid., 41. This view is disputed by Samuel Popkin, who pointed out that according to Scott's conception of the village, elites with unequal resources should never emerge in the first place. Samuel L. Popkin, *The Rational Peasant* (Berkeley: University of California Press, 1979), 61.

21. Lily Tsai, *Accountability without Democracy* (New York: Cambridge University Press, 2007).

22. Javier Auyero, "'From the Client's Point of View': How Poor People Perceive and Evaluate Political Clientelism," *Theory and Society* 28, no. 2 (1999): 297–334.

23. J. P. Olivier de Sardan, "A Moral Economy of Corruption in Africa?" *Journal of Modern African Studies* 37, no. 1 (1999): 25–52.

24. I use term collective rather than public to signify the fact that goods are targeted at specific communities and not intended for the benefit of the entire society. They can also be referred to as local club goods. See Kitschelt and Wilkinson, "Citizen-Politician Linkages: An Introduction," in *Patrons, Clients, and Policies*, 23.

sources of "investment." This expanded menu of options can be depicted as a typology along two dimensions: material vs. symbolic and collective vs. private.

This conceptualization captures the conventional and more visible material component of clientelism, but it also directs our attention to the cultural idiom in which it is provided, which is critical for securing public support. Symbolic gestures, whether independent of, or complementary to, material investments, can determine whether people perceive clientelist provision as beneficent or presumptuous. And because private patrons typically lack the institutional apparatus to monitor their clients' behavior that ruling parties often have, they do not wield a credible threat of punishment, so they must work to earn the genuine support of their followers to ensure their compliance.[25] The two dimensions of provision thus approximate the actual choices that confront aspiring patrons as they seek to reach into society. The typology of investment strategies, shown in table 4.1, along with specific examples, comes from fieldwork in Osh, Jalalabad, and Bishkek oblasts.

Autonomous elites decided in what proportion to invest in different forms of provision based, first, on the supply-side factor of the resources available for them to draw on. Those with money could purchase and donate goods that people lacked. If they could access and channel resources through a position in the legislature or ties with international organizations, they could steer funds or submit legislation targeted to their districts.[26] Those with personal charisma could use populist appeals and deploy cultural symbols to cultivate favorable reputations.

Demand-side considerations were also taken into account. Urban communities often desired the repair of degraded infrastructure and basic sanitation. People in rural areas preferred the construction of buildings and meeting venues. Conservative communities were more likely to demand religious facilities. Individuals would request cash handouts and loans for a variety of purposes such as medical care, home repair, and financing weddings.

Collective material contributions include facilities and infrastructure that are useful to the community but which states (or NGOs) fail to provide. Although more expensive than targeted private charity, collective projects benefit—and are observed by—many people at once, and stand as an enduring monument to the gift giver's generosity. In their choice of projects, Kyrgyz patrons would aim to

---

25. For examples of the symbolic element of clientelism in other contexts, see Shmuel N. Eisenstadt and Luis Roniger, eds., *Patrons, Clients and Friends: Interpersonal Relations and the Structure of Trust in Society* (Cambridge: Cambridge University Press, 1984); Frank O'Gorman, "Electoral Deference in 'Unreformed' England: 1760–1832," *Journal of Modern History* 56, no. 3 (1984): 392–429; Luis Roniger and Ayşe Güneş-Ayata, *Democracy, Clientelism, and Civil Society* (Boulder, Colo.: Lynne Rienner, 1994); Auyero, *Poor People's Politics*, chapter 4.

26. The term "district," when used in this chapter, refers to an electoral constituency (*izbiratel'nyi okrug*), and not a second-order administrative unit (raion) unless otherwise noted.

**Table 4.1** Typology of clientelist investment

|  | COLLECTIVE | PRIVATE |
|---|---|---|
| Material | • finance centrally located community projects<br>• fix decaying infrastructure<br>• contribute to local development projects funded by foreign aid organizations<br>• make contributions at life-cycle events | • distribute cash handouts<br>• give loans to individual suppliants<br>• award individual students for performance at school |
| Symbolic | • emphasize local origins and national authenticity<br>• champion local issues<br>• attend holiday celebrations and local life-cycle events<br>• publicize charitable deeds (e.g., rallies, ribbon-cutting ceremonies, interviews for newspapers) | • send representatives to make personal visits for congratulations and condolences (usually combined with private handouts) |

maximize the exposure of their charity and, where possible, to demonstrate their morality (sometimes seen as synonymous with religious piety) or their reverence for Kyrgyz tradition as a way of proving that they had not been corrupted by wealth or power. Thus, benefactors often built mosques because of their symbolic significance. Other common projects, because they were highly in demand, were schools, gymnasiums (*sportzaly*), bridges, and bathhouses (*bani*). Less expensive, but also material and collective, is the purchase of materials to use in these facilities, such as furniture, textbooks, and Korans. Finally, infrastructure improvements, a direct result of the withdrawal of the state, were often desired. In many cases, groups of neighbors requested—and elites provided—money to fix roads, water pipes, and electrical transformers.

Private material charity is less costly than collective donations and also produces positive externalities for the giver, since news of generosity can travel far by word-of-mouth. In many communities, poor people would arrive daily at the home or office of an elite (or his representatives) to request money. Some elites could afford to give a small amount ($5–$10) to all suppliants. They might grant larger sums for special requests, such as for an operation or help in traveling abroad to visit relatives. A popular institution with Soviet roots was to give out money to top students (*otlichniki*, in Russian parlance) at a local school, from which news was certain to circulate. Patrons with not as much cash at hand would give money only to those "who really deserve it" or, in rare cases, favor constituents from their own ethnic group.[27]

---

27. Interview, Kara-su (Osh Oblast), June 29, 2006.

A third type of charity is collective and symbolic. Giving of this sort is intended not to address people's material needs but instead to win their support by demonstrating solicitousness toward local issues. In some cases it is combined with collective material contributions. The wealthy, especially those who had moved to the capital and whose faithfulness to their roots was in some question, would work hard to prove their fidelity to, and knowledge of, Kyrgyz culture or Central Asian or Islamic traditions. They would make appearances on important holidays—including Soviet ones[28]—and sponsor events for the public, while often donating free food, usually including *plov*, and copious amounts of vodka.[29] To be true to Kyrgyz customs, they might provide sheep or—in mountainous regions—horses to slaughter. On Islamic holidays such as Hayit, which falls after a month of fasting for Ramadan, they would hand out meat and bags of flour to the poor, usually in collaboration with a local mosque. Patrons or their local representatives would also make appearances at funerals and weddings to provide small monetary contributions. Finally, they would endear themselves to youth and elders by sponsor traditional sporting events (usually wrestling or *ulak*, a local sport akin to polo, but using a sheep carcass as the ball) and award cash prizes to the winners. Parliamentary candidates running for office could be counted on to sponsor festivals or awards ceremonies in the period leading up to elections.

The final type of investment, private and symbolic, was less common than the others, as it required spending valuable time for a relatively small payoff.[30] More often, such personal visits would occur in the context of private material giving, during an election campaign, or in order to earn the support of an influential local opinion leader, such as an elder or religious figure.[31]

The types of activities witnessed in Kyrgyzstan, though expressed in local idioms, are in fact not uncommon in post-Soviet countries that have undergone economic reform. For example, Timothy Frye's survey of Russian entrepreneurs revealed that over 70 percent of firms in his sample have provided public goods ("support for educational and health institutions, aid to orphanages and

---

28. Including International Women's Day (March 8) and Victory Day (May 9).

29. Plov is a national dish made from rice and carrots. Vodka is in many ways a national drink, made from fermented grain and local river water.

30. A visit to a Kyrgyz home cannot be brief as the host is obligated to invite the guest (especially one performing a favor) in for at least tea, and more often for a full meal and several rounds of tea and vodka.

31. On the social influence of opinion leaders, see Ronald S. Burt, "The Social Capital of Opinion Leaders," *Annals of the American Academy of Political and Social Science* 566, no. 1 (1999): 37–54; Ronald S. Burt, *Brokerage and Closure: An Introduction to Social Capital* (Oxford: Oxford University Press, 2005), 84–86.

pensioners, and other forms of charity") for their region.[32] Georgi Derluguian notes that those who got rich from the shadow economy in the Caucasus would pave roads, build mosques, and send people on the hajj in order to boost their prestige.[33] Many so-called oligarchs in Russia and Ukraine, following in the footsteps of the American "robber barons" of the nineteenth century, established charitable foundations for a variety of causes in order to improve their reputations.[34] In these cases, as in Kyrgyzstan, the decline in government services left a void that entrepreneurs of various kinds—and for varying reasons—were able to fill.

## Mass Perceptions of Elites

In order for the efforts made by autonomous elites in Kyrgyzstan to pay off, the people whose allegiance is sought would need to perceive benefits from the elite's actions and respond with increased affection or support. Elites were successful in most but not all cases. The most prominent finding from fieldwork was that patrons' investment strategies succeeded in increasing their visibility; for better or worse, respondents would invariably recognize the name and have an opinion of the local elite-benefactor. Those who benefited personally or made use of charitable collective goods would develop favorable impressions of him.[35] In communities where an elite had made significant material contributions, he might come to be seen as indispensable. At other times, people might see only a cynical ploy. Whether people's lives actually improved—and whether they stood to gain by voting a local benefactor into parliament—is less certain.

In many cases, aspiring patrons were acting in a milieu in which co-villagers believed that the wealthy and powerful had a moral obligation to help. For example, numerous interviewees expected their parliamentary deputies to serve them not by passing legislation or directing transfers from the state budget (although

---

32. Timothy Frye, "Original Sin, Good Works, and Property Rights in Russia," *World Politics* 58, no. 4 (2006): 495.

33. Georgi M. Derluguian, *Bourdieu's Secret Admirer in the Caucasus: A World-System Biography* (Chicago: University of Chicago Press, 2005), 280.

34. Vladimir Pokrovsky, Andrey Allakhverdov, and Marina Astvatsaturyan, "Russian Billionaires Launch Science Fund," *Science* 291, 5510 (2001): 1878; Andrew York, "Business and Politics in Krasnoyrsk Krai," *Europe-Asia Studies* 55, no. 2 (2003): 246; Vladimir Popov, "Fiscal Federalism in Russia: Rules versus Electoral Politics," *Comparative Economic Studies* 46 (2004): 521; Marshall I. Goldman, "Putin and the Oligarchs," *Foreign Affairs* 83, no. 6 (2004): 33–44.

35. In other words, they would grant the giver enhanced prestige. William Josiah Goode, *The Celebration of Heroes: Prestige as a Social Control System* (Berkeley: University of California Press, 1978), 7. Lily Tsai calls this "moral standing." See Lily L. Tsai, "Solidarity Groups, Informal Accountability, and Local Public Goods Provision in Rural China," *American Political Science Review* 101, no. 2 (2007): 355–72.

MPs take advantage of that opportunity), but by spending their own money to help the district. When people would claim that their MP "helps" them, they usually meant that he donated his own money rather than assisted in the capacity of a public servant.[36] This expectation has been attributed to the inertial effects of the Soviet "nanny state," which inculcated dependence on the state to take care of people's problems.[37] Yet the belief that elected or prospective MPs should redistribute their personal wealth in exchange for support can also be seen as a legitimate desire for distributive justice in a political system in which money and politics are so intertwined—where most members of parliament are businessmen, where votes are purchased, and where politicians habitually avail themselves of the spoils of office.

Being aware of people's expectations and past experiences, patrons correctly discerned that charity, or the perception of it, could enhance their prestige. They worked hard to make their investments appear philanthropic and did little to discourage misperceptions that worked in their favor. In some cases, people I interviewed reported hearing that an elite had financed a project, such as a mosque or school, but could not recall when it was built or where it was located. Upon further investigation, it often turned out that the expenditure was far lower than the informant had believed. In several cases, credit was mistakenly given to an elite for single-handedly financing a new building project, when in fact it had been paid for by the government or an NGO.[38] Members of parliament could boost their prestige while saving money by steering funds through the state budget or lobbying NGOs to implement projects in their district. They could then claim to have donated the money out of their own pockets—or at least not correct the perception that they had—and reap the benefits without paying the costs.[39] Some interviewees spoke vaguely of an elite's charitable activities, saying, for example, "he always helps the poor," but could not recall a single concrete case of such giving.[40]

Despite an elite's best efforts at shaping public perceptions, sometimes cynicism prevailed. Respondents who were especially alienated by corruption in

---

36. Interviews, Osh, November 2, 2003; Aksy, April 10, 2004; Bishkek, June 16, 2005; Jalalabad, April 20, 2005, June 20, 2006.

37. See Sarah M. Terry, "Thinking about Post Communist Transitions: How Different Are They?" *Slavic Review* 52, no. 2 (1993): 333–37; Stephen Kotkin, "Modern Times: The Soviet Union and the Interwar Conjuncture," *Kritika: Explorations in Russian and Eurasian History* 2, no. 1 (2001): 111–64; Kelly McMann, "The Shrinking of the Welfare State: Central Asians' Assessments of Soviet and Post-Soviet Governance," in *Everyday Life in Central Asia*, ed. Jeff Sahadeo and Russell Zanca (Bloomington: Indiana University Press, 2007), 234.

38. Interviews, Kizil-too District, Jalalabad, June 21, 2006; Alai District, Osh, June 28, 2006.

39. Interviews, Jalalabad, June 20, 2006; Kizil-Too District, June 21, 2006.

40. Interviews, Kara-su District, Osh, June 29, 2006; Aravan District, Osh, June 30, 2006.

the political system projected their disgust onto all elites—including their putative benefactors—and highlighted the instrumental nature of their actions.
They noted that patrons visited frequently and built roads and schools in the
six months before an election, then disappeared for four years until the next
campaign season.[41] In some districts, people applied a double standard to patrons depending on their origins: where competing candidates came from different communities, voters would remain immune to the appeals of the nonlocal
candidate—for example, accusing him of trying to "buy" the election—while
imputing only the best of intentions on their local candidate, who was engaged
in the same activities.[42] Critical but pragmatic citizens understood the cynical
games that elites played to enhance their stature but acknowledged that their
community in fact derived some benefits in the process.

## Quantitative Evidence for Subversive Clientelism

How widespread was subversive clientelism? Was it particular only to Kyrgyzstan,
which privatized and partially opened its political system, or did it also occur in
Uzbekistan, despite its deficit of economic openness and political competition?
Results from my 2005 survey provide answers to these questions. Based on what
I argued in earlier chapters, the data should show that reliance on independent
elites for economic assistance is more widespread in Kyrgyzstan than in Uzbekistan. To this end, a series of questions was asked to determine whom people
turned to for financial and other assistance, highlighting the role of the state,
businessmen, and politicians. Data was also gathered on respondents' gender,
income, age, education, religiosity, urban or rural residence, and ethnicity, all
of which could plausibly account for variation in clientelism and are therefore
included as controls in the statistical analyses.[43]

41. Interviews, Osh, June 24, 2004; Bishkek, June 17, 2006, June 19, 2006; Jalalabad, April 17,
2005, June 23, 2006.

42. Interviews, Nariman District, Osh, April 29, 2005.

43. To ascertain income, respondents were asked, "Which of the following best describes the level
of well-being of your household?" (1) It is difficult for us to afford even basic goods and food, (2) We
can afford food, but it is difficult for us to pay for clothes and utilities, (3) We can afford food, clothing, and utilities, but we cannot afford such things as a new television or refrigerator, (4) We can afford food, clothing, utilities, and such things as a television or refrigerator, (5) We can buy everything
we need. Because a linear relationship cannot be assumed, the responses were included in the regres-
sions as dummy variables, Income2 to Income5, with the lowest category excluded. Income2 was
the second lowest income level and Income5 was the highest. Education is broken down into three
categories, with dummy variables included for secondary school and higher education, while the
category "less than secondary school" was excluded. Questions on religiosity were only asked of self-
declared Muslims, who comprised 95% of the Uzbekistan sample and 78% of the Kyrgyzstan sample,

The first question asked where people turn for a loan: "If you had a big project to do, such as repair a house, put on a wedding or send a relative abroad, and were short of cash, to whom would you turn for a loan?" Respondents were given a list of sources and asked to select their top three choices in order. I later coded those sources as state or non-state.[44] Given the diverging economic and political opportunities in Kyrgyzstan and Uzbekistan, we would expect respondents in Uzbekistan to be more reliant on the state than in Kyrgyzstan.[45] In fact, this is what we find: all else being equal, an Uzbek was 30 percent more likely than a Kyrgyz respondent to name a state entity as one of their top three choices, with a 95 percent confidence interval from 25 percent to 35 percent.[46] Secondary and higher education were negative and significant, and urban residence was positive and significant.

What about the tendency to turn to nonstate entities? Kyrgyz are significantly more likely than Uzbeks to do so. In particular, Kyrgyz are 9 percent more likely to name a businessman as one of three responses than Uzbeks, all else being equal (95 percent CI: 0–26).[47] Residence in a rural area is also highly significant.

---

which approximates officially reported proportions. The variable included in the analysis is an additive index of three questions: "How often do you pray?"; "How often do you attend mosque?"; and "How often do you fast?" The combined result ranged from 3 to 16, with a higher number indicating greater religious observance. For ethnicity, I coded respondents as 1 if they stated their nationality as Russian, Ukrainian, or Belorussian (Slavic), and 0 if other (mostly Central Asian).

44. Choices included local businessman, state organization, bank, village/city council, friend, relative, neighbor (who is neither friend nor relative), co-worker, mosque, and clan relation. State organization, bank, and village/city council were coded as state entities. Local businessman, friend, relative, neighbor, co-worker, mosque, and clan relation were coded as nonstate. Banks were coded as state in Uzbekistan and nonstate in Kyrgyzstan to reflect the dominant mode of private or state ownership. Mosques, even though highly regulated, were coded as nonstate, since loans, to the extent they took place, would likely occur "off the books" and be perceived by both parties as a private transaction. Changing the coding of banks or mosques does not alter the results.

45. In this discussion, I use "Kyrgyz" interchangeably with "resident of Kyrgyzstan" and "Uzbek" with "resident of Uzbekistan," and not as a reference to ethnicity.

46. I use a logit model because the dependent variable is dichotomous. For this and subsequent estimations, probabilities are the means of 1,000 simulated predicted probabilities estimated using the Zelig function of R. See Kosuke Imai, Gary King, and Olivia Lau, "Zelig: Everyone's Statistical Software," 2009, http://gking.harvard.edu/zelig; and Kosuke Imai, Gary King, and Olivia Lau, "Toward a Common Framework for Statistical Analysis and Development," *Journal of Computational and Graphical Statistics* 17, no. 4 (2008): 892–913. For simulations, I allowed the country variable to vary but set continuous explanatory variables at their means and dummy variables at their modes. I also ran an OLS regression using a weighted index of responses to the question as the dependent variable. Responses were weighted as follows: 3 points for a state entity as the first choice, 2 points for second, and 1 point for third. Then the three responses were summed so that the resulting variable ranged from 0 to 6. The results of the analysis are substantively the same as with logit.

47. Estimated using logit. Local businessman was coded as 1 and all other choices as 0. I also ran an ordered logit regression using as the dependent variable an index ranging from 0 to 3, weighted according to whether the respondent named a businessman as his/her first, second, or third response. The result was substantively the same.

A second question asked about influence: "Who do consider the most influ-ential person in your village/*mahalla*?" Respondents were asked to select one choice from a list of relevant positions, which I later coded as state or nonstate.[48] Here, as well, we would expect a significant national-level difference in terms of the weight of state vs. nonstate actors in daily life. As it turned out, Uzbeks were indeed more likely than Kyrgyz to name a state entity as influential: 6 per-cent more likely, holding other variables constant (95 percent CI: 1–10)—but perhaps surprisingly, respondents from both countries were statistically equally likely to cite a nonstate entity.[49] This may be because Uzbeks considered local (nonstate) actors influential based on cultural, religious, or moral authority, rather than because of their material resources. To check this, I also tested the propensity to name as the most influential person (1) a local businessman, and (2) a member of parliament (MP) (roughly 80 percent of whom in Kyrgyz-stan are wealthy and a source of revenue for a constituency[50]). Respondents in Kyrgyzstan turn out to be 5 percent more likely than Uzbeks to name a busi-nessmen (95 percent CI: 0–27) and 8 percent more likely to name their MP (95 percent CI: 0–60), despite being less likely than Uzbeks overall to cite any influential person.

The previous result could be interpreted to imply that parliamentary deputies are considered more influential in Kyrgyzstan only because parliament is more powerful vis-à-vis the president than its counterpart in Uzbekistan. To check this, another question probed more deeply into the reasons that people select their MPs. When asked to rank the qualities people considered most important in their MPs, Kyrgyz respondents were 5 percent more likely than Uzbeks to name prosperity as one of the three most important characteristics of their MP (95 percent CI: 3–9).[51]

---

48. Head of village committee/community leader, city mayor, district head, district police chief, head of a (state) enterprise, and urban community leader were coded as state. Member of parliament, elder (not government representative), local religious authority, local businessman, a respected per-son (educated, experienced, cultured, influential, and so forth) who is none of the above, and wealthy farmer were coded as nonstate.

49. This was possible because a number of respondents selected no one as influential. Thus, Uzbeks were in general more likely than Kyrgyz to identify an influential person.

50. Interview, National Democratic Institute, Bishkek, July 5, 2006.

51. Respondents were asked to rank, in order, the three most important qualities of an MP from the following list: personal acquaintance, blood relative, comes from a good family, honest, expe-rienced, hard-working, prosperous, poor, educated/intelligent, and member of a political party. In addition to the binomial logit analysis, I also ran an ordered logit estimation using a dependent vari-able that takes into account the order of the responses. If prosperity was given as a first choice it was weighted as 3, second choice as 2, third choice as 1, and no mention of prosperity was given a 0. The variable ranged from 0 to 3. The result of this estimation is substantively the same as with the dichotomous measure.

The results of the above logit analyses are displayed in table 4.2. Estimates of differences in predicted probabilities for residents of Kyrgyzstan and Uzbekistan are shown in table 4.3.

These results suggest the importance of independent sources of wealth in Kyrgyzstan as compared with Uzbekistan. Kyrgyz are significantly more likely than Uzbeks to seek loans from nonstate entities, especially businessmen; to perceive businessmen as influential; and to perceive wealth as an important attribute of their elected representatives. These insights are consistent with the argument that, where economic reforms were carried out (i.e., Kyrgyzstan), there was redistribution from the rich to the poor, and wealth can be converted into influence. Through their connections to autonomous elites—and their dependence on them—many people in Kyrgyzstan developed a stake in the continued prosperity of elites and access to the resources of those who were helping their community. In Uzbekistan, by contrast, there were few alternatives to the state as a means to solve problems, parliament did not represent a source of influence or aid, and, insofar as respondents knew of particular businessmen, they were not likely to see them as a source of financial assistance or influence.

# Profiles of Patrons in Kyrgyzstan

Whereas statistical analysis provided evidence of the greater prevalence of subversive clientelist networks in Kyrgyzstan than Uzbekistan, it is sufficient only to demonstrate the phenomenon at a high level of abstraction. To give a better sense of the substance of subversive clientelism, it is necessary to supplement the numbers with more detailed contextual evidence. Several brief biographies of elite benefactors will help fill in the picture.

The profiles that follow reveal the importance of the institutional context in the decisions of elites to invest in communities. They show how patrons emerged from within the economically and politically favorable setting of Kyrgyzstan in the 1990s, where privatization and minimal barriers to wealth creation played an essential role in the economic success of the new rich. They also highlight the fungibility of political and economic power, showing that a position in a ministry or close ties to those with access to state resources could help elites obtain the start-up capital or institutional access needed to generate wealth, which they could in turn parlay into independent political careers. Finally, the profiles hint at the subversive cast of clientelism, as autonomous elites were often aware of their role in substituting for state functions and knew that their actions gave them informal political influence, but they did not necessarily intend—at least openly—to use their power to oppose the regime.

**Table 4.2** Predictors of subversive clientelism

| | STATE LOAN | BUSINESS LOAN | INFLUENTIAL STATE ENTITY | INFLUENTIAL NONSTATE ENTITY | INFLUENTIAL BUSINESSMAN | INFLUENTIAL MEMBER OF PARLIAMENT | RICH MEMBER OF PARLIAMENT |
|---|---|---|---|---|---|---|---|
| Residence in Kyrgyzstan | -1.44*** | .97*** | -.23* | .05 | .79* | 2.77*** | .74*** |
| | (.13) | (.18) | (.10) | (.10) | (.38) | (.44) | (.19) |
| Male | -.24 | .15 | -.22* | .189 | -.19 | -.12 | -.05 |
| | (.13) | (.16) | (.10) | (.10) | (.36) | (.25) | (.18) |
| Income2[a] | -.12 | -.40 | .09 | -.01 | -.65 | -.27 | -.11 |
| | (.21) | (.26) | (.17) | (.16) | (.58) | (.49) | (.32) |
| Income3 | .11 | -.41 | .18 | -.11 | -.33 | -.09 | .04 |
| | (.20) | (.26) | (.17) | (.16) | (.54) | (.48) | (.31) |
| Income4 | .04 | -.52 | -.06 | .04 | -.54 | -.25 | -.10 |
| | (.27) | (.35) | (.22) | (.21) | (.76) | (.58) | (.40) |
| Income5 | .47 | -.74 | .57* | -.52 | -.65 | -15.50 | -15.22 |
| | (.35) | (.52) | (.29) | (.29) | (1.11) | (746.00) | (481.90) |
| Religiosity | -.09 | .66 | -.12 | .38 | .77 | -.57 | .81 |
| | (.37) | (.48) | (.30) | (.29) | (1.00) | (-.72) | (.53) |
| Slavic | .31 | -12.88 | 1.00 | -.65 | -12.47 | -15.30 | .19 |
| | (.71) | (385.97) | (.57) | (.57) | (655.49) | (1620.00) | (1.05) |
| Age | .01 | -.01 | .00 | -.00 | -.01 | .01 | -.03*** |
| | (.00) | (.01) | (.00) | (.00) | (.01) | (.01) | (.01) |
| Secondary education | -.66*** | .02 | .33* | -.22 | -.62 | -.39 | .44 |
| | (.20) | (.26) | (.16) | (.15) | (.49) | (.35) | (.27) |

Continued

**Table 4.2** Predictors of subversive clientelism (*Continued*)

| | STATE LOAN | BUSINESS LOAN | INFLUENTIAL STATE ENTITY | INFLUENTIAL NONSTATE ENTITY | INFLUENTIAL BUSINESSMAN | INFLUENTIAL MEMBER OF PARLIAMENT | RICH MEMBER OF PARLIAMENT |
|---|---|---|---|---|---|---|---|
| Higher | -.74** | -.19 | .26 | -.26 | -.54 | -.08 | -.33 |
| education | (.24) | (.32) | (.19) | (.19) | (.61) | (.41) | (.32) |
| Urban | .54*** | -1.48*** | -.19 | -.10 | .24 | .62* | -.15 |
| | (.13) | (.27) | (.11) | (.11) | (.39) | (.26) | (.21) |
| Constant | .17 | -2.05 | -.54 | .22 | -3.19*** | -5.00 | -1.69*** |
| | (.35) | (.46) | (.29) | (.28) | (.93) | (.79) | (.50) |
| N | 1365 | 1669 | 1670 | 1669 | 1670 | 1670 | 1670 |

*Notes*: All entries are logit estimates. Robust standard errors are in parentheses. Continuous variables are evaluated at their means and dummy variables other than country of residence are evaluated at their modes. *p<.05, **p<.1, ***p<.001

[a]Income1, as the reference category, is left out of the regression.

**Table 4.3**  First differences in expected values of subversive clientelism in Kyrgyzstan and Uzbekistan

| | KYRGYZSTAN | UZBEKISTAN | DIFFERENCE | 95% CONFIDENCE OF INTERVAL OF DIFFERENCES | |
|---|---|---|---|---|---|
| State loan | .18 | .48 | −.30 | −.35 | −.25 |
| Business loan | .28 | .19 | .09 | .00 | .26 |
| Influential state entity | .40 | .46 | −.06 | −.10 | −.01 |
| Influential nonstate entity | .52 | .51 | .01 | −.04 | .06 |
| Influential businessman | .25 | .20 | .05 | .00 | .27 |
| Influential member of parliament | .41 | .33 | .08 | .00 | .60 |
| Rich member of parliament | .11 | .06 | .05 | .03 | .09 |

In Osh, Kyrgyzstan's second city, plentiful economic opportunities coupled with low public goods provision gave rise to several major patrons, one of whom was Davran Sobirov.[52] Like many businessmen who made their fortunes in the 1990s, Sobirov took advantage of his influential position within the Communist Party hierarchy in the late Soviet period. Born in Osh in 1953, he studied civil engineering at the Tashkent Polytechnic Institute in the Uzbek Republic. Returning to Osh, he worked as a technician at the state gas company and was promoted to manager. In 1979, he was appointed deputy secretary of the city Communist Party committee (*gorkom*), and then head of the Communist Youth League (Komsomol) in Osh, with responsibility for thirty-five thousand members. In 1989, at the height of Gorbachev's reforms, Sobirov was appointed vice-mayor of Osh and the next year won a seat in the Kyrgyz Supreme Soviet in the republic's first competitive elections.[53]

In a more liberal economic environment and with access to the economic levers of power, he took up business in 1990, importing liquid natural gas from

52. On the economic opportunities available in Osh, see Kelly M. McMann, *Economic Autonomy and Democracy: Hybrid Regimes in Russia and Kyrgyzstan* (Cambridge: University Press, 2006), 157–62.

53. On the historic election, which led to Akaev's rise to the presidency, see Eugene Huskey, "Kyrgyzstan: The Fate of Political Liberalization," in *Conflict, Cleavage, and Change in Central Asia and the Caucasus*, ed. Karen Dawisha and Bruce Parrott (New York: Cambridge University Press, 1997), 253.

Russia and Kazakhstan. In 1991, he founded the Uzbek National Cultural Center, devoted to advancing the interests of Uzbeks in Kyrgyzstan, and created an Uzbek-language television station in 1995, marking his introduction as a patron and advocate of Osh's Uzbek community. In 1997, he became the head of the Osh city gas company (Gorgaz). After Uzbekistan stopped supplying gas to southern Kyrgyzstan over a pricing dispute, he negotiated with his old colleagues in Uzbekistan to continue deliveries, earning the public's respect in the process. In addition to his media concerns, he also purchased a hotel and a glass factory.

Sobirov used his wealth and influence in part for philanthropic ends, targeted mostly at the Uzbek community of Osh. As the head of Gorgaz, not only did he work out payment plans for people who were behind in their payments but he also occasionally made individual exceptions by forgiving debts entirely and paying the debt out of his own pocket. Over the years (and especially before elections) Sobirov financed the construction of buildings in Uzbek communities, including a mosque and a school.[54] For the opening of the latter, President Askar Akaev flew in to attend the ceremony, which was shown on Kyrgyz television. People in Sobirov's community, including community leaders, would appeal to Sobirov when a problem arose and money was required.[55]

In return for his largesse, Sobirov was elected to parliament four times and became one of the most influential politicians in Osh. With his advocacy of minority interests and his perceived authenticity as a native Uzbek speaker in a city where much of the intelligentsia preferred Russian, Sobirov attained the status of a near-cultlike figure among Osh Uzbeks, who constitute half of the city's population of 250,000.[56] He would later rely on this support to rescue his political career.[57]

---

54. Interview with Davran Sobirov, Osh, December 24, 2003.

55. Interviews, Osh, June 24, 2005, June 27, 2005, June 28, 2005.

56. A survey of Uzbeks carried out in 2002 by the Uzbek Cultural Center in Osh found that more respondents (71%) considered Davran the "leader" of Uzbeks than any other Uzbek elite.

57. In 2000, Sobirov's opponents for parliament had him preemptively disqualified as a result of a controversial television advertisement that violated a prohibition on ethnic incitement. In response, Sobirov hired a political activist who maintained close ties with the Osh elite to organize protests on his behalf. The activist convened a group of loyalists who went to designated parts of the city to spread word of Sobirov's case and urge people to take to the streets. Over several days, more than a thousand people protested on Sobirov's behalf, with the highest representation coming from Sobirov's *mahalla* and employees of his firm, Gorgaz. The unexpected show of numbers led the election commission to reverse the decision. A pensioner from Sobirov's neighborhood, when asked why people protested, explained that his community leader had walked around the neighborhood saying, "Davran Sobirov helped us, [so] we should support him." In the end, Sobirov was reinstated and easily won reelection. The episode indicated that latent public support, with minimal effort, could be converted into people power. Interviews, Muhammad, Osh, June 27, 2004; Tolqinbek, Osh, July 4, 2004.

Another pair of elite benefactors in Osh is Alisher and Hulkar Sobirov (neither related to Davran). Alisher began his career in the security services of the Ministry of Internal Affairs and used his position to move into business by investing in restaurants. He won his first seat in parliament in 1995. His wife, Hulkar, worked as an accountant in the Ministry of Trade before capitalizing on her husband's popularity and influence to win a seat on the Osh City Council in 2004. Both Sobirovs became increasingly philanthropic as they became wealthier. As I was conducting an interview in Alisher Sobirov's district, his lawyer came to assess the progress of a community gym that was under construction across the street, courtesy of a donation by Alisher. The community leader I was interviewing confessed that his *mahalla* was dependent on "the Sobirovs" because the state did not provide enough funds.[58]

In the run-up to the city council elections, Hulkar provided charity to her district. She started an organization (Elim Uchun, or "For My People") devoted to alleviating poverty; opened a sewing workshop that employed 75 workers and provided free sewing lessons to 37 local girls; donated 100,000 som ($2,500) for micro-credit in units of 3,000 som per person at 10 percent interest; and handed out the equivalent of welfare benefits to 120 poor residents of the community. Unsurprisingly, she won her seat with one of the highest vote counts in the city.[59]

A community benefactor outside of Osh, Zaibiddin, maintained a lower profile but exemplified the same relationship between philanthropy and political ambition of the previous examples.[60] Interview subjects in the neighborhood had told me that Zaibiddin was the most active member of the community. After locating his house, my assistant informed his wife that we wanted to speak with her husband. She immediately responded by asking whether we needed money. The house did not stand out from others, nor did the owner appear to have a car, which would be atypical for the "new rich" of the area. Yet Zaibiddin had managed to make major financial contributions to the community, in part through "rich friends"—as he put it—in his *gap*,[61] among them a factory director and several entrepreneurs. Zaibiddin himself appeared to be involved in trading at the nearby Kara-su bazaar, the largest in ex-Soviet Central Asia,[62] admitting that he regularly traveled to Iran and the Gulf states, though he did not reveal the source of his income.

---

58. Interview, Saidjon, Osh, November 2, 2003.

59. Interview with Hulkar Sobirova, Osh, June 20, 2004.

60. He requested that I not report his last name.

61. A *gap* is a social and material support network, usually of men, that meets regularly to share food and engage in discussion.

62. On the importance of the Kara-su bazaar, see Regine A. Spector, "Securing Property in Contemporary Kyrgyzstan," *Post-Soviet Affairs* 24, no. 2 (2008): 149–76.

Zaibiddin earned public support primarily by building and repairing local infrastructure. A former employee of the gas company, in 1994 he used connections to import pipes and gas from Uzbekistan to supply 460 people with gas. He lobbied to obtain two hectares from the district government to expand the local cemetery, negotiated with Andijan's governor to provide water pipes to channel water from the Kara-su River, and contributed to the repair of schools, mosques, and a kindergarten; financed weddings for the poor; built several houses; and settled people's gas and electricity debts with the city. Additionally, he helped negotiate the release of nine local men who had been arrested for suspected membership in Hizb ut-Tahrir.

When asked why he devoted so much time and money to help others, Zaibiddin answered, tersely, that he acts because the government does not, and because Islamic principles dictate that the rich help the poor. Along these lines, he argued that the government would better serve the people if it adopted the principles of Sharia, or Islamic law. Despite his outspoken distaste for the government, Zaibiddin had held political office, working as a community leader from 1990 to 1993, a deputy on the city council from 1999 to 2004, and as Akaev's local political representative (*doverennoe litso*) in the 1995 presidential election.[63] Since he had been active in community politics since 1990, it was not clear which came first—political influence or access to wealth. Clearly the two reinforced each other.

Examples of elite benefactors abounded in other regions of Kyrgyzstan. Outside of Jalalabad, Abdumutalip Hakimov, the owner of a large cotton factory who won a seat in parliament in 2005, built a mosque three years before the elections and paid for the construction of two bridges. He would regularly sponsor holiday celebrations and reward highly performing students with his own money. For his overall contributions, his constituents named the school that Hakimov attended, and the street where it stands, in honor of Hakimov's father.[64] In Barpy in the same region, Kamchibek Tashiev, the owner of a large chain of gas stations, ran for parliament unsuccessfully in 1995 and 2000. In the hope of increasing his popularity, Tashiev refurbished a school, paid to install a drinking water system in a village, lent out farming supplies without interest, and helped individual poor residents who asked for money, among other charitable ventures.[65] He ultimately succeeded in winning a seat.

Even in and near the capital, Bishkek, patrons stepped in to supplant an unresponsive state. Kubatbek Baibolov, formerly an official in the KGB who used his advantageous position to acquire part of a large shopping plaza, built a

63. Interview, Zaibiddin, Kara-su, June 29, 2004.
64. Interview, Suzak District, Jalalabad, June 22, 2006.
65. Interviews, Barpy District, Jalalabad, June 23, 2006.

community center with an engraving on the front entrance proclaiming that Baibolov had built it; regularly paid for repairs of transformers, water pipes, and roads; and threw lavish parties on holidays such as Navruz, which involved slaughtering a horse.[66] Baibolov later embarked on a political career and ran for parliament unopposed in his district. In Bishkek proper, Roman Shin, a Russian-speaking ethnic Korean who earned his wealth from casinos, opened a charitable fund through which he financed roads, funerals, and clothes for orphans, all of which he documented in brochures that he distributed during the 2005 parliamentary election campaign. He beat out four competitors to win a seat in the first round.[67]

## Potential Patrons in Uzbekistan

Because of the restrictive institutional setting in Uzbekistan, cases of nonstate charity are rarer than in Kyrgyzstan. This is the case because most wealth is concentrated in the hands of the state, which limits the opportunities for private business, and because the national legislature has little real authority. In my fieldwork in Uzbekistan, I was able to uncover examples of relatively prosperous small business owners (twenty employees or less) in major cities, and of nonwealthy individuals held in local esteem for various reasons, such as their moral or spiritual qualities, seniority, or family lineage. However, I came across no examples of individuals who possessed *both* independent wealth and a local support base in Tashkent, Namangan, or Karshi.

As chapter 3 explained, Uzbekistan operates a Soviet-style system of state control over agriculture and large enterprises, which not only provided few openings for nonstate actors to provide collective goods but also created disincentives for state officials to provide local charity "off-budget" and claim credit. State officials, such as directors of cooperative farms and the heads of city and village committees and *mahallas*, had some discretion in how to distribute resources—and a fair amount might end up in their private bank accounts—but they owed their livelihood and prospects for advancement to the state. As in the Soviet Union, the center rotated regional and district leaders to prevent their capture by local interest groups.[68] Given these constraints, defiant officials would have little to

---

66. Interviews, Bishkek, June 16, 2006, June 17, 2006.

67. Interview, journalist, Bishkek, June 15, 2006. His success came in spite of the fact that there are very few ethnic Koreans in Kyrgyzstan.

68. Alisher Ilkhamov, "The Limits of Centralization: Regional Challenges in Uzbekistan," in *The Transformation of Central Asia,* ed. Pauline Jones Luong (Ithaca: Cornell University Press, 2004), 169–70.

gain—and much to lose if suspected of subverting the regime—by developing their own support base.

When there was nonstate service delivery, it was provided by firms under pressure from local authorities and was not seen by the providers as an opportunity for self-promotion or advancement. Local officials operating with constrained budgets felt an obligation, partly as a legacy from the Soviet era, to provide social assistance to the poor and to prevent frustration from boiling over. In order to accomplish this, they often levied informal taxes on small and medium enterprises[69] or compelled heads of large enterprises to directly finance public projects, such as schools, swimming pools, and waste removal. In Uzbekistan's suffocating political economy, businessmen asked to sacrifice in this manner might see their contribution as an opportunity to please officials who have the power to tax and harass them rather than as an opportunity to earn public support.[70]

Other local actors had authority but few material resources. Almost every community I visited had *aksakals* (elders; literally "white beards") who had earned respect due to their seniority and sometimes the prestige of their profession. Some families enjoyed elevated status as descendents of the pre-Russian aristocracy (*ok suiak*—"white bone") or from reputed lineage from the Prophet.[71] A more contentious source of local authority is religious influence. In the independence period, as during the Soviet era, sometimes village imams led communities of believers who practiced Islam outside the state's supervision. The government, perceiving unofficial Islam as a threat, worked to co-opt, arrest, or exile popular imams before their influence could rise too high.

Uzbekistan prevented the advent of subversive clientelism through the creation of an institutional setting that ensured the dominance of the state in allocating resources. Small businessmen were preoccupied with avoiding the coercive power of the state in order to retain their revenues, which rarely grew to the level of some Kyrgyz private businesses. Others, who possessed informal authority in society, lacked independent means of earning income. As a result, the

---

69. Pauline Jones Luong, "Political Obstacles to Economic Reform in Uzbekistan, Kyrgyzstan, and Tajikistan: Strategies to Move Ahead," paper presented at the Lucerne Conference of the CIS-7 Initiative, January 20–22, 2003, 20.

70. Interviews, Karshi, May 8, 2004, May 11, 2004; Namangan, August 23, 2004, August 24, 2004.

71. See Sergei Abashin, "Ok suiak: musul'manskaia elita tsentral'noi Azii," *Central Asia and the Caucasus* 6 (2000); Anita Sengupta, *The Formation of the Uzbek Nation-state: A Study in Transition* (Lanham, Md.: Lexington Books, 2003), 60–61; Eric McGlinchey, "The Making of Militants: The State and Islam in Central Asia," *Comparative Studies of South Asia, Africa and the Middle East* 25, no. 3 (2005): 554–66.

overall configuration of power in Uzbekistan changed little from independence until 2005.[72]

In Kyrgyzstan, where the economic environment permitted the independent generation of revenue and the political system offered alternative paths to power, the environment was conducive to subversive clientelism. In many cases, new elites played the role of a surrogate state in their communities by providing material collective goods, such as roads, mosques, and electric lines, and making symbolic appeals emphasizing their morality and fidelity to local traditions. The result of patrons' partial substitution for state functions was not only beneficial to both elites and communities but was also subversive, in that it redirected citizens' allegiance from the regime to other actors. By contrast, in Uzbekistan, where the state strictly limited opportunities to generate wealth and accrue autonomous political support, the conditions were highly unfavorable to establishing subversive clientelist relationships. Although the Uzbek state, like Kyrgyzstan's, failed to meet people's needs, new ties between elites and ordinary citizens that might threaten the regime's hold on power were largely averted.

The contrast between the political configurations of Uzbekistan and Kyrgyzstan fifteen years after independence shows that economic policies can have major implications for the possibilities for political change. Some observers of the postsocialist region have argued, with a sense of resignation, that geography or culture are determinant in shaping political outcomes, enabling rapid democratization in the case of Central Europe and the Baltic states, while dooming Central Asia and, to a lesser extent, the Caucasus, to a fate of perpetual backwardness and tyranny.[73] The findings of the last three chapters suggest otherwise—agency, although not the only variable, can nonetheless heavily influence a country's political and economic development. Despite their shared geography, common predicaments in the late 1980s, and other surface similarities, by 2005 Uzbekistan and Kyrgyzstan differed in many respects. Kyrgyzstan, due to its

---

72. One prominent case in Uzbekistan saw philanthropy translate into social support, an exception that proved the rule. Twenty-three businessmen in the city of Andijan, who were later arrested and charged with membership in an extremist organization, had provided jobs, donated money to the poor, and built schools and orphanages for the community. After their arrest, thousands of people came out to protest, indicating that the businessmen, through their charity, had won significant public support. See chapter 7 for more detail.

73. See Patricia Carley, "The Soviet Legacy and the Prospects for Civil Society in Central Asia," in *Political Culture and Civil Society in Russia and the New States of Eurasia,* ed. Vladimir Tismaneanu (Armonk, N.Y.: M. E. Sharpe, 1995); Jeffrey S. Kopstein and David A. Reilly, "Geographic Diffusion and the Transformation of the Postcommunist World," *World Politics* 53, no. 1 (2000): 1–37; M. Steven Fish, "The Dynamics of Democratic Erosion," in *Postcommunism and the Theory of Democracy,* ed. Richard D. Anderson Jr., M. Steven Fish, Stephen E. Hanson, Philip G. Roeder (Princeton: Princeton University Press, 2001).

geopolitical location, was susceptible to antidemocratic influences from Russia and China, yet it nonetheless stood out from its neighbors. The fact that Kyrgyzstan was pluralistic, though not quite democratic, was a consequence of Akaev's policies, which altered the balance of power between the state and society in favor of the latter.

From here, the narrative turns to Kyrgyzstan alone, and the ability of autonomous elites who developed a support base to mobilize their communities in exigent situations. The perspective also shifts from a focus on the medium-term factors affecting the balance of power to an analysis of how the actors described in the last three chapters—independent elites and ordinary people—are capable of responding when their interests are threatened. To this end, the regime itself becomes an actor. The interaction of these three forces—the regime, independent embedded elites, and the poor—would determine whether antiregime mobilization would occur, and the extent to which it threatened the regime's survival.

# 5

# MOBILIZATION IN
# RURAL KYRGYZSTAN

The last three chapters have described the process whereby elites independent of the regime in Kyrgyzstan sought to defend their positions through the cultivation of support bases in poor communities—subversive clientelism—and through ad hoc collaboration with other elites. This chapter details the innovative and unlikely response of an elite with such a support base when faced with a challenge from above: a peaceful protest movement in rural Kyrgyzstan that involved nearly ten thousand people at its peak and continued for ten months. The Aksy protests can best be understood as the joint product of strategies adopted by communities to cope with collective problems, and the logic of self-preservation in uncertain institutional environments, which pushes insecure elites to seek out informal sources of protection from below.[1] In 2002, member of parliament (MP) Azimbek Beknazarov contested an abuse of power by the president by mobilizing his supporters, thus transforming community social networks into a political weapon.

This and the next chapter will illustrate how elites utilize community networks to bring about mobilization against the regime. This chapter, detailing the smaller of the two events, emphasizes processes within communities rather than links between them. Resource scarcity and shared adversity in Aksy's villages had led to the development of dense social capital, which binds people together and aids in problem solving. Beknazarov, who was born and raised in Aksy and

---

1. Aksy is a district (raion), the second tier of government in Kyrgyzstan.

was perceived as a benefactor there, tapped into that social capital when he was arrested and mobilized supporters in his defense.

The case study of the larger and more politically consequential Tulip Revolution in chapter 6 shows how local-level mobilization processes can be scaled up even further, thanks to cross-regional interelite ties and a provocation affecting numerous elites simultaneously. Candidates who lost parliamentary elections activated community networks, as in Aksy, but then confederated to generate a nationwide protest against the regime. Although the mobilization processes within these communities were similar to those in Aksy, the purpose of the chapter is to show how subversive clientelism and cross-regional elite networks *together* can threaten, and even topple, a government. The emphasis in the next chapter will therefore be on the strategic interaction among elites, and between elites and the regime.

In order to elucidate how elites can mobilize communities as leverage against more powerful actors, I examine the processes that led to successful mobilization in Aksy. I first analyze the economic and political environment in Kyrgyzstan and specifically in Aksy at the time the protests began and detail the formation, expansion, and institutionalization of the Aksy movement. I then analyze community dynamics, individual motivations, and protest organization within the framework of the theory from chapter 1. I also consider alternative explanations that could plausibly account for the emergence or expansion of mobilization in Aksy.

## Prelude to Mobilization

In the difficulties it faced in the 1990s—poverty, reduced public services, isolation, and sporadic but manageable levels of social conflict—Aksy was no different from many rural areas throughout the former Soviet Union, or for that matter, across the developing world. Yet unlike Uzbekistan, an authoritarian country with a state-controlled economy, Kyrgyzstan had made economic and political reforms that opened new avenues for contesting authority. The country's moderately free and fair parliamentary elections gave independent elites desiring a seat in parliament an incentive to court supporters, and gave people a channel to express their discontent.

### Hard Times

Aksy, like most of rural Kyrgyzstan, suffered declines in income, employment, and investment after independence. Rather than creating a new class of prosperous, independent farmers, the privatization of Aksy Raion's five collective farms, four state farms, and three forest preserves left people impoverished and lacking the means to extricate themselves.[2] Collective-farm administrators, who were politically connected and vested with the power to distribute resources, appropriated a disproportionate share of the land and sold equipment from dissolved farms on the black market.[3] In some villages, the average family was left with no more than 10 *sotka* (each the equivalent of 100 square meters, or one-hundredth of a hectare) of land on which to raise cattle or grow potatoes. Farmers, in need of cash and lacking experience managing their own land, sold off their livestock and lost potential future income. Educated professionals who had received adequate salaries in the Soviet system decided to pursue business and left Aksy in large numbers in search of better opportunities.

*corruption*

Low levels of public and private investment in the region after independence left its mark on the local economy. A cursory inspection of Aksy's villages betrays the absence of the kinds of economic activity that are otherwise common throughout Kyrgyzstan—the cafés, teahouses, bathhouses (*bani*), food kiosks, ice cream vendors, shoe repair stands, and stalls selling pirated DVDs. Most commerce takes place in Kerben, which, as the district center, enjoys higher investment and better transportation links than the rest of the district. Kerben also has a permanent functioning bazaar, while other villages are dependent on a "rotating" bazaar that sets up in different villages one day a week. Although the state never maintained a heavy presence in the rural areas of the Soviet Union,[4] after the collapse the state disengaged further from the countryside. By 2002, the only state employees that came into regular contact with residents of Aksy were tax inspectors and military recruiters (*voenkomat*).[5] Even law enforcement officers were rarely seen.[6]

---

2. B. O. Oruzbaeva, ed., *Oshskaia Oblast* (Frunze: glavnaia redaktsiia Kyrgyzskoi Sovestkoi entsiklopedii, 1987), 228.

3. See Peter C. Bloch, "Land Privatization and Land Market Development: The 'Unsuccessful Cases of Kyrgyzstan and Uzbekistan," in *Building Market Institutions in Post-communist Agriculture: Land, Credit, and Assistance,* ed. David A. J. Macey, William Pyle, and Stephen K. Wegren (Lanham, Md.: Lexington Books, 2004); Max Spoor, "Agrarian Transition in Former Soviet Central Asia: A Comparative Study of Uzbekistan and Kyrgystan," *Journal of Peasant Studies* 23, no. 1 (1995): 46–63.

4. Alfred Evans, "Equalization of Urban and Rural Living Levels in Soviet Society," *Soviet and Post-Soviet Review* 8, no. 1 (1981): 38–61; Cynthia Buckley, "Rural/Urban Differentials in Demographic Processes: The Central Asian States," *Population Research and Policy Review* 17, no. 1 (1998): 71–89; Stephen K. Wegren, "Russian Agrarian Reform and Rural Capitalism Reconsidered," *Journal of Peasant Studies* (1998): 82–111.

5. Interviews in Aksy: Turali, Kara-su village, April 11, 2004; Akmatali, Kizil-too, April 12, 2004.

6. Interviews, Asylbek, Foundation for Tolerance International (FTI), Kerben, April 6, 2004; Dosbaev, Kizil-too, April 13, 2004. Throughout this chapter, I refer to the protagonists I interviewed by last name, and supplemental interviewees by first name.

Villagers who suffered declines in their standard of living turned their experience into narratives of personal hardship and grievance. Almost without exception, my informants reported being poorer and less satisfied than they were during the Soviet era. Even those who supported Akaev—discreetly, because he was unpopular—were nostalgic for the material security of the Soviet system. Yet these refrains were common in all parts of Kyrgyzstan, as well as throughout Central Asia and other republics.

Can poverty in Aksy explain its protests? Table 5.1 shows several indicators for economic well-being of the eight raions in Jalalabad Oblast. Because data on income and wealth are not available for all raions, I include measures of higher education per population, industrial output per population, and irrigated land per rural population. As the table shows, Aksy has a relatively high number of people with higher education, but variation among the raions is small. Aksy fares less well on the two proxies for wealth, ranking second to last on both irrigated land and industrial output per capita. Whether this means it was likely to rebel depends on what determines the formation of grievances. If the *absolute* level of quality of life is the most important factor, then Aksy may have harbored grievances ever since the Soviet period because it has always lagged in development. However, if grievances reflect perceived changes in well-being,[7] then Aksy should be no more aggrieved than other raions, since there is nothing to suggest that its *relative* decline was more severe than its neighbors.[8]

Perhaps the relative poverty of villages can explain variation in protest *within* Aksy.[9] When asked how well off their village was compared to the other eleven villages, people in all case-study villages invariably considered theirs to be the most disadvantaged, citing the indicator that they believed placed their village in the worst light—unemployment, isolation, or scarcity of water and irrigated land. For example, residents of Kara-su and Kizil-too in the north claimed to have the lowest endowment of irrigated land, while others pointed out that northern villages earned unreported income from selling fruit and nuts from trees that grow in that area. In Kosh-tebe in the south, villagers noted that although they owned

---

7. On relative deprivation, see Ted Robert Gurr, *Why Men Rebel* (Princeton: Princeton University Press, 1970); Joan Neff Gurney and Kathleen J. Tierney, "Relative Deprivation and Social Movements: A Critical Look at Twenty Years of Theory and Research," *Sociological Quarterly* 23, no. 1 (1982): 33–47.

8. On the other hand, if people assess their situations on the basis of comparisons with their peers, Aksy might have cause for dissatisfaction due to its relative poverty within the region. Yet this would require that people possessed the means to make such comparisons with neighboring raions—an unwarranted assumption given people's limited mobility.

9. The villages are administrative areas, governed by an official village committee (*ayil okmotu*) and chairman. As described below, the administrative boundaries only partly correspond to natural geographic features.

**Table 5.1**    Indicators of well–being of raions in Jalalabad Oblast

| RAION | WITH HIGHER EDUCATION (AS PERCENT OF POPULATION 15 YEARS AND OVER)[a] | INDUSTRIAL OUTPUT (SOM PER PERSON)[b] | IRRIGATED LAND PER RURAL POPULATION (HECTARES)[c] |
|---|---|---|---|
| Aksy | 5.7 | 694 | .13 |
| Ala-Buka | 5.6 | 1,025 | .23 |
| Bazar-Kurgan | 5.6 | 2,552 | .14 |
| Nooken | 5.5 | 5,168 | .26 |
| Suzak | 5.1 | 2,020 | .17 |
| Toguz-Toro | 7.4 | 29,418 | .63 |
| Toktogul | 5.3 | 423 | .06 |
| Chatkal | 5.6 | 1,363 | .60 |

[a] *Jalalabadskaia Oblast: Itogi pervoi natsional'noi perepisi naseleniia Kyrgyzskoi respubliki 1999 goda* (Bishkek: National Statistical Committee of the Kyrgyz Republic, 2001), 116–19.
[b] *Kyrgyzskaia respublika i regiony,* vol. 2, 534 (Bishkek: National Statistical Committee of the Kyrgyz Republic, 2003), 72.
[c] Julia Bucknall, Irina Klytchnikova, Julian Lampietti, Mark Lundell, Monica Scatasta, and Mike Thurman, *Irrigation in Central Asia: Social, Economic, and Environmental Considerations* (Washington, D.C.: World Bank, 2003), annex 3, 30.

more land than the northern villages, their water supply had become unreliable since Uzbekistan cut off the downstream flow from their river after independence, causing them greater hardship.[10] The best available indicators that can be used to draw conclusions about the relative well-being of the villages are land per person and irrigated land per person. As table 5.2 shows, Kerben and Kara-su suffer from deficits of land, and Kara-su, Jangi-jol, and Ak-jol are the worst-off villages in terms of irrigated land. Yet of these only Kara-su had high levels of protest. The others were Kizil-too and Kara-Jigach, which are relatively poorly endowed, but not the worst off.

## Social Isolation and Interaction

Aksy Raion has long been cursed by geography. Perched astride a mountain range that divided the country in half, Aksy never considered itself fully "northern" or "southern."[11] Located in the foothills of the Tien Shan Mountains, it shares a tightly secured border with Uzbekistan in the south and is surrounded by the

---

10. Interview, Satilgan, Kosh-tebe, April 17, 2004.

11. Kyrgyzstan is bisected by a mountain range running east-west. This division historically coincided with tribal and cultural cleavages, which some have argued affect politics today. For an explanation of the salience of the north-south division, see Pauline Jones Luong, *Institutional Change and Political Continuity in Post-Soviet Central Asia* (New York: Cambridge University Press, 2002), 74–82.

**Table 5.2**   Characteristics of villages in Aksy, Kyrgyzstan

| VILLAGE | NUMBER OF HOUSEHOLDS[a] | POPULATION[a] | LAND PER PERSON (HECTARES)[b] | IRRIGATED LAND PER PERSON (HECTARES)[b] |
|---|---|---|---|---|
| Avletim | 2,430 | 9,340 | 0.829 | 0.013 |
| Ak-jol | 1,441 | 6,317 | 1.162 | 0.002 |
| Ak-su | 1,058 | 5,397 | 1.978 | 0.006 |
| Jangi-jol | 1,383 | 5,939 | 0.791 | 0.002 |
| Jerge-tal | 1,918 | 6,620 | 0.996 | 0.059 |
| Kara-jigach | 1,312 | 5,964 | 0.584 | 0.017 |
| Kashka-su | 1,878 | 7,748 | 0.733 | 0.008 |
| Kerben | 5,808 | 22,409 | 0.289 | 0.060 |
| Kosh-tebe | 2,380 | 11,664 | 0.725 | 0.083 |
| Kizil-too | 1,320 | 5,443 | 0.766 | 0.003 |
| Kara-su | 1,540 | 6,642 | 0.516 | 0.000 |
| Uch-korgon | 2,998 | 16,451 | 0.678 | 0.210 |
| **Average** | **2,122** | **9,161** | **0.837** | **0.039** |

[a] "Plan razvitiia Aksyiskogo raiona" (Kerben: UNDP, 2004).
[b] "Aksy raion boiuncha maalymat" [Information on Aksy raion], Aksy Raion Statistical Bureau, January 1, 2002.

Chatkal mountain range in the north and west, and the Naryn River in the east. The district capital, Kerben, is located in the western edge of the raion near the Uzbek border. To drive from Kerben to the regional capital of Jalalabad, a distance of 180 kilometers, takes four hours by taxi. The twenty-five-kilometer ride on the only road from Kerben to Avletim—paved with dirt and gravel—takes over an hour in an old Soviet car (or longer by bus), and the thirty kilometers to Kara-su takes ninety minutes. From Kerben to a southern village such as Kosh-tebe or Kashka-su is a forty-five-minute drive. Figure 5.1 depicts the locations of Aksy's twelve villages. The villages where I conducted fieldwork—Kizil-too, Kara-su, Kara-jigach, Kashka-su, Kerben, and Kosh-tebe—are shaded.

Social interaction is rich and dense within communities, but sparse between them. Aksy's twelve villages are arrayed in clusters, which are separated from one another by anywhere from several to many kilometers, and accessible only by bus or taxi. The northernmost cluster consists of Kizil-too, Kara-su, and Kara-jigach and is, for the most part, contiguously inhabited and small enough to be accessible on foot.[12] The other three villages in the northern half of the raion are

---

12. As defined in chapter 1, a community refers to a collectivity within contiguous geographic space sharing many-sided and direct relations. Clusters of villages described here can therefore be considered single communities. For example, Kara-su, Kizil-too, and Kara-jigach together comprise a community. The other communities are, clockwise: Jangi-jol/Ak-jol/Ak-su, Uch-korgon, Kosh-tebe,

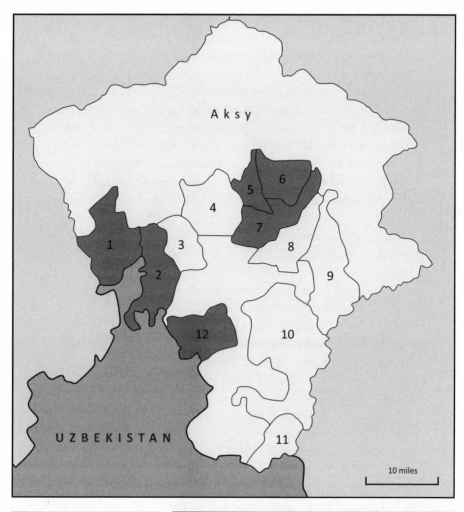

## Villages of Aksy

Fieldwork site

1. Kashka-Su
2. Kerben
3. Jerge-tal
4. Avletim
5. Kizil-too
6. Kara-su
7. Kara-jigach
8. Jangi-joi
9. Ak-jol
10. Ak-su
11. Uch-korgon
12. Kosh-tebe

**FIGURE 5.1.** Aksy Raion and its villages

Jangi-jol, Avletim, and Jerge-tal, which are not within walking distance of the first cluster. Within a village or cluster, locals typically know everybody of the same age cohort by name, and others by sight.

Interaction is far less frequent between communities. In part because of economic hardship, but also out of long-standing practice, informants reported that they rarely leave their village or cluster, where most of their family, friends, and relatives live. Due to the prohibitive cost of travel, people with relatives in other communities would visit only on occasions such as weddings and funerals. The most common destination outside one's community was Kerben, where people would go to obtain medical care or hire a taxi to travel to the oblast center, Jalalabad, to complete administrative tasks. There was no regular bus service to Jalalabad.

People were also effectively isolated due to the lack of information about villages outside their immediate vicinity, to the extent that they were sometimes better informed about events in the capital than in neighboring villages. Newspapers were available only in Kerben and often arrived late.[13] Yet, according to the UNDP, Aksy residents enjoyed access to the mass media: 78 percent of those surveyed reported watching television, and almost everyone owned a radio, although they were used infrequently due to poor reception.[14] Although this gave them the ability to learn of events taking place in Bishkek, they faced much steeper barriers in acquiring information about local matters—only one out of eight had a telephone line.[15]

In addition to geographic and communication barriers, Aksy faced social divides. The raion is split between two subtribes, a vestige of identity from Kyrgyz nomadic history prior to Russian colonization. As reported by respondents, Kyrgyz of the six villages in the northern part of the raion came from the Bagysh, while the Saruu predominated in the southern five villages and Kerben was mixed.[16] Yet tribal affiliation had no discernable impact in social, economic, or political life. Although people were aware of their tribal identity, their

Kerben, Jerge-tal, Kashka-su, and Avletim. The entirety of each village is not necessarily contiguous, because in some cases, sections of a village are separated by mountains or wooded areas.

13. Interview, Natasha, Kizil-too, April 13, 2004.

14. "Pervyi otchet rannego preduprezhdeniia na raionnom urovne: Jalalabadskaia Oblast, Aksyiskii raion" [First early warning report at the raion level: Jalalabad Oblast, Aksy Raion], (Aksy: United Nations Development Program, 2003), 10–11.

15. In 2003, there were 3,037 telephone lines in the raion for nearly twenty-four thousand households. Two villages—Kosh-tebe and Ak-su—had no working phone lines because the cables ran through Uzbek territory and had been disconnected or stolen. Ibid., 15.

16. Both are branches of a larger Sarybagysh tribe. Based on national tradition, tribal identity is passed on through patrilineal descent. Kyrgyz often admit, with a tinge of guilt, that although according to tribal custom they should be able to name their ancestors going back seven generations, usually they cannot. On the role of tribal identity in contemporary Kyrgyzstan, see David Gullette, "Kinship,

affiliation did not prevent all manner of cross-tribal interaction, from business to marriage.

## Political Opportunities and Challenges

By the early 2000s Kyrgyzstan had settled into a pattern typical of hybrid regimes in the former Soviet Union and elsewhere. A corrupt and self-aggrandizing executive intent on sustaining his rule used the levers of power to keep his ruling coalition intact and his opponents weak and divided. Although the citizenry was distrustful of the president and disillusioned with politics in general, it had few means to express its dissatisfaction and was, anyway, preoccupied with solving more immediate problems. An independent parliament and a semifree press provided the only dissent, but within limits. If the president's opponents crossed an assumed but unspecified threshold of criticism or obstruction of his initiatives, he had various tools at his disposal—the police, tax audits, and an obedient judiciary—to make them pay.

In 2000, Aksy elected as its deputy Azimbek Beknazarov, who won the post without the advantage of a prior position in the Communist Party apparatus or support from the Akaev regime. Raised in a poor family of shepherds in the village of Kara-su in Aksy, he excelled in school and took advantage of opportunities for mobility provided by the Soviet system by studying law in Tashkent. He had never studied or worked in Russia, had no ties to Western governments or NGOs, and remained predominantly Kyrgyz-speaking, a factor limiting his chances for national recognition but cementing his credentials with his home region.[17]

Instead, Beknazarov used other assets—authenticity, charisma, and diligence—to establish a political career. After independence, he rose through the ranks of Kyrgyzstan's legal system, first as chief investigator at the Jalalabad prosecutor's office, then as a judge on Bishkek's city court. His success also translated into financial well-being: his salary as a prosecutor, and later as an MP, along with the side payments his position conferred, far exceeded the meager incomes of his co-villagers.[18]

Beknazarov ran for parliament in 2000 on a populist platform, advocating the interests of poor farmers.[19] He railed against the land privatization process that

---

State, and 'Tribalism': The Genealogical Construction of the Kyrgyz Republic on the Role of Tribes in Kyrgyzstan" (PhD diss., Cambridge University, 2006).

17. Much of the ethnic Kyrgyz intelligentsia is more comfortable speaking Russian than Kyrgyz.

18. MPs received 25,000 som ($600) per month.

19. Populism refers to "a political strategy through which a personalistic leader seeks or exercises government power based on direct, unmediated, uninstitutionalized support from large numbers

had sent his co-villagers into penury, and linked their grievances with another issue of great resonance—a 1999 agreement in which Akaev had secretly agreed to transfer ninety thousand hectares of disputed territory to China without consulting parliament. Beknazarov accused Akaev of corruption and of selling out Kyrgyzstan's national interests. Even though the land ceded to China was not fertile and not in the vicinity of Aksy, his appeals resonated and he won his seat in the lower house of the Jogorku Kenesh, the Kyrgyz parliament.[20] Beknazarov's was a classic case of a local hero who managed to ascend to the national stage against all odds. He represented the hopes of his impoverished region and was rewarded with local prestige.

Ironically, Beknazarov's populism was also his undoing. In 2001, when Akaev was at a low point in popular support, as reflected in parliamentary opposition to his policies, Beknazarov brought impeachment charges against him.[21] This decision, though popular in his district, did not sit well with the president. Akaev responded by striking back in typical fashion for a post-Soviet leader, using compromising material or *kompromat* against his adversary.[22] In January 2002, he had Beknazarov arrested and charged with abuse of power for releasing a murder suspect without proper cause while he was an investigator with a prosecutor's office in 1995.[23] In most cases of this kind, the president would have successfully disposed of his adversary and that would have ended the matter.

## In Beknazarov's Defense

Mobilization was neither an inevitable, nor an expected, response to Beknazarov's arrest. In Kyrgyzstan, a powerful president appeared to tower over an emasculated

---

of mostly unorganized followers." Kurt Weyland, "Clarifying a Contested Concept: Populism in the Study of Latin American Politics," *Comparative Politics* 34, no. 1 (2001): 14.

20. On the controversial transfer of territory to China, see "Central Asia: Border Disputes and Conflict Potential," International Crisis Group, April 4, 2002, 17. It was widely rumored that Beknazarov's constituents had pooled money to buy his parliamentary seat, an investment they could expect to recoup through legislative action and private transfers. Interview, NGO leader, Kerben, April 5, 2004.

21. "Kyrgyzstan at Ten: Trouble in the 'Island' of Democracy," International Crisis Group, August 28, 2001, 8–10; Lola Sigaeva, "Impichment v obmen territorii" [Impeachment in exchange for territory], *Gazeta SNG*, May 13, 2002.

22. On *kompromat*, see Anna Ledeneva, *How Russia Really Works* (Ithaca: Cornell University Press, 2006), 58–90; Andrew Wilson, *Virtual Politics: Faking Democracy in the Post-Soviet World* (New Haven: Yale University Press, 2005), 70–71.

23. "Summary of the Work of the State Committee for Study of the Reasons and Conditions Enabling the Tragic Events of 17 March 2002," General Prosecutor, Jalalabad Oblast (2002), 7. An independent committee investigating the events would later determine that the charges against Beknazarov were unfounded. Ibid., 8–10.

and docile society; Akaev had ruled continuously since 1991, having successfully weakened challengers without facing significant opposition. Beknazarov's legislative powers were removed when he was charged, and there were no obvious (constitutional) remedies available to his supporters. The people of Aksy, poor and isolated in the mountains of the south, had no history of political activism and, ostensibly, no capacity to resist authority. Yet these presumptions were proved false when Beknazarov, through his network of campaign operatives, exploited his popularity to build a movement dedicated to securing his freedom.

## Mobilizing the Community

Beknazarov and his closest associates originated the idea of mobilizing his social support base—the residents of Aksy—to put pressure on the government. It took only one day for news of his arrest to spread throughout his village, Kara-su. The same day, two of Beknazarov's closest confidants met with him in the Jalala-bad prison where was being held. One was Janysh Kurbanov, an art teacher and Beknazarov's childhood friend, neighbor, and political operative in Kara-su. The other was his assistant Tajimamat Turaliev, a lawyer from Kosh-tebe village and a colleague of Beknazarov's from the prosecutor's office. Following the meeting with Beknazarov, Kurbanov returned home to Kara-su and Turaliev to his office in the district capital, Kerben, where they began contacting sympathetic people and announced that Beknazarov had begun a hunger strike in prison. Kurbanov recruited two former classmates—Tabalde Dosbaev and Begimkul Seetkulov, both unemployed former teachers—who immediately agreed to help.[24] Turaliev met with friends of Beknazarov and anti-Akaev "rights defenders"[25] in Bishkek, and Seetkulov sent the first of many updates about Beknazarov's status to Radio Liberty's Kyrgyz service.[26]

On the advice of sympathetic parliamentarians in Bishkek, Beknazarov's associates planned a public demonstration in the district center, Kerben, on January 14, the day charges were formally brought against Beknazarov.[27] Not knowing how to conduct a demonstration, Kurbanov instructed the other participants to hold up signs, stand still, and remain silent. Several dozen protesters, who arrived

---

24. Interviews, Dosbaev, April 13, 2004; Seetkulov, Kara-su, April 10, 2004.

25. Rights defenders (*pravozashchitniki*) are lawyers often associated with the NGO community.

26. Interview, Seetkulov, April 10, 2004. Radio Liberty is a station funded by the U.S. Congress that broadcasts in local languages throughout the former Soviet Union, the Balkans, and the Middle East.

27. Throughout the course of the events, Beknazarov's supporters received advice from a group of sympathetic MPs, including Adahan Madumarov, Omurbek Tekebaev, Absamat Masaliev, Duishenkul Chotonov, and Bektur Asanov. Interviews with several participants; *Aksyiskii dnevnik* [Aksy journal] (Bishkek: Institute of War and Peace Reporting, 2002), 6.

at the mayor's office on public minibuses, were met by police and ordered to disperse. They returned home that night as ordered, but came back to Kerben the following morning. As they approached the building, they were met by a larger contingent of police and soldiers, who broke up the demonstration and arrested its putative leaders. Most were released immediately but five were detained for several days.[28]

In order to elicit participation from a wider circle of people, most of whom could not afford to travel to Kerben, Beknazarov's supporters announced measures that would be less costly and time-intensive: signing petitions, stopping their children from attending school, and conducting hunger strikes. By January 16, volunteers had gathered fifty-three hundred signatures demanding that Beknazarov be freed, and sent copies to the press.[29] Around the same time, Beknazarov's supporters in Bishkek, including human rights activists, journalists, and sympathetic MPs, announced that they were beginning a hunger strike.[30] Following their lead, Kurbanov and other leaders in Kara-su announced that they too would begin a hunger strike, and persuaded three hundred others to follow. Those who participated were examined by doctors, and updates on their status were then sent to Radio Liberty. The strike continued intermittently for nearly two months.[31] In mid-February, the group began a boycott of local primary schools, which lasted until early April.[32]

## Activating Beknazarov's Network

It soon occurred to Beknazarov and his supporters that their protests would be more effective if they involved people from outside Kara-su. On Kurbanov's initiative, the organizers contacted Beknazarov's political operatives who had worked on his campaign throughout the district and invited them and some co-villagers to attend an informal assembly in Kara-su.[33] At the assembly, each village

---

28. Interviews, Dosbaev, April 13, 2004; Seetkulov, April 10, 2004.

29. Interview, Seetkulov, April 10, 2004; *Aksyiskii dnevnik,* 5. Dosbaev claimed that they had gathered seventeen thousand signatures, which were stolen by the intelligence services (SNB), compelling them to start over. Interview, Dosbaev, April 13, 2004; *Aksyiskii dnevnik,* 11.

30. "Hunger Strike in Kyrgyzstan to Defend Jailed Politician," Agence France-Presse, January 16, 2002.

31. Interview, Turaliev, Kerben, April 6, 2004; Seetkulov, April 10, 2004.

32. Interview, Tursunbek, Kara-su, April 15, 2004; *Aksyiskii dnevnik,* 15.

33. In the course of a political campaign, a candidate typically assembles a group of close associates to act as political operatives, called *doverennye litsa,* roughly translated as "trusted agents." These agents are tasked to organize rallies, handle logistics for the candidate's travel, pass out flyers and "gifts" (food, vodka, and money), and go door-to-door on election day to get out the vote. Since candidates usually assign at least one agent to work in each village, a candidate may have up to twenty or thirty agents to cover a whole district. If they win the election, parliamentarians can draw on this

was told to select a representative to serve on a new steering committee created to coordinate protest actions, which they called the Committee to Defend Beknazarov (CDB). After some debate, the initiators in Kara-su decided to appoint three of their own—the core organizers—to the committee, so the CDB would have fourteen members in all. Most of Beknazarov's village-level political operatives agreed to serve; those who declined out of fear or lack of free time asked neighbors or associates to serve instead. Some CDB members, such as those who had worked on the campaign together, had met previously. Others, having joined through their co-villager/political operative, did not know anybody on the committee and had never met Beknazarov in person.[34] Yet Beknazarov was now the common reference point shared by all village representatives.

The CDB planned, organized, and publicized all subsequent acts of protest. As Beknazarov's personal assistants or their designated alternates, CDB members were seen by most villagers as his legitimate representatives. Yet they were also politically naïve and had no experience in social movement leadership or tactics. Kurbanov and Turaliev, though improvising, ran the meetings. At the first meeting, they devised a division of labor, assigning each member a task such as taking minutes or communicating with the media. They resolved to meet weekly at Turaliev's office in Kerben, after which each representative would return to his home village and inform people about the place and time of the next protest action. In this way, mobilization would involve participants from all villages in the district.

In February, members of the CDB established subcommittees within their respective villages to disseminate information more efficiently. Kurbanov created a committee in Kara-su, to which the main instigators appointed themselves and additional volunteers to act as liaisons to the village's eight subdivisions.[35]

---

network as their office staff or as go-betweens to remain connected with their district. Most candidates recruit personal acquaintances—co-workers, schoolmates, friends from military service, and relatives—to work as political operatives. Because candidates prefer articulate and disciplined people to run their campaigns, operatives tend to be more educated and better off financially than average residents of the district.

34. Interview, Kurbanov, Kara-su, April 15, 2004.

35. Ibid. A village is subdivided into sections (*uchastki*), each of which has an unpaid unofficial representative, the *juz-boshi* (literally "head of one hundred"—hereafter, JB), who is usually an older and respected informal leader of the community. Those representatives meet weekly with the village council chairman and are in turn assisted by several *un-boshi*, or "heads of ten," who implement decisions made by the village council and inform and mobilize citizens. This system emerged from local self-government initiatives that were introduced in the mid-1990s at the urging of international donor organizations, in order to decentralize decision making and revenue collection with the intention of bolstering accountability and responsiveness, satisfying local demands for public goods, and compensating for budget shortfalls at higher levels of government. See Emil Alymkulov and Marat Kulatov, *Local Governments in Eastern Europe, the Caucasus, and Central Asia* (Budapest: Soros Foundation, 2000), 545–46; Pranab Bardhan, "Decentralization of Governance and Development," *Journal of Economic Perspectives* 16, no. 4 (2002): 185–205.

Others villages followed suit. Because active citizens in most villages had already begun disseminating information and organizing protests, most committees simply formalized their roles. Many of these active members were well known, respected, and had experience organizing people for other tasks, such as gathering money or working on NGO projects.[36]

## Confrontation with the Government

The Akaev regime had lost legitimacy in Aksy long before mobilization began, but this only became apparent to the government when the number of protesters increased and it attempted to put an end to the unrest. A telling incident occurred on February 17: in response to rumors that Beknazarov had been beaten in prison, a crowd of several thousand people gathered in Kara-su. Eight raion-level officials, including the governor (*akim*), his deputy, and the head of the security services, the SNB, were sent to dispel the rumor. However, the crowd was not reassured and responded by kidnapping the officials.[37] Although they were released unharmed when the rumors were checked and refuted, the incident signaled to the state that it was no longer in control in Aksy.

Relations between the government and the protesters deteriorated further when Beknazarov's trial began, on March 11. On that day, 250 people began a march to the courthouse in Toktogul, a distance of approximately two hundred kilometers, while three hundred gathered in Kara-su and twenty traveled to Bishkek.[38] On March 13, when the presiding judge called a five-day recess, the CDB planned a march and demonstration for March 17. Attempting to preempt a large turnout when the trial resumed, police were sent to arrest the CDB's representative in Kara-jigach, only to be chased away by an angry crowd of demonstrators. When word of this provocation spread, a crowd gathered in Kara-jigach to demand an apology from the government. Jalalabad's governor promised to apologize in person on March 15, but when he failed to appear, this further inflamed the protesters.[39] On the morning of the 17th, the protesters planned to

---

36. While I was there, the U.S. Agency for International Development (USAID) and the United Nations Development Programme (UNDP) had several ongoing projects emphasizing social mobilization, for which a recipient community was required to solicit widespread participation and contribute to the overall cost of the project. The year 2004 was, in fact, designated by the government as the "year of social mobilization and good governance." "Kyrgyz Republic: Poverty Reduction Strategy Paper Progress Report," International Monetary Fund (Washington, D.C.: April 2004), 5.

37. Interview, Seetkulov, April 10, 2004; *Aksyiskii dnevnik*, 15. A similar situation, in which the masses took police officers hostage in exchange for releasing protesters under custody, took place in September. *Respublika*, September 10, 2002.

38. *Aksyiskii dnevnik*, 20.

39. Reported by Kadrali, ex-teacher and JB (later member of CDB), Kara-jigach, April 14, 2004; *Aksyiskii dnevnik*, 21.

make a major statement. They met in Kara-su and split into two groups: three hundred marched toward Kerben to demonstrate at the mayor's office, while twenty-five hundred set off for the courthouse in Toktogul.

The violence that occurred on March 17, which later became known by the euphemism "Aksy events," was the result of raucous crowds, nervous and inexperienced security forces, and the mutual distrust between the two sides. Having learned in advance of the plan to march on Kerben, the government posted soldiers on the road thirteen kilometers outside Kerben in the town of Bospiek to signal that it was drawing a line in the sand. When the protesters reached the blockade, they stopped; some unpacked their bags and started to eat lunch. The soldiers then demanded that the crowd hand over Tursunbek Akunov, a "rights defender" from Bishkek who had been advising the protesters and who was accused of inciting disobedience. When Seetkulov, the group's leader for that day, refused to hand him over, the soldiers began to penetrate the crowd. As people in the front rows instinctively fought them off, a scuffle began. When people reputedly tried to grab a soldier's gun, several shots rang out and scattered the crowd. Once the chaos subsided, six people lay dead and several dozen had been wounded.[40]

News of the shootings quickly spread around Aksy. Many people who had never participated in protests did so after being informed by indignant friends and neighbors. An hour after the shooting, when the dead and wounded in Bospiek had been taken away, Seetkulov and most of the marchers decided to continue toward Kerben. When they arrived, they began a sit-in in the central square, where they were joined over the next two days by a constant stream of people, totaling six thousand people by the 18th and eight thousand by the 19th.[41]

The mushrooming crowd, with participants from all twelve villages, put unprecedented pressure on the government. The situation threatened to descend into violence as young men threw stones at police, who in turn beat and seriously wounded a number of bystanders.[42] Seeing no way to end the escalating tensions without causing massive bloodshed, officials began to negotiate in earnest. On the 19th, the regional chief of the Ministry of Internal Affairs and Prime Minister Kurmanbek Bakiev met with protest leaders Seetkulov, Akunov, and a CDB member from Kara-jigach, pleading with them to restore order and

---

40. "Informatsiia o situatsyii v Aksyiskom raione Jalalabadskoi oblasti za period 17–19 marta 2002 goda" [Information about the situation in Aksy Raion, Jalalabad Oblast in the period of March 17–19], Foundation for Tolerance International (FTI), reported twelve wounded. Sigaeva, "Impichment v obmen territorii," reported eighty injured. Sultan Jumagulov, "Bishkek Braces for Aksy Anniversary," IWPR, March 4, 2003 reports 60.

41. Figures from FTI. Higher figures in the range of fifteen thousand were provided by an NGO leader, Kerben, April 5, 2004; Seetkulov, April 10, 2004.

42. *Aksyiskii dnevnik*, 25.

send the crowd home. In exchange, Bakiev, under orders from Akaev, agreed to free Beknazarov. That night Beknazarov was released, though not relieved of the charges against him. He entered the square in Kerben to a hero's welcome, accompanied by Turaliev and Kurbanov.

## Institutionalization of the Movement

Mobilization in Aksy did not end at that point, however, because Beknazarov's case was still unresolved and the movement had begun to take on a life of its own, spawning new demands to help justify its existence.[43] On April 8, the CDB issued a new ultimatum—to punish the perpetrators of the Bospiek "massacre."[44] On April 12, thousands of protesters met in Kara-jigach, where the CDB called for an independent commission to investigate the shootings. Nearly two thousand gathered in various locales in Aksy on May 5; over three thousand on May 6; and six thousand on May 7.[45] On May 13, 2–3,000 protesters launched a new and disruptive tactic: lying in the road to block traffic on the only highway connecting northern and southern Kyrgyzstan, thus obstructing commerce in the country for twelve days.[46] That month, the CDB began demanding that President Akaev resign.

Planning for the long haul, the CDB determined to consolidate control over the expanding movement. Before March 17, the core organizers had developed a sense of camaraderie and could monitor newcomers, who came predominantly from northern villages, with relative ease. After the shootings there was a surge of new and mostly unfamiliar recruits who, the organizers feared, might unnecessarily provoke the authorities and weaken the ability of the group to act cohesively. In early April, the CDB introduced new measures to monitor protesters and punish inappropriate behavior. It created a pyramidal structure of supervision with the CDB at the peak. The system, based on traditional Kyrgyz nomadic governance, consisted of nested divisions in which each CDB member appointed trusted associates (usually village subcommittee members), who in

---

43. Kathleen Thelen calls this process "functional conversion": "a situation in which exogenous processes or shocks produce or empower new actors, who–rather than challenging existing institutions outright—harness existing organizational forms in the service of new ends." Kathleen Thelen, "Timing and Temporality in the Analysis of Institutional Evolution and Change," *Studies in American Political Development* 14 (2000): 105. See also Stephen D. Krasner, "Sovereignty: An Institutional Perspective," *Comparative Political Studies* 21 (1988): 66–94.

44. All participants I talked to were convinced that the decision to shoot protesters was deliberate and had been ordered from above. Their primary evidence was that hospitals had apparently been informed in advance to prepare extra staff and store blood for transfusions on March 17. However, even if true, this only suggests that the government thought bloodshed was a possibility, given the danger of a confrontation between soldiers and an unruly crowd.

45. *Aksyiskii dnevnik, chast' II*, 2.

46. Interview, Kadrali, April 14, 2004.

turned supervised and took responsibility for the actions of one hundred, fifty, or ten people they knew personally.

The system made it possible to account for every participant by enabling organizers to identify unfamiliar individuals, presumed to be from outside Aksy, whom they could single out and interrogate.[47] Supervisors were held accountable for the people under their watch, with their reputations on the line. As an additional precaution, the CDB passed a resolution prohibiting consumption of alcohol during protests on pain of one hundred lashes with a horsewhip—another symbol from Kyrgyz tradition.[48]

By early summer 2002, the movement was both large and resilient, and had honed its ability to disrupt normal politics and extract concessions from the government. It embarked on another round of protests after May 24, when the court gave Beknazarov a one-year suspended sentence, which would require him to surrender his seat in parliament. Beknazarov decided to appeal the sentence in order to regain his seat. Several days prior to his hearing, scheduled for June 18, over one thousand people left Aksy on a march to the courthouse in Jalalabad city. By the time the protesters reached Jalalabad, the prosecutor abruptly decided to move the court proceedings to Toktogul, which the marchers would not be able to reach by the beginning of the hearing.[49] Frustrated, eight hundred people began marching south toward the city of Osh.[50] Fearing that if the demonstrators entered Osh, they might provoke tensions with ethnic Uzbeks, Osh's governor halted them outside the city and pleaded with them to turn around.[51] The demonstrators responded that unless their demands were met within three days, they would enter the city.[52] Facing a dangerous escalation, the government backed down: Akaev flew back from a meeting in China and agreed to overturn the verdict against Beknazarov and reinstate his seat in parliament. Even though only one of their demands had been met, the crowd relented and returned home on June 25.[53]

---

47. CDB members claimed that they caught government "spies" using this method. Interviews, Kurbanov, April 15, 2004; Kadrali, April 14, 2004.

48. Interviews, Seetkulov, April 10, 2004; Toktogul, Kosh-tebe, April 17, 2004; Kurbanov, April 15, 2004. This punishment was never actually carried out, although Seetkulov brought his whip to the meeting to substantiate the threat.

49. *Aksyiskii dnevnik, chast' II*, 24; Filip Noubel, "Protests in Kyrgyzstan Gather Force and Focus," eurasianet.org, June 21, 2002.

50. Interview, Kadrali, April 14, 2004.

51. Osh had been the scene of interethnic rioting between Kyrgyz and Uzbeks in 1990 that led to the death of several hundred on each side.

52. Their demands now included (1) dropping all charges against Beknazarov, (2) punishing those responsible for the March 17 shootings, and (3) Akaev's resignation.

53. Interview, Kudrat, Osh, October 22, 2003.

However, the movement succumbed to inertia as protesters responded indignantly to a general amnesty of those involved in the March 17 shooting. The first of two major marches took place over eight days in September, as two thousand marched toward Bishkek. Halfway there, they were met be a government delegation and four hundred counterdemonstrators sent by the government, most of whom were state employees.[54] Five days of negotiations ensued, after which the government agreed to prosecute a number of district-level officials and the opposition acquiesced to a two-month moratorium on protest actions.[55] Yet even before the pact was set to expire, several hundred marchers set off from Aksy to Bishkek to demand Akaev's resignation.[56] However, most did not have the stamina or the provisions to reach their destination and the handful that made it to Bishkek (having used various forms of transportation along the way) were summarily loaded onto buses by police and driven home.

After this last push, protests decreased in size and frequency. Since most of the movement's demands had been met and the wider public, initially supportive, had grown weary of ceaseless demonstrations, the leaders decided to demobilize. In the end, several thousand people from throughout the district had sustained the mobilization for eight months, proving that citizen action, when properly organized and sustained, could have major political ramifications. They had won back Beknazarov's freedom, restored his parliamentary seat, secured a trial of the officials involved in the Aksy events, and forced the resignation of Prime Minister Bakiev. Members of the CDB, having established close working relationships, chose not to disband, however, and continued to meet periodically. One of their last resolutions warned that if Akaev were to run for a constitutionally prohibited fourth term as president or engineer a succession within his family, they would again bring large numbers of people out into the streets.

## Breaking Down Mobilization Dynamics

Aksy is a case study of how social ties can be converted into an instrument of political resistance with the proper stimulus. Beknazarov's allies harnessed the power of society to turn an otherwise ordinary confrontation between the

---

54. *Respublika*, September 10, 2002. Many of these people came from Bishkek and were threatened with losing their jobs if they did not participate. Alexei Sukhov, "Dva dnia iz Zhizni Demonstrantov" [Two days in the lives of demonstrators], *Kommersant*, September 2, 2002.

55. Bert Herman, "Kyrgyz Opposition Gives Government until Mid-November to Sentence Those Behind the Protest Shootings That Galvanized Country," Associated Press, September 15, 2002.

56. "Armistice between Aksy People and Government Ends on November 15," Kabar News Agency, October 11, 2002.

president and a political opponent into an issue of widespread public significance. Beknazarov had many supporters, but few would have demonstrated spontaneously as isolated individuals. However, in their social context, with persuasive appeals and proper coordination, thousands of people were mobilized as a single, cohesive movement.

Beknazarov's arrest set a string of processes in motion: first, the activation of horizontal ties within a contiguous set of villages; second, the coalescence of Beknazarov's political network; and third, the expansion to villages throughout the district. Beknazarov, even while sitting in prison, acted as a focal point for his assistants to coordinate and broker between villages. Once representatives from all twelve villages had come together and agreed on a common set of goals and tactics, they began simultaneous processes of local mobilization throughout the district. These two processes—the activation of community networks and brokerage—worked in tandem.

## The Central Role of Community Networks

Aksy cannot be understood in isolation from the history of the local investments people had made in their communities in the course of everyday life. Most people did not decide to participate based solely on their attitudes toward Beknazarov or Akaev. Instead, they looked around to see what their neighbors, friends, relatives, classmates, and colleagues were doing and saying. Prior to mobilization, people not only knew who their neighbors were; they were aware of intimate details of one another's lives and would meet and exchange information at venues such as the street, the pasture, the bazaar, and the square in front of the town hall (*ayil okmoti*). Once the protests began, participants would interact with the same people at the same venues, only with a unique purpose.[57]

In the initial stages of mobilization, the concentration of direct ties with Beknazarov determined where mobilization occurred. Thus, Kara-su, the home of Beknazarov's neighbors and extended family, had a higher density of zealots—those with "an excess of incentive to contribute to the common cause"[58]—and

---

57. Participants were generally middle age and older, with comparable numbers of men and women. Young women typically remained at home with their children but older women were active and vocal supporters of Beknazarov. However, men were more likely to play leadership roles; all members of the CDB were men.

58. James S. Coleman, "Free Riders and Zealots: The Role of Social Networks," *Sociological Theory* 6, no. 1 (1988): 53; Mark Irving Lichbach, *The Rebel's Dilemma* (Ann Arbor: University of Michigan, 1995), 36–38. They have also been called "instigators" (Mark Granovetter, "Threshold Models of Collective Behavior," *American Journal of Sociology* 83, no. 6 [1978]: 1420–43) and "first actors" (Roger D. Petersen, *Resistance and Rebellion* [New York: Cambridge University Press, 2001], chapter 9, 272–95).

saw more initial protests than other villages. The organizers in Kara-su did not have to expend great effort to persuade people to join. Villagers identified with Beknazarov and did not hesitate to support him. They only needed to be informed of the place and time of an event to appear.

Outside of Beknazarov's immediate social and geographic circles, people had a weaker sense of attachment or, before March 17, were simply unaware of events unfolding in Kara-su and Kerben. Beknazarov's political operatives, loyal to the MP and (for the most part) underemployed, took the initiative of working to expand mobilization beyond Kara-su. They recruited their neighbors, relatives, former classmates, and co-workers in their respective villages, but participation was still most intense within networks spanning the community comprising Kara-su and the two neighboring northern villages—Kizil-too and Kara-jigach. In those villages, even those without direct ties to Beknazarov joined after being solicited by relatives and neighbors. Outside of this cluster, few people seriously considered joining a demonstration even though they were impoverished and upset at government corruption.[59]

This dynamic changed after the shootings. Hearing of the "massacre" (the term people used, even though it was accidental rather than intentional) turned many who had paid little attention up to that point—or who had privately sympathized with the government—into activists. In fact, the government could not done anything that would have galvanized the opposition more effectively than by shooting unarmed protesters, thus transforming Beknazarov into a symbol representing the people of Aksy against an oppressive regime. News of the March 17 shootings reached even the most isolated and previously uninformed peasants, whereupon many became receptive to protest appeals. Even villages in the south of Aksy now became involved. One interviewee, a bus driver from Kosh-tebe who had previously been indifferent to the protests in the north, was stopped and questioned by soldiers on March 17 while driving his usual route to Kerben. When he arrived at the raion center, he learned of the shootings from the thousands of people occupying the square. Returning home, he saw groups of people walking toward Kerben from Kosh-tebe and other southern villages and offered to transport them at no charge.[60]

---

59. The events were of less significance in villages such as Kosh-tebe and Jangi-jol. Whereas uninterested parties in Kara-su were pressured into going to Kerben by their leaders and neighbors, in other villages only those who were in networks with the initiators or highly motivated participated, while the majority could remain at home without fear of retribution. Interviews, Kosh-tebe, April 17, 2004; Kashka-su, April 18, 2004.

60. Interview, Satilgan, April 17, 2004.

## Explaining Individual Motivations

At the individual level, how did people decide whether to participate? According to a strict application of the logic of collective action, an individual would weigh the (material or other) incentives against the potential costs. In Aksy, most people's decisions were heavily influenced by other people in their social networks. A higher level of participation among one's neighbors did not necessarily increase the benefits of participating, but it significantly raised the anticipated (social) costs of staying home.[61]

Appeals to aid Beknazarov traveled through horizontal networks, and were made more effective by the bonds that hold communities together, especially in difficult times—norms of reciprocity, reputation, and occasionally, the threat of coercion.[62] In Aksy, good relations with one's neighbors were essential to survive the grinding poverty of post-Soviet life. The desire to maintain standing in the eyes of the village resulted in conformity of behaviors and stated attitudes. Although most participants in the three northern villages joined protests enthusiastically out of identification with Beknazarov, even people who were otherwise indifferent were compelled to participate in order to prevent damage to their reputations. When, in March and April, discourses in a number of villages fixated on the need to support Aksy's native son, it was impossible to stand on the sidelines.

By all accounts, after March 17 the only nonparticipants in the most active villages were government employees who risked losing their jobs; businessmen, who spent much of their time traveling outside of Aksy and were less dependent on the community; and devoted opponents of Beknazarov. One visibly wealthy individual, who had built an ostentatious neocolonial-style house on a hill in Kizil-too, claimed he was busy during the time of the protests and had no opinion on the matter.[63] Supporters of Beknazarov's 2000 opponent for parliament, Malabek Toktobulatov, had a harder time. His political representative in Kara-su refused to participate and was ostracized and maligned by neighbors for some time.[64] In other villages it was possible to openly oppose the mobilization and (God forbid) express support for Akaev.[65] In Kara-jigach, where a large

---

61. For a similar dynamic in the Paris Commune of 1871, see Roger V. Gould, *Insurgent Identities* (Chicago: University of Chicago Press, 1995), 171–81.

62. Coercion was threatened in Kara-su after the shootings, when people who were reluctant to march with the majority were branded "enemies of the people." Mentioned by two sources, Kara-su, April 13 and April 19, 2004. At other times, there were isolated threats against perceived shirkers.

63. Interview, Rashibek, Kizil-too, April 12, 2004.

64. Interview, Saparbek, Kara-su, April 19, 2004.

65. Interviews, Mirzabek, JB, former sovkhoz chauffer; Mairam, Kizil-too, April 12, 2004.

proportion participated, Toktobulatov's representative remained at home but was not harassed, since people understood his allegiances.[66]

Reputational incentives continued to function during marches and demonstrations, and were used to prevent disorder. The CDB was small enough to monitor itself. Villages, in which everyone knew everyone else, marched together as a group and held one another accountable. The new post–March 17 rules broke monitoring down into small groups, in which the heads of ten, fifty, or one hundred people supervised people in their villages and answered to a leader at a higher level. Thus, a system of reciprocal monitoring let everyone know their actions were under scrutiny by others: participants knew that they would be recognized and shamed if they drank excessively or destroyed property, supervisors knew their reputations would suffer if disobedience occurred during their watch, and CDB members knew that their counterparts on the committee would disapprove of them if their subordinates could not prevent untoward behavior.

Individuals deciding whether to participate did not have to reckon with high potential costs to their physical well-being.[67] Unlike insurgency or civil war, the anticipated cost of participation in protests in Aksy was minimal.[68] Even on the day of the greatest violence, when six people were killed, the participants had no inkling that marching could become dangerous; people knew their government was corrupt, but they also knew from past experience that it was not prone to use excessive physical force.

At the same time, there were also few anticipated material benefits from protesting. The organizers provided no selective incentives;[69] local merchants and residents of Aksy were urged to contribute to a fund to buy provisions for long marches and sit-ins, but individual participants were not remunerated for their efforts. Even those with longer time horizons could not reasonably expect to

---

66. Interview, Akbarali, Kara-jigach, April 14, 2004.

67. However, the government harassed and intimidated CDB members and their families on numerous occasions. For example, on February 18 the police came to harass Seetkulov but were mobbed by local people and forced to flee. Later they arrested his brother and held him for six days. On June 8, near Tashkumir, seven members of the CDB were arrested, sent to the Jalalabad internal affairs office, and later freed. Turaliev was arrested and released several times. Kurbanov was twice fired from his teaching job and rehired. In another case an elder who had been a spiritual leader in the movement met with Akaev and agreed to join a government commission on the Beknazarov affair, after which he ceased his protest activities. Rumor had it that the government had threatened to punish his sons, both of whom held high positions in Kyrgyz universities. Turaliev, April 6, 2004; Kadrali, April 14, 2004; Kustarbek, Kizil-too, April 13, 2004.

68. On the perceived risks of joining an insurgency, see Petersen, *Resistance and Rebellion,* 18; Elisabeth Jean Wood, *Insurgent Collective Action and Civil War in El Salvador* (New York: Cambridge University Press, 2003), 12, 119; Steven Pfaff, *Exit-Voice Dynamics and the Collapse of East Germany* (Durham: Duke University Press, 2006), 9–10.

69. See Mancur Olson, *The Logic of Collective Action* (Cambridge: Harvard University Press, 1965), 72; Samuel L. Popkin, *The Rational Peasant* (Berkeley: University of California Press, 1979), 252–59.

receive private payoffs; Beknazarov, though well off for Aksy, was unable to reward any but his closest and most loyal supporters, through the possibility of employment. A more common opinion was that Beknazarov had to be defended because he was "one of us." If freed, supporters believed, his advocacy of district interests would continue to benefit everyone.

Counterintuitively, more people participated *after* the March 17 shootings than before them—once it was revealed that the government was prepared to use violence to stifle resistance. Conventional wisdom, expressed in game-theoretic terminology as "assurance games" or "tipping" posits that, when mobilization carries potential costs, people will calculate the likelihood of being harmed as a function of the expected size of the crowd.[70] The government's demonstrated willingness to use violence should, at least temporarily, suppress the urge to mobilize and the size of crowds. Yet, when people heard of the shootings, they headed for Kerben's central square seemingly without heed of the consequences.

Speaking with people whose first involvement in the movement was to join their compatriots in the square on the day of the shooting revealed that they understood their participation in support of Beknazarov as an expression of support for fellow citizens. Yet like in earlier protesters, they did not join as isolated individuals and were not simply captive to their emotions. Their outrage was necessary but not sufficient; people who joined that day were *brought* by someone they knew. That is, their decision was mediated by their social networks. On that day, recruitment took place more rapidly, penetrated more deeply into communities, and occurred on a far wider scale than on any previous day. Newcomers may not have been informed of the shooting or been compelled to join had their co-villagers not already been immersed in the movement.

## Establishing the Missing Link: Brokerage

When mobilization occurs through clientelist ties, autonomous elites can act as brokers linking communities or regions. In this instance, Beknazarov was the only elite directly affected by a challenge from above. Beknazarov enjoyed greater access to material and political resources than other people in Aksy thanks to his formal position as a member of parliament and his informal network of elites in Bishkek and other regions.[71] The network that he had built in Aksy while running

---

70. Timur Kuran, "Now Out of Never: The Element of Surprise in the East European Revolution of 1989," *World Politics* 44 (1991): 7–48; Susanne Lohmann, "The Dynamics of Information Cascades: The Monday Demonstrations in Leipzig, East Germany, 1989–1991," *World Politics* 47 (1994): 42–101.

71. On the ability of brokers or gatekeepers to access valued resources, see Javier Auyero, *Poor People's Politics* (Durham: Duke University Press, 2000), 94–98; Ronald S. Burt, *Brokerage and Closure: An Introduction to Social Capital* (Oxford: Oxford University Press, 2005).

for and winning a seat in parliament was put to use in mobilizing communities and brokering between them—but only within the raion, which is as far as his network extended.

The people who became the organizers of protest emerged haphazardly but always through prior relationships, initially through ties to Beknazarov himself. The most common characteristic of organizers was to have been one of his village campaign representatives. This cohort responded enthusiastically to Kurbanov and Turaliev's call to action, and many served on the committee. They believed in Beknazarov and associated his well-being with their own.

Another way of ending up on the CDB or a subcommittee was to be a close associate of one of the first-tier organizers. It was not necessary to have a personal connection to Beknazarov, or even to have been a supporter; the recommendation of an existing committee member was sufficient. Even the initial organizers from Kara-su were not equally close to Beknazarov, having been chosen by Kurbanov through his alumni network. Likewise, Turaliev, the CDB representative in Kashka-su, chose a former classmate to replace him when he decided to quit the committee under pressure from the government.[72]

Before mobilization began, its organizers would not have qualified as elites, being neither significantly wealthier nor more powerful than the people they led in protest. Since Aksy's social structure had been decapitated when its already meager number of entrepreneurs, Communist Party bosses, and aspiring politicians (including Beknazarov himself) moved to other cities in the 1990s, people of less influential status remained to fill the void. This can be seen in the relatively humble backgrounds of those on the CDB: teachers, agronomists, petty traders, and technicians.[73] They came predominantly from the rural intelligentsia, the stratum of the population from the Soviet countryside that possessed professional skills and had the ability to speak articulately and to manage subordinates.[74] In the course of mobilization, people from this cohort augmented their status by drawing on Beknazarov's resources: his personal prestige, his influential contacts in Bishkek, and his role as a focal point for people across the region.[75] Another motivation amid conditions of poverty and high unemployment was

---

72. Interview, Kashka-su, April 18, 2004.

73. Teachers, though not usually considered politically influential, are the closest most villages have to an intelligentsia, by virtue of their speaking and leadership skills and the fact that the profession is widely respected. On the role of village teachers in the Vietnamese rebellion, see Samuel L. Popkin, "Political Entrepreneurs and Peasant Movements in Vietnam," in *Rationality and Revolution*, ed. Michael Taylor (Cambridge: Cambridge University Press, 1988), 9–62.

74. See L. G. Churchward, *The Soviet Intelligentsia: An Essay on the Social Structure and Roles of Soviet Intellectuals during the 1960s* (Boston: Routledge, 1973), 24.

75. This observation corresponds to Wood's account of the South African and Salvadoran insurgencies, whose "leaders were elite *only* by virtue of their leadership of powerful insurgent organiza-

the prospect of finding work. Some rightly reasoned that Beknazarov would use his connections to help those who secured his release to find employment in Kerben or Bishkek.[76]

Beneath the CDB, activists within villages also enjoyed heightened prestige during the protests. Many were semiofficial community leaders who worked in village governments (JBs—"heads of one hundred"). In ordinary times, they would contribute significant time and energy to solving local problems without compensation. They used their everyday legitimacy to facilitate mobilization, by convening street meetings, recruiting people door-to-door, volunteering to work on subcommittees, and supervising protesters during marches.[77] Despite having been selected by the chairman of the village council, a state employee, they none-theless felt vindicated in working on behalf of the movement, since they suffered the same hardships as ordinary people. Also, because mobilization was broadly popular, they earned the community's respect in the process.

## Alternative Explanations

This chapter has argued that the outbreak of mobilization in Aksy and the varia-tion in the rates of participation by village can best be explained by the level of support for Beknazarov and the processes of horizontal recruitment within communities and brokerage between them. But what about other types of net-works and affiliations that could, in theory, have produced the same outcome? For example, it has been conjectured that the clan membership is the most po-litically relevant identity in Central Asia, and that Aksy was actually a clan- or tribe-based conflict.[78] Clan and tribe were in fact powerful bases of social and political organization in Central Asia historically, but generations of Russian and

---

tions." Elisabeth Jean Wood, *Forging Democracy from Below* (New York: Cambridge University Press, 2000), 12.

76. In Kyrgyzstan, ambitious members of political campaign teams can gain lucrative positions on the deputy's staff or find a government job if the candidate wins. This possibility is especially attractive to assistants in rural areas who otherwise lack job opportunities or contacts in big cities. Thus Kurbanov, having become an opposition activist after the Aksy events, later became the deputy governor of Jalalabad after the Tulip Revolution. After the revolution, Turaliev briefly served as the *akim* of Aksy Raion.

77. They functioned as opinion leaders. See Ronald S. Burt, "The Social Capital of Opinion Leaders," *Annals of the American Academy of Political and Social Science* 566 (1999): 37–54; and Ronald S. Burt, *Brokerage and Closure: An Introduction to Social Capital* (Oxford: Oxford University Press, 2005).

78. Alisher Khamidov, "Kyrgyzstan's Unrest Linked to Clan Rivalries," Eurasianet.org, June 5, 2002. For a clan-based argument about general Kyrgyz or Central Asian politics, see Vladimir Kha-nin, "Ethnic Pluralism and Political Conflict," *Central Asia and the Caucasus* (2000); Kathleen Collins, "The Political Role of Clans in Central Asia," *Comparative Politics* 35, no. 2 (2003): 171–90.

then Soviet rule, along with purges, collectivization, and industrialization, have made social life in the region much more complex.

Although the first-movers in Kara-su self-identified as one tribe, Saruu, their participation was overdetermined since they were more likely to know Beknazarov personally, to be relatives of Beknazarov or his wife, and to come into frequent contact with him and his relatives. Because these affiliations overlap, tribe cannot be isolated as the unique cause of people's involvement. Later, when the protests expanded beyond the northern cluster, new recruits came from villages that were predominantly Bagysh. Finally, six of the fourteen CDB members, including Turaliev, Beknazarov's closest advisor, were Bagysh, and not Beknazarov's Saruu. Today, people in Kyrgyzstan know that they "belong" to a tribe or clan, but the identity exists in the form of mythology and memory, and it neither enables nor inhibits mobilization.

Another possibility is that civil society, in the form of Western-funded NGOs, may have provided inspiration, advice, or resources for mobilization. NGOs in Kyrgyzstan are almost entirely dependent on international donor aid to survive, which would appear to make them inviting channels for Western governments to influence politics. Indeed, Aksy did have a small number of NGOs, mostly concentrated in Kerben, dedicated to such causes as defending human rights, protecting women, and providing legal assistance. In other villages, I came across a "society of invalids" and a nascent microlending group, with seventy-eight and twenty-five beneficiaries, respectively.[79] Yet NGOs in Aksy lacked the organizational reach and financial resources to facilitate the recruitment for or funding of mobilization. The main protest leaders lived in villages far from Kerben and had no ties to NGOs.

The NGO community in Bishkek did, however, exercise an indirect effect on the movement, by instructing participants on the tactics of the U.S. civil rights movement, such as school boycotts, marches, and hunger strikes.[80] Two lawyers—Tursunbek Akunov and Topchubek Turgunaliev—were members of Bishkek's network of civic organizations and had been part of the liberal opposition to Akaev since the early 1990s. These activists, who were close to Beknazarov's allies in parliament, became associated with the movement in mid-January. Over the next several months, they would visit Aksy to train organizers in the mechanics of various kinds of protest actions and inform demonstrators of their constitutional rights.[81] They also aroused the ire of the government; Akunov would later become notorious for his unrelenting (and opportunistic) advocacy

---

79. Interviews, Mudalbek, Kizil-too, April 12, 2004; Nurdolyt, Kizil-too, April 13, 2004.

80. See Dennis Chong, *Collective Action and the Civil Rights Movement* (Chicago: University of Chicago Press, 1991).

81. Interview, Kadrali, April 14, 2004.

of Beknazarov's cause. The desire to apprehend him was the spark that led to violence in March 17. However, these activists did not play a role in initiating, organizing, or expanding the movement.

In this chapter I have analyzed mobilization in rural Kyrgyzstan to demonstrate how an embedded independent elite and member of parliament was able to activate communities to defend himself against a challenge by the executive. Beknazarov, though not wealthy enough to contribute substantial material goods, had convinced his constituents over time that he was indispensable to ensuring their interests. His immediate supporters, a cohort from the rural intelligentsia, initiated mobilization within his village, formed a central committee to coordinate protest actions, and oversaw a web of subcommittees in the twelve villages. Yet the deeper source of connectivity lay within the communities where people lived, worked, and socialized. These dense networks suffused with social capital were the building blocks of mass mobilization—on their own, they were useful in solving local collective action problems, but when activated and aggregated, they were a formidable vehicle for challenging authority.

The Aksy mobilization demonstrated the importance of low levels of public goods and political and economic liberalization in generating subversive clientelism. Beknazarov was able to make populist appeals based on the idea that the state (and by implication, the Akaev regime) had abandoned its constituents. Yet a precondition for making these appeals was his ability to survive as a political entrepreneur autonomous of the regime—a role that would be impossible to play in Uzbekistan.

Beknazarov's example shows the crucial intermediary role played by independent elites in a hybrid political system such as Kyrgyzstan's. Many such elites are embedded in the fabric of community life yet possess access to resources that allows them to compete in high-level political struggles.[82] They can empower communities by lending their prestige and material resources to nonelites and mediating between previously unacquainted associates to facilitate collective action. In extraordinary circumstances, they can transform the energies of otherwise apolitical citizens into a political weapon.

In the final analysis, the Aksy movement had effects beyond the partial victory that it won in 2002. It brought together opposition activists who shared a

---

82. Beknazarov conforms to Wolf's definition of brokers: "people who mediate between community-oriented groups in communities and nation-oriented groups which operate primarily through national institutions. . . . They stand guard over the crucial junctures or synapses of relationships which connect the local system to the larger whole." Eric R. Wolf, "Aspects of Group Relations in a Complex Society: Mexico," *American Anthropologist* 58, no. 6 (1956): 1075.

formative experience and established ties that they could activate in the future. It proved that ordinary people, with a little bit of help, could take matters into their own hands and bring about political change. By openly challenging Akaev, the movement proved that the regime was ill-prepared to deal with organized peaceful opposition and was perhaps more vulnerable than many had assumed. These developments helped pave the way for a far more massive mobilization in 2005 that would bring down Akaev's government.

# 6

# ELITE NETWORKS AND THE TULIP REVOLUTION

Following the peaceful transfers of power that took place after mass protests in Serbia, Georgia, and Ukraine in the early 2000s, few analysts expected the "wave" to reach Central Asia. Whereas the European cases may have possessed the necessary social, cultural, and political preconditions for a peaceful popular uprising, the Central Asian states lagged on critical indicators such as income per capita and civil society. In the unlikely event that an uprising took place, some predicted, it would be led or exploited by Islamic radicals and accompanied by violence.[1] Yet Kyrgyzstan confounded the skeptics: in March 2005 over forty thousand Kyrgyz citizens across six provinces (oblasts) and the capital participated in a series of peaceful protests and exposed the brittle façade of the Askar Akaev regime, which collapsed with little resistance. The event—the so-called Tulip Revolution—marked the first, albeit extraconstitutional, change of power in Central Asia since the period of transition from Soviet rule.[2]

The Tulip Revolution was a result of the interlocking subversive clientelist and horizontal networks—the mass mobilization infrastructure—that had developed over the previous years. The catalysts were autonomous elites (wealthy businessmen, former government officials, former or active parliamentarians)

---

1. See Anara Tabyshalieva, "Hizb ut-Tahrir's Increasing Activity in Central Asia," *Central Asia-Caucasus Institute Analyst* (2004); Tyler Rauert, "The Next Threat from Central Asia," *Journal of International Security Affairs* 9 (2005); "Kyrgyzstan: Would Reformist Gains Spark Change in Other Central Asian States?" Radio Free Europe/Radio Liberty, February 23, 2005.

2. Along the lines of the earlier "rose" and "orange" revolutions, the event earned a popular sobriquet, so named because tulips are the national flower of Kyrgyzstan.

who were bound to ordinary citizens through clientelist ties and linked to other elites through preexisting networks. When a number of embedded elites who were running for parliament failed to win in the first round of the elections, they contested the results outside institutional channels in the manner they thought would be most effective: mobilizing street demonstrations. In numerous locales across the country, losing candidates mobilized community networks, as in the Aksy movement. The candidates' supporters then occupied the central square of the district or provincial capital to pressure officials to reexamine or overturn the results of the disputed election.

Up to this point, the dynamics were similar to those of the Aksy protests, a peaceful rural uprising that, thanks to its scope and duration, extracted concessions from the Akaev government. However, in 2005, mobilizing candidates had an additional source of leverage to apply. Drawing on informal horizontal networks, rebellious elites from different oblasts confederated, expanding the scale of mobilization beyond that witnessed in Aksy, and posing a challenge to the regime's survival. Ultimately, a national-level opposition alliance under a single leadership took control of the protests and forged a movement with a common objective: securing President Akaev's resignation. When the movement became too large and dispersed to counter effectively with force, the regime was unable to offer acceptable concessions, and Akaev's government collapsed. The revolution highlighted the importance of the relatively permissive institutional context in Kyrgyzstan, in which elites independent of the regime were not only able to win the allegiance of people in their communities but also managed to establish crucial cross-village and cross-regional ties to other elites, which solved a problem posed by the absence of other cross-regional networks.

In this chapter, I detail how the Tulip Revolution began and unfolded. I provide a background to the political situation in Kyrgyzstan before the 2005 elections, and then trace the process of protest outbreak and expansion in three regions: Jalalabad, Osh, and Bishkek. I then analyze the March events in terms of the vertical and horizontal components of Kyrgyzstan's mass mobilization infrastructure and explain variations in participation on the district and village levels, before considering alternate explanations.[3]

## Semidemocratic Elections in Kyrgyzstan

In the 2005 parliamentary elections, President Askar Akaev attempted to secure a majority of seats for candidates loyal to him. Two years previously, Akaev had

---

3. In this chapter, "district" refers to an electoral constituency (*izbiratel'nyi okrug*), not to an administrative district (raion).

created a new party, Alga Kyrgyzstan (Forward Kyrgyzstan), in order to consolidate pro-presidential forces and provide favored candidates with *administrativnye resursy*—financial and other assistance—to help them win elections.[4] Alga fielded candidates in twenty-seven out of Kyrgyzstan's seventy-five electoral districts. In addition, some furtively pro-presidential candidates ran as independents in order to distance themselves from Akaev, who had become increasingly unpopular.[5] Akaev also ensured that his son and daughter ran in districts where they were likely to win: Akaev's hometown of Kemin and the Kyrgyz State University district in Bishkek, where university employees could be mobilized to get out the vote.[6]

Akaev's government worked to weaken the opposition by manipulating the eligibility requirements for candidates. The most controversial move was made against Roza Otunbaeva, a popular former member of the nomenklatura, foreign minister, and ambassador, who had recently declared her opposition to Akaev. Fearing the threat she posed if elected, the government instituted a requirement that, to be eligible for parliament, candidates must reside in Kyrgyzstan for five years before running. As Otunbaeva had recently returned from a diplomatic post, she was automatically disqualified.[7] A compliant supreme court affirmed the decision. Other preemptive disqualifications on dubious grounds took place throughout the country.[8]

Yet the president was unable to provide sufficient resources to guarantee his allies a decisive advantage over their opponents, leading candidates of all persuasions to engage in hard-fought campaigns that involved both innovative and crude means of winning votes. One election observer called pre-election vote buying the worst she had seen in fifteen years of Kyrgyz elections.[9] Some candidates paid voters in cash.[10] Others distributed baskets of food and sacks of flour to needy families. One candidate reputedly gave out packages containing clothes,

---

4. Mira Karybaeva, "Development of a Multiparty System in Central Asia," *Central Asia and the Caucasus* 2, no. 32 (2005). On the euphemism of "administrative resources" in post-Soviet elections, see Andrew Wilson, *Virtual Politics: Faking Democracy in the Post-Soviet World* (New Haven: Yale University Press, 2005), chapter 4, 73–88.

5. "Kyrgyzstan: After the Revolution," International Crisis Group, May 4, 2005.

6. Erica Marat, "Upcoming Elections in Kyrgyzstan: Breakthrough or Sheer Ritual?" *Central Asia-Caucasus Institute Analyst,* February 23 (2005).

7. "Kyrgyzstan Opposition Strong, Lacks Unity," Associated Press, March 22, 2005.

8. "Repression in Advance of Elections: Letter to Kyrgyz President Akaev," Human Rights Watch, February 13, 2005, http://www.hrw.org/en/news/2005/02/13/repression-advance-elections.

9. Interview, election observer, Coalition for Civil Society and Democracy, Jalalabad, June 26, 2006.

10. Payments for votes sometimes reached up to $25 where there was stiff opposition. To ensure that the voter kept his side of the bargain, many used the "carousel" method, in which a voter is issued a premarked ballot and must exit the voting booth with a blank ballot. Interview, Sultan Kunazarov, Radio Liberty Kyrgyz Service, Bishkek, June 15, 2006.

tea, soap, and a towel to twelve thousand people.[11] In a frigid, mountainous region, a candidate distributed three sacks of coal to each family in the constituency.[12] Vodka was poured liberally, especially for local elders, whose ability to influence other voters was disproportionately large.[13] A more direct way to sway electoral outcomes was to bribe the district's election commission, which tallies votes and certifies the winner. Candidates were rumored to have paid commission members up to 100,000 som ($2,500) to curry favor, but even this did not guarantee a victory.[14]

Whereas the president presided over a cohesive party organization, albeit of recent vintage, Kyrgyzstan's fragmented opposition had made only superficial efforts to unite. As chapter 3 argued, Kyrgyzstan's many parties were best understood as vehicles for ambitious actors—democracy activists, wealthy local elites, and defectors from the regime—to promote their own political fortunes. Most parties were highly personalistic, possessed little organizational capacity, and lacked branches outside the leader's home region. Yet the unique circumstances surrounding the election increased the incentives for cooperation: Akaev was constitutionally required to step down in October 2005, so the March elections were seen by the opposition as the first battle in a struggle to prevent Akaev from choosing his successor. Thus, the months before the elections saw a flurry of new parties, alliances between parties, and alliances between alliances, impeded only by the half-hearted harassment of opposition figures. One such "party," the Civic Union for Fair Elections, united several longtime oppositionists and recent defectors from both the north and south of the country. It had no platform beyond what its name implied, but its membership made it the most formidable opposition network to that point.[15]

In late 2004, a new coalition, the People's Movement of Kyrgyzstan (PMK), unified nine ineffectual parties that were limited in support to individual regions.[16]

---

11. Interview, election observer in Kochkor, Bishkek, July 4, 2006.

12. Interview, Kial Tuksonbaev, nephew of an elder who distributed the coal, National Democratic Institute, Bishkek, June 16, 2006.

13. Interviews, Kubanych Joldoshov, Radio Liberty Kyrgyz Service, Osh, July 1, 2006; election observer, July 4, 2004.

14. Interview, Jybek Joroeva, chief editor of *Alai* newspaper, Gulchi village, Osh, June 28, 2006.

15. From the north were both businessmen and former regime officials: journalist Melis Eshimkanov, former education minister Ishengul Boljorova, businessman Almaz Atambaev, and the former head of the Security Council, Misir Ashirkulov. Opposition MPs Omurbek Tekebaev and Adahan Madumarov represented the south. "Political Transition in Kyrgyzstan," International Crisis Group (ICG), August 11, 2004, 15; Leila Saralaeva, "Changing Sides in Kyrgyzstan," Institute of War and Peace Reporting (IWPR), June 7, 2004.

16. These parties are the Party of Communists, the Communist Party, the Republican Party, Asaba, the Democratic Movement of Kyrgyzstan, Kairan El ("ill-fated people"), New Kyrgyzstan, Erkin ("free") Kyrgyzstan, and Erkindik ("freedom").

Soon after its founding, it too formed an alliance with three other opposition co-alitions.[17] This new umbrella organization had the potential to project significant strength, not from grassroots membership or ideological coherence, but from the union of individual opposition figures from both the north and south of the country—in particular Kurmanbek Bakiev (who was chosen to head the PMK) and Roza Otunbaeva (who had founded her own party, Ata-Jurt—fatherland—which then joined with the PMK)—and less influential elites from the country-side. This was a powerful alliance: Bakiev, Otunbaeva, and other party leaders contributed experience in government, ties to the business community and inter-national sector in the capital, and an understanding of public relations, while local elites maintained ties with their communities and possessed an aura of authentic-ity that more cosmopolitan ex-politicians lacked. The PMK had little in the way of a common platform beyond supporting fair elections and urging that Akaev follow through on his pledge to step down in October 2005, and it lacked a char-ismatic figure comparable to Mikheil Saakashvili or Viktor Yushchenko from the Georgian and Ukrainian "revolutions."[18] Instead, its influence came from linking several powerful personalities with local elites in rural areas around the country.

Despite Akaev's belated attempts to consolidate power, pluralism in Kyrgyz-stan's political system prevailed in the 2005 elections, as a diverse group of nearly four hundred candidates competed for seventy-five seats.[19] Ironically, the first round of voting, which sparked the protests that eventually led to Akaev's ouster, was probably the freest and fairest election in Central Asia to that point. Accord-ing to the Organization for Security and Cooperation in Europe (OSCE), it was "more competitive than earlier elections, [though it] fell short of OSCE commit-ments and other international standards for democratic elections in a number of areas."[20] Violations included government manipulation of the media in the period before the elections, denial of access to diverse sources of information,

---

17. "Zaiavlenie ob'edineniia politicheskikh sil 'narodnoe dvijenie Kyrgyzstana'" [Announcement of the union of political forces 'people's movement of Kyrgyzstan'], MCH Online, September 29, 2004, http://www.msn.kg/ru/news/8067/; Nazgul Baktybekova, "Next Revolution: Kyrgyzstan?" *Central Asia-Caucasus Institute Analyst*, January 12, 2005; Saralaeva, "Changing Sides." Because the PMK was the most influential of these groups—and essentially absorbed the others—I refer to the whole coalition as the PMK.

18. See Michael McFaul, "Transitions from Postcommunism," *Journal of Democracy* 16 (2005): 5–19.

19. The 2005 elections saw the inauguration of a unicameral legislature, with all legislators cho-sen from single-member districts. Runoffs were held between the top two vote recipients if no one could win a majority in the first round. Previously the Kyrgyz parliament had been comprised of an upper house of forty-five members and a lower house of sixty members.

20. Daniel Kimmage, "Analysis: Kyrgyz, Tajik Elections Present Familiar Issues, New Context," Radio Free Europe/Radio Liberty (RFE/RL), March 2, 2005. This endorsement, though tepid, was stronger than previous ones.

and manipulation of the eligibility requirements to run for parliament.[21] Many losing candidates additionally complained of widespread corruption during the campaign, including the use of vote buying by pro-government candidates.

The initial results were not favorable to the opposition. Out of seventy-five seats in parliament, thirty-two races were won outright in the first round. Of these, only two went to the opposition, while the remainder were won by openly pro-government or independent candidates.[22] In the second round on March 13, opposition figures won another eight seats.[23]

The results suggested that money and government support were helpful in securing a seat. Two factors—running as Alga, Akaev's party, and being one of the one hundred richest people in Kyrgyzstan[24]—greatly increased the likelihood of winning. Twenty-seven Alga candidates and forty-eight of the wealthiest one hundred Kyrgyz ran for parliament. The Alga candidates won twenty seats, a 74 percent success rate. Of the seven defeated Alga candidates, five advanced to the second round before losing. Three of those seven suffered defeats to candidates on the "wealthiest" list.

For their part, twenty-eight of the wealthiest prevailed in their contests, a 58 percent success rate—sixteen in the first round and twelve in the second.[25] Of the twenty losers, six defeats came to other wealthy candidates. Only eight of those twenty lost to somebody who was neither in the Alga Party nor on the "wealthiest" list. The most formidable candidates were those on both lists—all eight who were on the "100 wealthiest" list *and* represented Alga won their elections.

## National Mobilization in Kyrgyzstan

The first protests occurred long before election day on February 27. On January 6, when Otunbaeva's candidacy was rejected, several dozen activists from NGOs and youth groups in Bishkek mounted protests in her defense. Daily demonstrations continued over the next two weeks in front of parliament, but did not succeed in reinstating her candidacy. Beginning in mid-February, candidates in

---

21. "Missiia BDIPCh/OBSE po-prezhnomu otmechaet nalichie znachitel'nykh nedostatkov vo vtorom ture vyborov JK KR" [Bureau of Democratic Institutions and Human Rights/OSCE mission notes as earlier significant flaws in the second round of elections to the parliament of the Kyrgyz Republic], http://www.akipress.org, March 14, 2005.

22. Michael A. Weinstein, "Kyrgyzstan's Chronic Complications," Eurasianet.org, March 18, 2005.

23. RFE/RL Newsline 5(12), April 5, 2005.

24. From an unscientific 2004 survey conducted by the regional newspaper *Fergana*, in which readers were asked to nominate people to the list and experts from around the country winnowed it to one hundred. It was conducted three years straight, and 80% of the names from the 2003 list appeared again in 2004.

25. Put another way, the wealthiest were 6.7% of the candidates, but won 37.3% of the seats.

other regions who had been disqualified due to alleged violations of campaign rules challenged the decisions, both through the courts and in the streets. Protests ranging in size from several dozen to several thousand took place in late February in the provinces of Osh, Jalalabad, Naryn, Issyk Kul, Talas, and Bishkek. Protesters held signs, demonstrated in front of election commission offices, blocked roads, and forcibly entered several government buildings.

After the first round of voting, the number and size of the protests increased. Supporters of candidates who had lost or, in some cases, failed to win a majority in the first round—whether legitimately or as a result of cheating—turned out to protest. The day after the election, on February 28, people began gathering in Aravan in Osh Oblast. The next day, protests broke out in Kara-su—also in Osh Oblast—and in Naryn. Then demonstrations occurred outside of Jalalabad City and in Toktogul in Jalalabad Oblast; in Uzgen, Kurshab, and Osh City in Osh Oblast; and in the northern provinces of Issyk Kul, Talas, Chui, and Bishkek.

Why did they protest? In some cases, losing candidates believed that a fraud had been committed and that demonstrating was the only way to have their case examined. In other instances, candidates who lost outright in the first round—even if they believed the result to be legitimate—may have claimed fraud in order to save face after an embarrassing defeat. For those who made it to the second round but received fewer votes than expected, protests could be used to intimidate their rivals and, if there were legitimate suspicions of first-round fraud, to deter second-round manipulation.[26] Once protests had broken out in several places, the potential costs of mobilizing one's supporters declined, whereas the benefits increased: leading demonstrations was now seen as an act of heroism and could attract media attention. Better yet, it qualified a candidate to become a leader in a putative post-Akaev government.

Who were the candidates involved in mobilization? They did not fit a single description, but two characteristics increased the likelihood that a candidate would lead protests: wealth and a history of opposition activism. Of the twenty-eight candidates who led protests, eight were also on the list of the one hundred wealthiest Kyrgyz. Ten to twelve can be considered active oppositionists. The majority of mobilizing elites were wealthy but not among the one hundred wealthiest people. Most (all but two or three), including those in opposition, owned businesses. Tables 6.1 and 6.2 list mobilizing candidates along with their backgrounds, affiliation at the time of the election, protest tactics, opponents, and the outcome of each election. Figure 6.1 shows where protests occurred.

---

26. On protesting as signaling, see Katrin Uba, "Political Protest and Policy Change: The Direct Impacts of Indian Anti-Privatization Mobilizations, 1990–2003," *Mobilization: An International Quarterly* 10, no. 3 (2005): 383–96; Jessica Weiss, "Powerful Patriots: Nationalism, Diplomacy, and the Strategic Logic of Anti-Foreign Protest" (PhD diss., University of California, San Diego, 2008).

**Table 6.1** Major preelection protests, Kyrgyzstan, 2005

| DATE | DISTRICT[a] (OBLAST) | CANDIDATE | PROFESSION | AFFILIATION | OPPONENT/TARGET | TACTIC | RESULT |
|---|---|---|---|---|---|---|---|
| January 6 | University (Bishkek) | Roza Otunbaeva | Former foreign minister, former ambassador | Opposition | Election commission; Bermet Akaeva, President Akaev's daughter | Demonstrated at parliament with student organizations | Disqualified |
| February 10 | Osh | Achahan Turgunbaeva | Leader of Ellet Party | Independent | Election commission; MP Alisher Sobirov | 200 blocked road | Disqualified |
| February 20 | Tiup (Issyk Kul) | Sadyr Japarov | Managing director of oil and natural gas company | Pro-government | Kurmanbek Namazaliev, director of construction company, akim of Tiup Raion; Ukon Isaeva, President Akaev's sister-in-law | Blocked roads | Disqualified and reinstated; won in 2nd round |
| February 21 | Ton (Issyk Kul) | Arslanbek Maliev* | MP | Independent | Askarbek Aliev, director, Center for Land and Agricultural Reform, brother of governor of Issyk Kul | 2,500 blocked road | Disqualified; eventually won after court decision |
| February 21 | Bakait (Talas) | Ravshan Jeenbekov* | Former chairman of the State Committee for the Management of State Property | Pro-government until 2004 | Jusup Imanaliev, head of agricultural cooperative | February 21, 2,000 demonstrated; March 14, 5,000 demonstrated, blocked roads, occupied buildings, (March 15 kidnapped governor) | Disqualified and reinstated; lost in 2nd round |

| February 22 | Kochkor (Naryn) | Beishenbek Bolotbekov; Akylbek Japarov | Bolotbekov: director of Center for Direct Investment; Japarov: former head of tax collection in Ministry of Finance, MP | Bolotbekov: opposition; Japarov: independent | Naryn governor Shamshybek Medetbekov; candidate Turdakun Usubaliev (Communist Party) | ~5,000 blocked road | Disqualified; vote against all candidates |
|---|---|---|---|---|---|---|---|
| February 22 | Kara-Unkur (Jalalabad) | Kurmanbek Bakiev* | MP, leader of PMK | Opposition | Police, who closed Bakiev's campaign headquarters | 500 demonstrated | Lost in 2nd round |

*Sources for tables 6.1 and 6.2:* Radio Free Europe/Radio Liberty; http://www.akipress.org; http://www.shailoo.gov.kg; http://www.centrasia.ru, and "Kyrgyzstan: After the Revolution," International Crisis Group, May 4, 2005.

*Notes:* Tables 6.1 and 6.2 contain protest events that were reported in the press and involved at least one hundred people. Names marked with an asterisk were on the list of 100 wealthiest Kyrgyz. Candidates who were members of the pro-presidential party, Alga, are noted in the "Opponent" column.

[a] Districts encompassed numerous villages and were drawn to include 30,000–35,000 eligible voters.

**Table 6.2** Major postelection protests, Kyrgyzstan, 2005

| DATE | DISTRICT[a] (OBLAST) | CANDIDATE | PROFESSION | AFFILIATION | OPPONENT | TACTIC | RESULT |
|---|---|---|---|---|---|---|---|
| February 28 | Aravan (Osh) | Tursunbai Alimov | Head of Aravan village council | Independent | Muhamedjan Mamasaidov, director, Kyrgyz-Uzbek University in Osh, Alga | 1,000–3,000 blocked highway | Lost in 1st round |
| February 28 | Nooken (Jalalabad) | Dooronbek Sadyrbaev | MP, leader of Kairan-El Party | Opposition | Jeneshbek Eshenkulov, MP | ~5,000 demonstrated, blocked road, joined Jalalabad demonstrations March 13 | Won in 2nd round |
| February 28 | Kara-su (Osh) | Arap Tolonov | Head of agricultural cooperative | Independent | Bayysh Yusupov, head of Ak-Altin village council, Alga | Captured admin. building March 7, disbanded March 10 | Lost in 1st round; later won after court decision |
| March 1 | Kara-Kulja (Osh) | Duishenkul Chotonov | MP, deputy chairman of Ata-Meken Party | Opposition | Soorunbai Jeenbekov, MP | 200 demonstrated in Osh | Lost in 1st round |
| March 2 | Kogart (Jalalabad) | Jusupbek Jeenbekov | Head of Osh city committee for external economic ties | Independent | Rashid Tagaev, head of Jalalabad regional police department | 400 demonstrated | Lost in 2nd round |
| March 4 | At-Bashy (Naryn) | Naken Kasiev* | Governor of Osh Oblast | Independent | Askar Salymbekov, businessman, governor of Naryn Oblast, Alga | 300 demonstrated | Lost in 1st round |
| March 4 | Jalalabad City | Jusupbek Bakiev | MP | Opposition | Kadyrjon Batyrov*, businessman, president of Batyr-avia airlines | ~1,000 demonstrated | Lost in 1st round |

| Date | District | Name | Position | Affiliation | Opponent | Demonstration | Outcome |
|---|---|---|---|---|---|---|---|
| March 4 | Kizil-too (Jalalabad) | Bektur Asanov | MP, leader of Erkin Kyrgyzstan Party | Opposition | Ergesh Torobaev, managing director of the Jalalabad Elektro joint stock company, Alga; Marat Kaipov, former chairman of constitutional court | Several hundred demonstrated in Jalalabad City | Lost in 1st round |
| March 6 | Naryn (Naryn) | Ishenbai Kadyrbekov | MP | Opposition | Karganbek Samakov*, businessman, MP | 500 blocked highway | Disqualified and reinstated; lost in 2nd round |
| March 6 | Nariman (Osh) | Anvar Artykov | Former MP, director of ORP Credit-Technical Assistance | Opposition | Inom Abdurasulov, head of Kashgar-Kishtak village council | 100–150 demonstrated in Osh | Lost in 1st round |
| March 12 | Chui (Chui) | Turatbek Andashev | President of tourism complex in Issyk Kul | Independent | Aidarbek Kerimkulov, MP, Alga | 500 demonstrated in Ivanovka village | Disqualified for vote-buying |
| March 13 | Kurshab (Osh) | Adahan Madumarov | MP, cochairman of Ata-Jurt Party | Opposition | Mamat Orozbaev*, former MP, businessman | ~2,000 captured admin. building | Lost in 2nd round, then won after appeal |
| March 13 | Alay (Osh) | Marat Sultanov* | MP, former finance minister | Independent | Abdygany Erkebaev, MP, parliamentary speaker | 500 blocked road | Lost in 2nd round |
| March 14 | Toktogul (Naryn) | Toktosun Madiarov* | President of the Azamat Oil Corporation | Independent | Tairbek Sarpashev, MP, businessman, Alga | 5,000 blocked road; later captured building | Lost in 2nd round |

Continued

**Table 6.2** Major postelection protests, Kyrgyzstan, 2005 (*Continued*)

| DATE | DISTRICT[a] (OBLAST) | CANDIDATE | PROFESSION | AFFILIATION | OPPONENT | TACTIC | RESULT |
|------|------------------|-----------|------------|-------------|----------|--------|--------|
| March 16 | Asanbai (Bishkek) | Melis Eshimkanov | Editor-in-chief of *Agym* newspaper | Opposition | Sharipa Sadybakasova*, chairperson of Kyrgyzstan Commercial Bank | 500 demonstrated near the Bishkek Oktiabrskaia district admin. building | Lost in 2nd round |
| March 16 | University District (Bishkek) | Bolot Maripov | Editor of *Obshchestvennyi Reiting* newspaper | Opposition | Bermet Akaeva | 1,000–2,000 demonstrated in Bishkek | Lost in 2nd round |
| March 16 | Kara Unkur (Jalalabad) | Kurmanbek Bakiev* (second time) | MP, leader of PMK | Opposition | Saidulla Nyshanov, businessman | 500 captured Bazar-Kurgan admin. building | Lost in 2nd round |
| March 16 | Tunduk (Bishkek) | Janysh Rustenbekov* | MP, former governor of Osh, former head of presidential administration | Independent | Jyrgalbek Surabaldiev, head of Association of Kyrgyz Businessmen | Supporters blocked road | Lost in 2nd round |
| March 19 | Asanbai (Bishkek) | Noncandidates Almaz Atambaev* (leader of Soc-Dem Party), Japar Jeksheev (leader of Dem. Movement of Kyrgyzstan Party), Murat Imanaliev (leader of Jangi Bagyt Party) | Businessmen/party leaders | All opposition | N/A | ~3,000 demonstrated in Bishkek | N/A |

*Sources and notes:* See table 6.1.

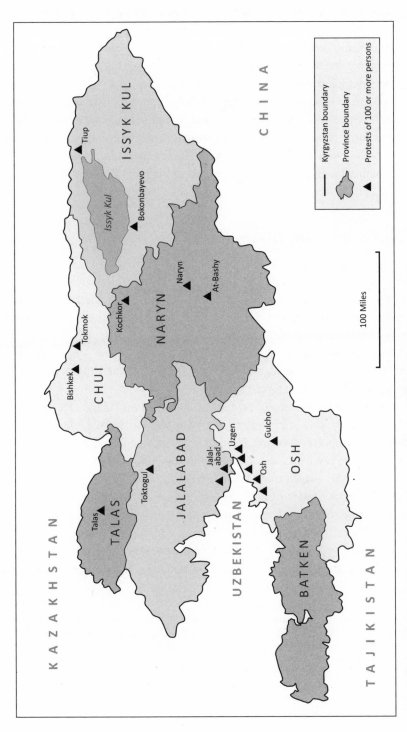

**FIGURE 6.1.** Locations of major protests in Kyrgyzstan, February–March 2005

Two additional factors should also be noted from the tables. First, most pre-election protests ended before the first round of voting, whereas postelection protests continued until the government collapsed.[27] This difference stems from a new dynamic that took hold after the elections, when separate protests merged and candidates jumped on the opposition's bandwagon.

Second, protests began and ended in Bishkek, but did not take place there in the middle. Oppositionists and NGOs in the capital were unable to attract the grassroots support needed to build a movement themselves. Only when candidate-led mobilization in the south turned out large crowds and caused the overthrow of a number of provincial governments did significant protests appear in Bishkek.

## Stirrings in the South: Jalalabad

The origins of mobilization in Jalalabad lay in the grievances of parliamentary candidates disappointed by first-round election results. On March 3, two to three hundred supporters of candidate Jusupbek Jeenbekov gathered to protest in front of the Kogart District election commission headquarters, a short ride from the regional capital, Jalalabad. They claimed that the campaign of the first-place finisher—the pro-presidential candidate, Rashid Tagaev[28]—had tried to intimidate Jeenbekov's campaign staff prior to the voting, when Tagaev defeated Jeenbekov 36–27 percent to force a runoff.

Jeenbekov was not wealthy or prominent outside of his village. However, he was the younger brother of a popular deceased opposition figure, Satybaldi Jeenbekov. Equally important, his son, Bahtior, was a successful businessman working in Russia who headed an association for labor migrants that hired exclusively from Vin-Sovkhoz—which translates as "state wine farm"—and ran a charitable fund that helped residents of the village.[29] Vin-Sovkhoz stands out from its neighbors in the striking and open displays of wealth of its residents, including two-story houses, new mosques, paved roads, and a modern drainage system.[30] The Jeenbekovs' importance to their community translated directly into public support. One participant told how Jeenbekov's son had gathered people in the

---

27. Analysts have noted that unrest in the typically docile north should have been a warning signal to Akaev about the extensiveness of the opposition. However, one can draw the opposite conclusion—that the relative calm in the south implied that elections would come off smoothly. See ICG, "After the Revolution."

28. Tagaev was the head of the Jalalabad Interior Ministry.

29. Interview, Cholpon Ergesheva, Jalalabad; residents of Vin-Sovkhoz village, Kogart District, Jalalabad, June 26, 2006.

30. Author's personal observation, Vin-Sovkhoz, June 26, 2006.

center of the village and told them to demonstrate for his father.[31] A member of Jeenbekov's campaign staff, a schoolteacher named Roza, explained that she helped round up 30–40 campaign volunteers and friends from throughout the village to protest.[32] This initial cohort from Vin-Sovkhoz became part of a movement that would later involve people from other parts of the oblast.

Jeenbekov's complaint became a regional matter after the election commission refused to address his claim. The demonstrators moved en masse to the central square in Jalalabad on March 4, where they protested the election results in front of the regional-administrative building and demanded an audience with the governor. They were soon joined by several hundred supporters of other candidates from the surrounding area who had lost in the first round, including Jusupbek Bakiev, the younger brother of Kurmanbek, head of the PMK.[33] Another was Bektur Asanov, an opposition deputy from an outlying village who had finished behind both Marat Kaipov, a former justice on the constitutional court, and Ergesh Torobaev, a wealthy energy magnate representing Alga.[34] Asanov, through his Erkin Kyrgyzstan Party (a constituent party of the PMK), paid for and distributed four thousand leaflets in his and a neighboring district encouraging people to join the protests.[35] These different contingents, expressing similar but independent local grievances, pooled their forces into upwards of one thousand people and planted themselves for a sit-in in the central square of Jalalabad.

Developments in Jalalabad attracted broader attention when the demonstrators made a provocative move. After three hundred protesters approached the regional-administrative building to demand a meeting with the governor and were stopped by police, a scuffle ensued. The crowd then forced its way into the office building (most of whose occupants had left) and began to ransack it.[36] For the next two weeks, small groups of protesters continually occupied the building. As the sit-in continued into March, candidate Dooronbek Sadyrbaev, whose

---

31. Interview, Vin-Sovkhoz, June 26, 2006.

32. Interview, Roza, Vin-Sovkhoz, April 17, 2005.

33. Two losing candidates from Jeenbekov's district, Samagan Mamatov and Bakytbek Sydykov, also brought their supporters to the square. Interview, election commission official, Bazar-Kurgan-Suzak District headquarters, April 18, 2005. A longtime Communist Party activist from Oktiabrskaia village in Kogart District, Tagaibek Jarkynbaev, also joined at this time but had few followers.

34. Asanov had briefly taken part in the Aksy mobilization of 2002.

35. Interviews, Bektur Asanov, Jalalabad, June 23, 2006; residents, Kizil-too District, Jalalabad, June 21, 2006.

36. It is unclear whether the siege happened spontaneously or by design. Some reports asserted that the Bakiev brothers, along with Bektur Asanov, had planned the storming in advance and persuaded the police to stand aside. "V Jalalabade mitinguiushchie zakhvatili zdanie oblgosadministratsii" [In Jalalabad demonstrators seized the regional government administration building], March 4, 2005. Asanov also claimed it was his idea. Interview, Asanov, Jalalabad, June 23, 2006.

supporters had been blocking the road in his district forty kilometers away to protest alleged campaign violations, sent several thousand people to Jalalabad after winning in the second round.[37] Emboldened, the leaders began demanding Akaev's resignation.

Not long after protesters had begun gathering in Jalalabad's central square, well-connected elites appropriated the movement from the initiators. Whereas the first candidates to mobilize, such as Jeenbekov, were well known within their communities but lacked wider political connections, the new leaders had national recognition and experience. This cohort included two more of Kurmanbek Bakiev's brothers, who not only enjoyed the prestige of being close to the leader of the PMK but were also influential professionally[38]; and Medir Usenov, an opposition activist from Jalalabad who had founded, along with Azimbek Beknazarov (from chapter 5), an organization called Erk (freedom) that was dedicated to Akaev's ouster. The Bakievs worked with leaders in Jalalabad who possessed only local support and communicated through their brother with the PMK leadership in Bishkek. On the national level, Kurmanbek Bakiev and other leaders of the PMK visited Jalalabad but retained their headquarters in Bishkek throughout the month.[39] The now-demoted local candidates, who had been the first to mobilize, concentrated on winning the second round of voting or worked with their associates to recruit more protesters and coordinate transportation between the villages and the square.[40]

Candidates and their associates cooperated in organizing and policing the crowds occupying Jalalabad, which totaled 1,500–2,000 by March 7.[41] They set up an ad hoc coordinating committee (*koordinatsionnyi sovet*) that supervised the collection of money, which was solicited from local business owners and villagers who came to the square; the provision of food, which they purchased from the bazaar or local restaurants and cafes (*chaihonas*) and then distributed to informal

---

37. Tellingly, the posters and slogans of Sadyrbaev's supporters were directed against the local authorities (*akims*) and called for fair elections. Only later did they begin shouting slogans against Akaev. Interview, Erkin Salimjanov, Sadyrbaev's nephew and chief representative, Nooken District, Jalalabad, June 24, 2006.

38. His three brothers worked as the director of the legal department of the Ministry of Justice; a budget manager in the Ministry of Emergency Situations; and a high-ranking official in the Ministry of Interior. *Kommersant* 53 (3137), March 26, 2005.

39. Kurmanbek Bakiev, who had been in Bishkek, made a surprise appearance with another opposition leader from the south, Usen Sydykov, on March 6. "V Jalalabade Kurmanbek Bakiev prizyvaet k smene vlasti" [Kurmanbek Bakiev calls for a change of power in Jalalabad], http://www.akipress.org/, March 6, 2005.

40. They were later rewarded for their efforts: after the change in power, Jeenbekov became governor of Jalalabad and Jarkynbaev became mayor (*akim*) of Suzak Raion.

41. "Mitingi v Jalalabade prodolzhaiutsia [Protests in Jalalabad continue]," http://www.akipress.org/, March 7, 2005.

village leaders; and monitoring, by recording the names of participating villages and the number and names of individual protesters.[42] Several activists spontane-ously created a "defense militia" (*otriad oborony*) to police the crowd and deter disruptive behavior. It consisted of two groups of twelve young men, equipped with red armbands to identify them and megaphones to communicate.[43]

At the village level, social ties facilitated recruiting and led to a surprisingly sophisticated level of organization. Far from the chaos that stereotypes of rebel-lious peasants evoke, participants organized themselves into small groups and willingly subordinated themselves to the informal hierarchy that was develop-ing. Villagers selected leaders who would coordinate transportation between the village and the square, convey to Jalalabad's coordinating committee how many protesters they had brought and the amount of food they required, and answer for the group's conduct. In the village of Ok-took in Asanov's district, a retired physical education teacher, Kubanych, was chosen to lead the 15–20 protesters in the village and liaise with the committee. Beginning on March 6, people would gather in front of his house each morning to ride a bus thirty kilometers to the city, and then return home each afternoon. Several times Kubanych slept over at a park near the square in Jalalabad and worked out a schedule to alternate over-night stays with other men.[44] From a nearby village, a farmer and mother of ten children (honored for that accomplishment in the Soviet era as a *mat'-geroina*, or mother-heroine) was selected as the head of her cohort. Such patterns of vil-lage self-organization were reproduced throughout that and other districts in the region.[45]

Cross-regional interelite ties expanded the scale of mobilization by subsum-ing Jalalabad's protests into a national structure. A week after the first round of elections, the PMK began improvising a national-level operation from Bishkek.

---

42. Interviews with committee members and participants, Jalalabad, April 2005.

43. Interviews, Gamal, Jalalabad, April 20, 2005; Keres, Jalalabad, April 15, 2005.

44. Interview, Kubanych, Ok-took village, Kizil-too District, Jalalabad, April 23, 2005.

45. Interview, Guli-opa, Kizil-too District, April 23, 2005. Where did this organizational initia-tive originate? The organizers claimed that they had received no instructions to choose leaders. How-ever, it is unlikely that people in scattered villages would all adopt the same means of organization spontaneously. A more likely explanation is that once people from different villages began associating at the square in early March, the idea diffused from one group to another and was brought back to the villages. The mode of organization that emerged had the advantage of being culturally familiar. The pyramidal and hierarchical structure, in which leaders are put in charge of a small group and answer to leaders at a higher level, was based on traditional Kyrgyz nomadic organization, similar to that used in Aksy. Using a repertoire—a shared set of routines—from Kyrgyz history helped facilitate diffusion of the innovation. On protest repertoires, see Sidney Tarrow, *Power in Movement* (New York: Cambridge University Press, 1994), 30–32. On diffusion of protest repertoires, see Sarah A. Soule, "Diffusion Processes within and across Movements," in *The Blackwell Companion to So-cial Movements*, ed. David A. Snow, Sarah Soule, and Hanspeter Kriesi (Malden, Mass.: Blackwell, 2004), 294–310.

Bakiev and Otunbaeva communicated from Bishkek with leaders in Jalalabad and Osh, respectively, to direct their activities. By virtue of being the first whose administration building was occupied, Jalalabad was seen as the vanguard of a national struggle that now encompassed demonstrations taking place in the central squares of Osh, Talas, and Naryn Oblasts, and in a handful of peripheral areas. To increase media exposure and signal the movement's strength to the government, the PMK organized a party congress (*kurultai*) in Jalalabad on March 15, consisting of delegates from all parties in the alliance and representing most regions of the country. To this end, a reported four to six thousand delegates came to Jalalabad. A "people's committee" (*narodnyi kenesh*), consisting of a new governor, deputy governor, and district mayors, was selected as a shadow government. By this time, politicians who doubted the chances of the opposition risked being left out of any future government should the opposition succeed.

For most of the period of protest, the government had taken a cautious approach, but when it unexpectedly tried to retake control, its actions backfired and weakened its position. After protesters in Osh had seized its administrative headquarters on March 18 in emulation of Jalalabad, President Akaev decided to seize the initiative and restore his waning authority. Early in the morning on March 20, soldiers stormed Jalalabad's administrative building, disgorged its occupants, and arrested opposition leaders. News of this provocation quickly spread from protesters who witnessed the raid to co-villagers, replete with rumors exaggerating the event (that women were thrown from third-story windows; that special forces [OMONovtsy] were drunk and had beaten unarmed women and children). Asanov, one of the on-site organizers, decided to exploit the opportunity by announcing a demonstration for later that day at a junction of several roads near the entrance to the city. Large portions of villages, outraged at the news or dragged out by their neighbors, were seen walking together along Kyrgyzstan's main highway in groups of five or six hundred people.[46] As contingents from different villages converged on Jalalabad, some city residents joined that day for the first time,[47] including much of the bazaar, whose merchants were from outlying villages but who had previously chosen to continue working rather than protest.[48] Independent candidates who won their elections and had therefore been neutral toward (or opposed to) mobilization before March 20, now found it expedient to mobilize their followers as well.[49] In all, ten to twenty thousand people

---

46. Interview, Abdumajid, Barpy District, Jalalabad, April 22, 2005.
47. Interview, Aibek, Jalalabad, April 15, 2005.
48. See the methodological appendix for notes on interviews with bazaar merchants.
49. Interviews, Asylbek, Jalalabad, April 19, 2005; Kochkor-aka, Barpy District, Jalalabad, April 22, 2005.

(depending on the source), many carrying rocks, sticks, and Molotov cocktails, assembled and prepared for confrontation.

After overrunning a line of soldiers, people converged on the central square, burned down the district Interior Ministry headquarters (ROVD), reoccupied the administration building, and seized the airport. The "people's committee" declared itself the legitimate government in Jalalabad and called for sending the "revolution" to Bishkek. Immediately, the committee arranged for buses to send demonstrators to Osh and Bishkek, where standoffs with the government were continuing.

## Onward to Osh

The conditions for mobilization in Jalalabad were also present in Osh, Kyrgyzstan's second city. On the whole, the events in Osh were less dramatic than in Jalalabad: there were fewer protesters, most of whom came from two locales, as opposed to the wide array of candidates and villages that participated in Jalalabad. Yet the dynamics underlying mobilization in Osh had much in common with its neighbor to the north. The movement began as the expression of grievances by individual losing candidates, who acted through their operatives to initiate mobilization within communities. Leaders in Osh established a coordinating committee to monitor the central square, and were then absorbed by the national-level PMK network. Finally, the government stormed Osh's administration building and disgorged its occupants, an action that stimulated the recruitment of new protesters, who overpowered local law enforcement and proclaimed themselves the new government.

In Osh Oblast, as in Jalalabad, many losing candidates protested after the first round to district-level election commissions. In Kara-su, six hundred supporters of Arap Tolonov, director of an agricultural cooperative (former collective farm) with twenty-one thousand people, protested in front of the Kara-su courthouse where his case against a pro-government candidate was being heard. In nearby Aravan, five hundred supporters of village council chairman (equivalent of mayor) Tursonbai Alimov blocked the Osh-Aravan highway in protest of the first-round victory of his pro-government opponent. In mountainous Alai to the east, several thousand supporters of wealthy banking magnate Marat Sultanov blocked the main road.

However, the catalysts for mobilization in Osh City came from farther away, near the Chinese border, in Kara-kulja. On March 6, over two hundred supporters of Duishenkul Chotonov, an MP, deputy chairman of the opposition Ata-Meken Party (which was not part of the PMK), and a participant in the Aksy protests of 2002, began a two-day journey to the administrative center of Osh where they were to remain for twelve days.

The protesters in Kara-kulja are a case study of the activation of local net-works. When Chotonov lost in the first round to pro-government candidate Sooronbai Jeenbekov (no relation to Jalalabad's Jeenbekov), Chotonov and two of his aides—who later became deputy governors of Osh—began contacting other members of his campaign team. While Chotonov coordinated from the center of Kara-Kulja, his assistants went door-to-door to mobilize people in vil-lages throughout the district, some separated by up to one hundred kilometers.[50] The majority of recruits came from the district's center, Alai-kul, and most of those were from Koch-ati village, where Chotonov was born and his family re-sided—a small but committed portion of the total population.[51]

On March 11, Chotonov's group was joined by the supporters of Anvar Ar-tykov, an ethnic Uzbek businessman and former MP, and member of Otunbae-va's Ata-Jurt Party from Shark, seven kilometers outside of Osh. The two groups formed an unlikely alliance. Chotonov's ethnic Kyrgyz neighbors and relatives from Kara-Kulja came from an isolated and pastoral region in the foothills of the Tien Shan Mountains. Artykov's 100–150 supporters—mostly *his* neighbors and relatives—were ethnic Uzbeks from a collective farm just outside Osh city. Hav-ing heard of Chotonov's protest, Artykov's advisors persuaded him to join after he lost his court case.[52] When Artykov and his supporters arrived in Osh, they acquiesced to the leadership of Chotonov's committee, which had already been organizing at the square.[53]

Shark's residents recruited and organized through community social ties, as occurred so many times in Jalalabad. Artykov's supporters, mostly pensioners, held him in high esteem because of his influential family ties—his uncle had been the head of the collective farm and his father the head of the district Com-munist Party (*raikom*). They claimed to support him because he was "our boy",[54] because he "helps us," and because he was "familiar with agriculture."[55] Artykov's early supporters then canvassed their villages to recruit more participants and established a routine for commuting to the square; participants would meet in small groups, usually with friends, catch a public minibus (*marshrutka*) at 9 a.m. into the city, and return each day at 4 p.m.

---

50. Interview, Abdumamat, Chotonov's aide, Osh, April 29, 2005.

51. Interview, Zamir, candidate from Kara-Kulja District, Osh, April 30, 2005.

52. Interview, Muhammadjon, Shark Village, Osh, April 29, 2005.

53. One reason for Artykov's keeping a low profile may be his nationality. Uzbeks in southern Kyrgyzstan had been notoriously apolitical, and many feared that political activism on the part of Uzbeks might be exploited by the authorities to cast the conflict as ethnic rather than antigovern-ment. Despite the participation of several hundred Uzbeks, ethnic Kyrgyz remained the majority of oppositionists in Osh.

54. Interview, Muhbabahon, Shark Village, Osh, April 29, 2005.

55. Interview, Urinboi-aka, Shark Village, Osh, April 29, 2005.

Yet most residents of Shark—like Kara-Kulja—did not join; despite a general tendency to exaggerate numbers, my informants from Shark never claimed there were more than 150 protesters before March 21, out of twenty-four thousand eligible voters in the district.[56] One reason for the low level of activism was that most people were supporters of Artykov's rival, the victorious, wealthier, and reputedly pro-government candidate, Inom Abdurasulov.[57] During the postelection period, this division vitiated neighborly relations in Shark: when supporters of the rival candidates came into contact, they would greet one another but not speak on the same friendly terms as before. Some streets were split down the middle. Artykov's supporters bitterly accused Abdurasulov of buying votes and opportunistically running in Shark after having lost in another district. Presumably the resentment was mutual.[58]

The small operation in Osh was facilitated by ties to wealthy elites who joined the opposition when they sensed the government's weakness. The greatest contribution came from two businessmen and former wrestlers, Timur Kamchibekov and Bayaman Erkinbaev. Both had converted their athletic talents into successful business careers. Kamchibekov, at the age of twenty-seven, owned fifteen enterprises including sports clubs, where he cultivated a crew of young sportsmen committed to supporting him. Erkinbaev owned a large stake in Central Asia's largest bazaar. His network of young followers, unlike Kamchibekov's, stretched throughout the entire southern part of the country. In a fluid situation where muscle and money could make a difference, both men lent their assets with an eye toward gaining political influence.[59]

The wrestlers compensated for the low numbers that hindered Osh's opposition. Kamchibekov, after running unsuccessfully for parliament, contributed a truck with a loudspeaker, money for distributing leaflets, and over one hundred young men.[60] Erkinbaev, a relative of Chotonov's by marriage, joined the opposition despite having won his parliamentary seat in the first round. He used his personal fortune to help finance transportation, food, leaflets, and small cash handouts for protesters staying at the square.[61] He also appeared in Jalalabad after the transfer of power, announcing a gift of 20,000 som ($500) and supplying

---

56. www.shailoo.gov.kg.

57. Interview, Kubanych Joldoshov, Radio Liberty Kyrgyz Service, Osh, July 1, 2006.

58. Interviews, Shark Village, Osh, April 29, 2005.

59. On the influence of sportsmen in Russia and the Caucasus, see Vadim Volkov, *Violent Entrepreneurs: The Use of Force in the Making of Russian Capitalism* (Ithaca: Cornell University Press, 2002), 7–11; Georgi M. Derluguian, *Bourdieu's Secret Admirer in the Caucasus: A World-System Biography* (Chicago: University of Chicago Press, 2005), 266, 268.

60. Interview, Kushtar, Osh, April 30, 2005.

61. Interviews in Osh: Alisher T., April 28, 2005; Sharopat, April 28, 2005; Kushtar, April 30, 2005.

fifteen minibuses to send protesters to Bishkek.[62] Kamchibekov and Erkinbaev's followers instigated confrontations with armed police forces, providing physical strength and boldness (or stupidity) that most protesters lacked. In the chaos that followed the collapse of the government in Osh, Erkinbaev had his men patrol the streets to restore order, perhaps with the intention of remaining in control of the city after Akaev's downfall.[63]

Elite brokering, from Artykov to Otunbaeva in Bishkek and from Chotonov to Asanov in Jalalabad, connected Osh with other cities as part of an emerging national movement. Otunbaeva shuttled between Bishkek and Osh to strategize with Osh's leaders, while Bakiev coordinated from Bishkek with his brothers in Jalalabad.[64] At least once each day, leaders in Osh spoke with leaders in Jalalabad by mobile phone.[65]

Despite becoming part of a national movement, the overall number of protesters in Osh remained small. Candidates such as Arap Tolonov and Tursunbai Alimov had been protesting in nearby towns but, because they were still focused on contesting the results of their elections, did not join the sit-in in Osh.[66] When the administration building in Jalalabad was seized, leaders in Osh intended to follow suit, but there appeared to be too few people to overwhelm the police. In a desperate effort to increase their numbers, Chotonov's assistants and another losing opposition candidate from Kara-kulja canvassed nearby villages, only to find that few people were willing to participate.[67] As a result, Chotonov was forced to reach an agreement with the authorities: the governor and head of the Interior Ministry assured Chotonov that they would review his case, while Chotonov agreed to restrain his followers as they continued to demonstrate in front of the building, and a tense standoff ensued.[68]

Chotonov's pledge to hold the line was a tactical concession, to be reneged on when word came from Bishkek to seize the initiative. After the party congress in Jalalabad on March 15, to which the Osh contingent sent thirty delegates,[69] the PMK planned a second assembly for Osh four days later. Not wanting to play second fiddle to Jalalabad, Chotonov and Artykov decided to storm the administration building on the 18th. Since the Osh protesters lacked enough manpower, the wrestler Kamchibekov's men proved crucial. Tipped off in advance that the

---

62. Interviews with students, Medir Usenov, Jalalabad, April 20, 2005.

63. Interview, Alisher Saipov, Osh, April 26, 2005.

64. Ibid.

65. Interview, Alisher T., April 28, 2005.

66. Both were running against pro-presidential Alga candidates, but neither had a history of opposition activism or had served in parliament.

67. Interview, Zamir, Osh, April 30, 2005.

68. Ibid.

69. Interview, Muhammedjon, Shark Village, Osh, April 29, 2005.

police were prepared to stand aside in the face of an attack, his posse stormed the building and captured it without incident. The assembly took place the next day and, as in Jalalabad, a "people's committee" was chosen to serve as a shadow government. Two more contingents joined the crowds—those of Arap Tolonov and Adahan Madumarov, whose supporters had been protesting nearby in Kara-su and Uzgen.[70]

The government's storming of the Osh administration building on March 20, simultaneous with its raid in Jalalabad, provided the pretext for Osh's leaders to make a final pitch for mass participation. In an effort to involve city dwellers, Erkinbaev planned to shut down the bazaar and all restaurants and cafes the next day so that people would have nowhere else to go.[71] Several protest organizers persuaded the vice-rector of Osh State University to allow students, who had previously been forbidden to participate, to join.[72] To the opposition's good fortune, March 21 was Navruz, a holiday marking the vernal equinox, on which people typically stroll around the city to attend outdoor events; many people came by the square to watch the proceedings out of curiosity and some decided to join the crowd.[73] Bazaar merchants reported hearing rumors of gangs of marauders on the streets, so most closed their shops; some went home and others joined the protests. Additionally, after seizing Jalalabad on March 20, activists there had sent at least two hundred people on six buses to Osh to share their experience. With momentum on the opposition's side and the police sympathetic, the outcome was hardly in doubt.[74] The mobilized masses advanced behind the vanguard of young fighters from Kamchibekov's sports club, with Kamchibekov himself leading the charge—on a horse—for the television cameras to capture.[75] It did not take long for the protesters to recover the seat of power in southern Kyrgyzstan.

## Back to Bishkek

Only after the fate of the government was sealed in the south did the PMK plan protest actions in Bishkek. The situation in Bishkek before March 20 was

---

70. Tolonov's activists sent one thousand people from Kara-su on March 18 on eight buses financed by Bayaman Erkinbaev (Tolonov's godson) and Kurmanbek Bakiev. Interview, Raisa, election observer and assistant to Tolonov since 1991, Kara-su District, Osh, June 29, 2006. Alimov's sit-in had ended after five days without success due to a lack of funds to feed the protesters. Interview, Muhammadshukur Alimov, Tursonbai Alimov's son, Aravan District, Osh, June 30, 2006.

71. Interviews, Kushtar, Timur's assistant, Osh, April 30, 2005; Zamir, Osh, April 30, 2005.

72. Interview, Zamir, Osh, April 30, 2005.

73. Ibid.

74. Interviews, Medir Usenov, Jalalabad, April 20, 2005; Kerem, New Kyrgyzstan Party official, Osh, May 2, 2005.

75. Interview, Kushtar, Osh, April 30, 2005.

puzzling. It had Kyrgyzstan's most educated and mobile population, a wide variety of groups with diverse interests, and a high concentration of NGOs. Yet until the opposition captured the south, there were relatively few demonstrations in the city. The movement arrived in Bishkek only when embedded elites—not all of them candidates—brought their supporters.

After the capture of Osh, the country's attention—and the opposition's cumulative material and human resources—turned to the capital. PMK leaders hastily cobbled together an alliance of opposition parliamentarians, independent politicians, local businessmen, NGO activists, and mobilizing elites from other regions. Some opposition leaders with popular bases in the south, such as Omurbek Tekebaev, Azimbek Beknazarov, and Adahan Madumarov, arrived in Bishkek but did not bring along supporters. Other elites maintained support bases in the capital, including Jenishbek Nazaraliev, a world-renowned psychiatrist and multimillionaire; Bolot Maripov, a journalist and (defeated) opponent of the president's daughter; and newspaper owner Melis Eshimkanov and businessman Almaz Atambaev from the outskirts of Bishkek.[76] Prominent lawyers (*pravozashchitniki*) and NGOs such as the Coalition for Democracy and Civil Society had preexisting ties to opposition figures and helped disseminate information, but brought few protesters of their own. A first attempt to bring these diverse groups together on March 23 attracted 1,000–1,500 people and was broken up by the police.[77]

On March 24, better coordination and the arrival of fifteen hundred protesters from Naryn and Talas,[78] along with new contingents from Osh and Jalalabad, vastly increased the size of the crowd. The opposition divided and held rallies at 9 a.m. at two points in the city, following which the contingents were to march toward the center and converge on Ala-Too Square in front of the government administration building, or White House. The PMK planned to amass fifty thousand people, including ten thousand from the south, in the center of Bishkek and mount a long-term sit-in along the lines of the revolutionaries in Georgia and Ukraine.[79]

---

76. "Oppozitsiia provela v Bishkeke mnogotysiachnyi miting" [The opposition conducted a demonstration in Bishkek of many thousands], http://www.akipress.org/, March 19, 2005. Maripov's supporters had begun protesting independently in mid-March and joined with the PMK only after the fall of the south. Interview, Bolot Maripov, Bishkek, May 7, 2005.

77. Daniel Kimmage, "Kyrgyzstan: How Bishkek's Revolution Happened So Fast," RFE/RL, April 4, 2005.

78. These were the contingents of Akylbek Japarov and Ravshan Jeenbekov, who had taken over their respective regional government headquarters. "Storonniki eks-kandidata A. Japarova osvobodili zdanie kochkorskoi raiadministratsii" [Supporters of ex-candidate A. Japarov freed the Kochkor regional administrative building], March 21, 2005.

79. Hundreds of protesters being bused in from Osh and Jalalabad did not arrive in time to participate in Bishkek's "revolution," so the PMK's grand plan had no chance of materializing. Interviews, Zamir, Osh, April 30, 2005; Aziza, democratic activist, Bishkek, May 6, 2005.

The crowds that gathered on March 24 and marched to the center were not as massive as expected but gained strength along the way. Nazaraliev's clinic, where half the protesters assembled, was located near Bishkek's Osh Bazaar, where many merchants of southern origin worked. The bazaar closed in late morning in anticipation of unrest and its workers either went home or joined demonstrators from the same region. At noon the Nazaraliev contingent ended its rally and headed toward the White House, arriving two hours later with around five thousand people, including up to two thousand who had joined from the bazaar.[80] An equivalent number had begun marching from the other side of the city and arrived shortly after.[81]

For all intents and purposes, the scuffle at the White House was inconsequential—with half the country in the hands of the opposition and over ten thousand people gathered in Bishkek's central square, the Akaev regime had lost the initiative. The only question was whether Akaev would use force to break up the protest. As it happened, the denouement came so rapidly that he scarcely had time to ponder the decision.[82] Once the two groups of marchers converged, they were thwarted by police and soldiers who sealed off the entrance to the White House. A praetorian guard of several hundred men in civilian clothes and white hats, carrying clubs and shields, emerged from behind the White House gates and began pushing the crowd back. After first retreating, elements from the crowd surged forward only to be repulsed again. Eventually, the protesters penetrated the line of security forces and flooded into the building, sealing President Akaev's fate. He fled the country and resigned ten days later.[83]

## Mass Mobilization through Vertical and Horizontal Networks

Looking at the Tulip Revolution as a whole, a number of puzzling occurrences, at odds with the notion of a grassroots revolution, were observed as mobilization unfolded. For example, the people who took part in the revolution tended

---

80. Observers at the square later reported that a large portion of he crowd appeared to be from outside Bishkek, including a group of several hundred young men—holding posters with the word "Osh"—that later led an attack on soldiers guarding the White House.

81. Interviews in Bishkek: Askat, May 9, 2005; Bolot, May 7, 2005.

82. Akaev claimed that he never considered using force against protesters. His interior minister seconded the claim. See "Kyrgyzstan: How Bishkek's Revolution Happened So Fast," and "Kyrgyzstan: Deposed President Discusses his Ouster," RFE/RL, March 25, 2006.

83. For other accounts of March 24, see "Kyrgyzstan: After the Revolution"; Bolot Maripov, "Ot pervogo litsa" [From an eyewitness], Obshchestvennyi Reiting, March 31, 2005; Jean-Christophe Peuch, "Kyrgyzstan: Eyewitness to the Revolution," RFE/RL, March 24, 2005.

to respond to local and particularistic appeals rather than national or ideological ones. The distribution of protests was patchy, reflecting the fact that most communities and most individuals did not participate, even in the most active regions. The presence of mobilization correlated with the location of losing candidates who decided to protest, not with any demographic characteristics of the population. A thorough explanation for the event must account for the selective mobilization of communities, the decision of certain individuals but not others to join protests, and the belated but successful aggregation of protests across regions. An examination of the vertical and horizontal networks that had developed before 2005 can help to account for these occurrences, while also shedding light on the underlying social and political structures in Kyrgyzstan.

## Activating Subversive Clientelist Ties

Most candidates who mobilized in 2005 had already established networks of support within their communities, most visibly through material contributions, such as repairing infrastructure and distributing aid throughout the district.[84] Elites who were not among the wealthiest in the country could compensate in other ways, by making appeals based on their credentials as advocates of local interests and targeting their assistance toward close circles in their home village rather than to potential supporters dispersed throughout the district. Candidates who were already MPs could reward their districts by using their influence— providing jobs for residents, steering funds from the state budget and claiming credit for the results, and solving miscellaneous constituent problems.[85] A smaller number of those leading the mobilization, who were unable to make significant material investments in their districts and lacked a parliamentary seat to build districtwide popularity, relied on their charisma and family ties alone to mobilize supporters.[86]

In surveying the political landscape at the time of the election, who would mobilize was not foreordained. In order for a candidate to mobilize people, it was necessary that he or she have both the capability and the incentive to do so, yet a candidate with one was unlikely to possess the other. Those with the greatest capabilities to bring about collective action—the wealthiest—were more likely to win their elections than the nonwealthy, and therefore had little incentive to

---

84. A local analyst estimated that 80% of the members of the 2000 parliament owned their own businesses. Interview, National Democratic Institute, Bishkek, July 5, 2006.

85. Tekebaev (who did not mobilize) and Sadyrbaev (who did) were especially known in their districts for their work as MPs.

86. Maripov in Bishkek fell into this category.

protest. Conversely, those with the greatest incentive to mobilize—the election's losers—tended to have less capability to do so, or else they would have made greater investments to win the election in the first place. Mobilization was therefore the preferred strategy of the subset of candidates possessing these contradictory attributes: making the requisite investments in a social support base and losing an election.[87]

Two additional factors made a losing candidate more likely to mobilize: a history of opposition activism, especially if the candidate was enmeshed in networks of opposition leaders who had collaborated in the past;[88] and an election in which a pro-government candidate won by a small margin.[89] Pro-government candidates, on the other hand, typically did not mobilize when they lost. They had counted on the government's assistance and could not credibly turn against it after their loss.

Elite candidates initiated mobilization from the top down, following which their associates recruited through community networks—from the inside out—as far as the candidate's financial and social capital allowed. Within communities, a candidate's campaign team, which was well suited for acting collectively on short notice, handled recruitment. Having just concluded a campaign that involved close interaction with village residents, it was able to quickly round up a number of activists. Depending on a candidate's resources and popularity, his operatives might be able to mobilize several hundred to several thousand people.

The operatives' appeals were intended to evoke a sense of solidarity with the embedded elite. They would remind people how important the candidate was to the community. They would accuse the candidate's opponent(s) of cheating, charging them with violating campaign rules and receiving clandestine support from local officials.[90] Activists understood that it was easier to rally people in response to a common affront from an immediate target—the candidate's rival(s)—than to play on grievances against the regime. The former was concrete;

---

87. Of course, this explanation assumes that the official vote count approximated the actual vote. It may also be the case that the government was more likely to rig elections to prevent its most formidable opponents, such as Bakiev and Madumarov, from winning seats in parliament, making mobilization endogenous to previous opposition activism in some cases. If this was the case, then the government miscalculated in not foreseeing that such candidates had both the ability and, as a result of losing under suspicious circumstances, an extra incentive to mobilize.

88. The high number of opposition candidates who lost may lend support to the notion that the government targeted their elections to rig.

89. Examples of close and fiercely contested races include Orozbaev-Madumarov in Kurshab (49.27%–48.54%); Sadybakasov-Eshimkanov in Bishkek (46.60–46.24); and Yusupov-Tolonov in Kara-su (49.37–46.79).

90. Many protesters could recite a list of reputed campaign violations (some of which were documented by independent observers as well) over a year later. Interviews in Jalalabad, Aravan, Kara-su, and Alai, June 2006.

the latter, abstract. Thus, the picket signs used in rallies and the slogans that people initially shouted called for "fair elections" and "justice" for their candidate.[91] Even in cases where the government was rumored to have assisted the winner, whether through Alga or indirectly, people directed their anger at the winning candidate rather than at President Akaev.

Interviews with ordinary participants confirmed the strength of clientelist ties to candidates. For the most part, people did not look beyond local elites or their neighbors for cues about how to act. Protesters passionately expressed support for "their" (*svoi*) candidate and had little trouble recalling charitable contributions that the candidate had made in the district—even if mistaken. When I asked participants concretely what had led them to join, they rarely made reference to national- or even regional-level issues, and instead referred to their own politicians. In Jalalabad, Jusupbek Jeenbekov, through his son, had provided lucrative jobs and contributed large amounts of charity to his village. Asked why they mobilized, his co-villagers would respond "because he's *ours*" in the same breath as they described how he had helped the community. Sadyrbaev, a film director and three-term MP, had raised money to build mosques through contacts in the United Arab Emirates, handed out cash to the poor, and lobbied the government to provide new ambulances.[92] A supporter noted his "clean past" and said it was impossible for the government to find *kompromat*—compromising material—on him.[93]

Like the protesters who occupied the central squares of Jalalabad and Osh, those who came out into the streets in provincial parts of Osh Oblast were motivated first and foremost by the opportunity to help their candidate. Arap Tolonov of Kara-su, in addition to being the owner of a farming cooperative and the largest employer in his district, was said to have installed water pipes, built roofs for homes, spent one million som ($25,000) on roads and electricity, and given numerous handouts to the poor in his district.[94] His supporters referred to him as a "simple person" (*prostoi chelovek*),[95] despite the fact that he was obviously very wealthy, and a "decent guy" (*normal'nyi muzhik*).[96] Marat Sultanov from Alai had purchased furniture and computers for schools, built three mosques, given out stipends to poor students, secured passports for residents of a village recently transferred from Tajikistan, and paid 20 percent of the expenses of a development project to drain a swamp. He was also known to appear often in person,

91. Interviews, Jalalabad, April 13, 2005; Alai District, Osh, June 28, 2006; Raisa, Kara-su District, Osh, June 29, 2006; election observer, Bishkek, July 4, 2006.

92. Interview, Erkin, Nooken District, Jalalabad, June 24, 2006.

93. Interview, Sovetali, Nooken District, Jalalabad, June 25, 2006.

94. Interviews with residents of Kara-su District, Osh, June 29, 2006.

95. Interview, Raisa, Kara-su District, Osh, June 29, 2006.

96. Interview, Oibek, National Democratic Institute, Kara-su District, Osh, June 29, 2006.

despite living in Bishkek.[97] His supporters claimed to have protested because "he passed many bills in parliament [second only to Tekebaev], he's honest, and helps people," "we're proud of him," and "his father [a former high Communist Party official] was honest...and helped Alai's people."[98]

## Variation by Region, District, and Village

Regional (oblast-level) variation in the size of the crowds and the geographic scope of villages that protesters came from was largely a function of the number of candidates protesting the election in that region.[99] Where there was no perceived challenge, there were few protesters. Although some isolated individuals from districts without a mobilizing candidate may have joined spontaneously, they were too few to make an impact.[100] The size of protests would increase considerably only when a new candidate brought his contingent.

It also important to take into account bandwagon effects within oblasts, as the initial mobilizing candidates were joined by sympathetic and opportunistic local elites. Jusupbek Jeenbekov, the first to mobilize in Jalalabad, had no prior history of opposition politics, but his deceased brother, Satybaldi, had been a well-known activist (see chapter 3). When Bektur Asanov and Jusupbek Bakiev mobilized as well, they triggered further participation, as less influential elites and nonelites, who resented Akaev or who simply wanted to be part of the action, joined in the capacity of organizers. In Osh, independent elites and sportsmen Erkinbaev and Kamchibekov, sensing an opportunity to boost their prestige, joined as well, even though the former had won his parliamentary race. Other elites who had not run for parliament joined individually or helped to encourage others to contribute.[101]

---

97. Interviews with residents of Alai District, Osh, June 28, 2006.

98. Interviews, Alai District, Osh, June 28, 2006. These statements are not meant to imply that support for Sultanov—or any other candidate—was universal. In almost every case, other respondents would criticize the same elites for being corrupt, selfish, and aloof. These critics were obviously not likely to support losing candidates by protesting.

99. The largest crowds of demonstrators occurred in Jalalabad, where the numbers may have reached fifteen thousand on March 20. Bishkek and Osh Oblast may have attracted ten thousand people each at their peak. There were up to five thousand in Talas, three thousand in Naryn, twenty-five hundred in Issyk Kul, several hundred reported in Chui, and a negligible number in Batken.

100. The only protests in this period that did not occur in support of a candidate were progovernment demonstrations by government employees in Jalalabad and Bishkek. Circumstantial evidence suggested that they were not spontaneous, but rather cases of coerced mobilization by the authorities. Interviews, Jalalabad and Bishkek, April 2005 and June 2006.

101. Included are activists such as Usen Sydykov from Kara-kulja District in Osh and Tagaibak Jarkynbaev from Bazar-Kurgan-Suzak District in Jalalabad. Interviews, Kerem, Osh, May 2, 2005; Alisher T., Osh, April 28, 2005.

Within oblasts, participation did not correspond smoothly to geography. In the midst of concentrated activity were places where people did not participate. The obvious reason for this was that most parliamentary races were not controversial—there were no accusations of impropriety and the candidate favored by the majority of voters was declared the winner. Such was the case in Aksy, where people had mobilized in the past, but because Azimbek Beknazarov was elected without incident with 55 percent of the vote, Aksy remained passive. Beknazarov was embedded in opposition networks, remained in close contact with PMK leaders, and spoke at the party congress in Jalalabad, but he did not incite residents of Aksy to protest in Jalalabad or anywhere else.[102]

Another reason for nonparticipation within districts was some people's *opposition* to opposition candidates. Despite Akaev's unpopularity, many progovernment candidates were individually popular, for the same reasons that other candidates were popular. In Osh, for example, pro-government candidate Alisher Sobirov ran unopposed and won 80 percent in the first round. His putative opponent, Achahan Turgunbaeva, had been disqualified from running after being charged with buying votes.[103] She mobilized two hundred people in a protest that gained little notice and quickly dissipated because Sobirov, who had already served two terms in parliament, was popular in his district. In some cases, as in Nariman, the district was split between villages that supported the government's candidate, Abdurasulov, and the opposition candidate, Artykov.[104] The pull that some felt toward mobilization was mirrored on the other side by pressure against participating.

The spatial patterns resulting from these forces are clearly demonstrated in Jalalabad Oblast. The largest contingent of participants came from two districts—Kizil-too and Kogart—which accounted for 70–80 percent of protesters in Jalalabad's central square for the first two weeks, according to the estimates of participants and leaders. The most intense participation came from the candidates' home villages—Vin-Sovkhoz for Jeenbekov, Ak-selik for Asanov, and Nooken for Sadyrbaev—where people reported that at least one person from every household participated.[105] Only in these villages did pressure to mobilize

102. Interviews, Tagaibek Jarkynbaev, Bazar-Kurgan-Suzak District, Jalalabad, April 18, 2005; Medir Usenov, Jalalabad, April 20, 2005.

103. Interview, director of human rights NGO, Osh, July 1, 2006.

104. Artykov obtained most of his support from his home village of Shark. Abdurasulov's support came mostly from *his* hometown of Kashgar-Kishtak in the same district.

105. Interviews in Jalalabad: Vin-Sovkhoz village, Kogart District, June 26, 2006; Ak-Selik village, Kizil-too District, June 22, 2006; Erkin, Nooken District, June 24, 2006. There were similarly high concentrations from the home villages of candidates who protested at local courthouses but did not join the larger mobilizations at the oblast center. These include the districts of Aravan, Alai, and Uzgen in Osh.

reach a fever pitch similar to that in Aksy's Kara-su, where social obligations demanded full participation.

By contrast, few protesters came from the districts of Barpy, Bazar-Kurgan-Suzak, and Jalalabad city, even though they were very close to (or overlapped with) the center of activity. This is because wealthy, philanthropic candidates capable of mobilizing won in the first round in those districts. One student from Barpy, seven kilometers from Jalalabad, explained that the winning candidate, Kamchibek Tashiev, specifically held people back from participating until March 21 when speakers at the square goaded Tashiev into joining.[106] The student obeyed Tashiev because, "We look up to him, we respect what he says. He's like the president for us. He has done so many things for our village."[107] Another constituent lauded him for having built roads and donating money to the poor in the village.[108] Abdumutalip Hakimov, the director of a cotton factory that employed twelve hundred people, was the dominant and most philanthropic elite in Bazar-Kurgan-Suzak District; he won 76 percent of the vote in the first round. Residents of his district could list his accomplishments and cited the importance of his factory to the town's economy.[109] In Jalalabad proper, Kadyrjon Batyrov, a wealthy magnate who founded a six-million-dollar university for ethnic Uzbeks, won in the first round. His opponent, Jusupbek Bakiev, mobilized through his campaign team, but his supporters comprised a negligible part of the population of Jalalabad.[110] See figure 6.2 for a map of Jalalabad Oblast indicating the average rates of protest participation by district in the period from the first demonstrations until the day Jalalabad was captured by the opposition. It shows that participation rates did not correspond to geography, but were higher in districts with mobilizing candidates, and very high in those candidates' villages.[111]

## The Ties That Bind

At the local level, it is impossible to explain who joined in the March events and why without reference to the centrality of community in Kyrgyzstan and the

---

106. Interview, Asylbek, Barpy District, Jalalabad, April 20, 2005. Tashiev was the owner of a chain of petrol stations across southern Kyrgyzstan, and had won with 63% in the first round.

107. Interview, Barpy District, April 20, 2005.

108. Interview, Barpy District, April 22, 2005.

109. Interviews, Bazar-Kurgan-Suzak District, Jalalabad, June 22, 2006.

110. Interview, Sultan Kunazarov, Radio Liberty correspondent, Bishkek, June 15, 2006.

111. I collected data by driving through the districts of Nooken, Bazar-Kurgan-Suzak, Kizil-too, Barpy, Jalalabad, and Kogart and interviewing randomly selected people about whether they and people they knew participated in protests. I spoke with a total of forty-four people over seven days. I compared these responses with the assessments of numerous participants and observers I interviewed in Jalalabad city. I corroborated my data with six local experts who had observed the demonstrations and spoken with participants.

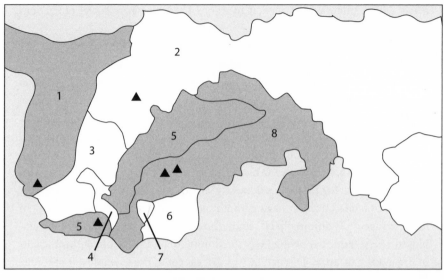

**FIGURE 6.2.**   Protest participation rates in Jalalabad Oblast, March 2005

tendency to identify with those from the same village or neighborhood. Some scholars have argued that clans are the most salient identity in Central Asia.[112] However, this meso-level of analysis cannot explain variation in mobilization at the village level. Community networks, on the other hand, structure the behavior of ordinary people in their daily lives and provide the means to carry out collective action. In the Tulip Revolution, social ties did not imply automatic solidarity among everybody in the village—people could be divided over a number of issues, including their support for different candidates. But, all else equal,

---

112. Edward Schatz, *Modern Clan Politics* (Seattle: University of Washington Press, 2004); Kathleen Collins, *Clan Politics and Regime Transition in Central Asia* (New York: Cambridge University Press, 2006).

individuals were more willing to give their time and accept risk when they saw their neighbors making a contribution.

Only after the government's countermobilizational raids in Jalalabad on March 20 did people join without a direct appeal from a candidate, his associates, or a neighbor. That day, many came with little encouragement, as exaggerated news of the attack diffused across communities by word of mouth and activated latent network ties. As in Aksy in 2002, when soldiers shot and killed six demonstrators, the storming of Jalalabad's administration building and rumors of violence evoked outrage, which protesters immediately rushed back to their villages to convey. In Osh, the assault on the administrative building also evoked outrage, but because there were fewer candidates and therefore fewer protesters to spread the news, it had less of a galvanizing effect.

Strong, inward-looking local attachments thus made for a potent political weapon, but also demonstrated inherent limitations. Individuals were motivated to act in support of local elites and neighbors, but were less prone to mobilize on behalf of issues or actors located outside their community. In all instances of mobilization in both Jalalabad and Osh oblasts, protesters initially limited their demands to investigating election fraud or rerunning the election. Only after the oppositions widened with their demands still unmet did candidates begin calling for the resignation of Akaev. Even when large numbers of people in Jalalabad responded to the government's raid by converging on the central square, they were motivated not by aspirations for democracy, but by a rational, if also emotional, sense of obligation to support their fellow villagers. The ties that facilitated cooperation within communities did not extend outside them, which begs the question of how dispersed protest participants could coordinate effectively on a national scale. To answer this question, it is necessary to identify networks that transcend the village and oblast.

## Making the Leap to a National Movement

Could mass mobilization have resulted from a broad-based uprising of the middle class seeking a greater role in determining the direction of the country?[113] The makeup of the protesters suggests not. On the contrary, most participants were rural and poor. They worked as petty or subsistence farmers, or were retired or

---

113. Seymour Martin Lipset, *Political Man: The Social Bases of Politics* (Baltimore: Johns Hopkins University Press, 1981); Ross E. Burkhart and Michael S. Lewis-Beck, "Comparative Democracy: The Economic Development Thesis," *American Political Science Review* 88 (1994): 903–10; William Easterly, "The Middle Class Consensus and Economic Development," *Journal of Economic Growth* 6, no. 4 (2001): 317–35.

unemployed. Demonstrators occupying Jalalabad and Osh were not from the city center, where most businessmen and professionals live, but rather from outlying farms and villages. Kyrgyzstan's small middle class occupied a fragile niche under Akaev and was reluctant to risk the uncertainty of regime change.[114] It also had no social incentives to join protests, as it was not dependent on wealthy elites or parliamentary deputies, and had little in common with most participants.

If the middle class had little incentive to mobilize, perhaps the working class provided the spark.[115] Although it is an important actor in industrialized societies with a history of labor activism, most labor in Kyrgyzstan is organized according to a corporatist arrangement that is a direct successor of the Soviet system of labor regulation. The percentage of the workforce employed in agriculture is nearly 50 percent, while the share working in industry, most of which is concentrated in Bishkek, declined from 27 percent in 1990 to 12 percent in 2005.[116] Workers in manufacturing and trade, if they mobilized, did so through community ties rather than through their workplace. Employees of government enterprises risked being fired for insubordination if they were to protest.[117] The passivity of labor in Kyrgyzstan is echoed in findings from across the postcommunist region.[118]

What about NGO networks? From the time of its independence, Kyrgyzstan was fertile ground for the proliferation of NGOs: as of 2007, eleven thousand were registered with the Justice Ministry.[119] Democratic activists from Bishkek's urban intelligentsia prepared for the 2005 elections by sponsoring seminars and conferences, working with opposition candidates, and increasing awareness about the quality of elections. In the March events, however, NGOs played a smaller role than would at first appear. Although NGO leaders were vocal critics of Akaev, they played no part in mobilizing people in Jalalabad or Osh, and only a minor one in Bishkek.[120] Once the sit-ins in the south began, NGO activists arrived from Bishkek and instructed leaders on how to conduct demonstrations in accordance with the law.[121] In Bishkek, democratic activists acted as liaisons

---

114. ICG, "Political Transition in Kyrgyzstan," 4.

115. Dietrich Rueschemeyer, Evelyne Huber Stephens, and John Stephens, *Capitalist Development and Democracy* (Chicago: University of Chicago Press, 1992).

116. "Kyrgyz Republic: Poverty Assessment, Volume 2: Labor Market Dimensions of Poverty," World Bank Poverty Reduction and Economic Management Unit, Europe and Central Asian Region, September 12, 2007.

117. See Kelly M. McMann, *Economic Autonomy and Democracy: Hybrid Regimes in Russia and Kyrgyzstan* (Cambridge: University Press, 2006).

118. Stephen Crowley, "Explaining Labor Weakness in Post-Communist Europe: Historical Legacies and Comparative Perspective," *East European Politics & Societies* 18, no. 3 (2004): 394–429.

119. "NGOs to Discuss Greater Input into Politics," IWPR, May 10, 2007.

120. Interview, Aziza, Bishkek, May 6, 2005.

121. Interview, Burul, youth activist, Bishkek, May 10, 2005.

between the PMK and other leaders, and helped organize the rallies on March 23 and 24.[122] But the organizations affiliated with these activists, such as the umbrella NGO in Bishkek—the Coalition for Civil Society and Democracy—were not deeply rooted in society and could not serve as a structure through which ordinary people could mobilize.[123]

Other organizations that might have facilitated cross-regional networks—such as universities or mosques—were controlled or monitored by the state, a legacy of the Soviet system. Unlike in the other color revolutions, youth activists played a negligible role in Kyrgyzstan. Students in every area of my research reported being warned by university administrations and teachers not to join the demonstrations on pain of expulsion. Several brave students called their bluff and joined anyway, and none I talked to suffered any reprisals, in most cases because the leadership of the institute was replaced after the transfer of power. Yet most students, though probably eager to participate, were too frightened to do so.

Mosques also played no role in mobilizing people. Kyrgyzstan's imams are vetted by the state and closely supervised to ensure that they do not meddle in politics or use their influence to spread subversive ideas. Although such figures may have participated discreetly, they did not help organize or provide spiritual guidance to the movement. The only mention respondents made of religious authorities was of a village mullah who exhorted protesters to be peaceful on their march to the city center.[124] Neither did Islam act as a mobilizing ideology. The influence of political Islam in the Middle East has only weakly penetrated Kyrgyzstan, and radical ideologies have largely fallen on deaf ears.[125] To have answered fraudulent elections with a call to jihad would have struck most Kyrgyzstanis as ridiculous. Knowing that they lacked a receptive audience, Islamist activists, such as they were, decided to lie low during the mobilization and refrained from making religion-based appeals.[126]

The network that ultimately transformed local power struggles into a national movement was an interregional alliance of autonomous elites. The creation of

---

122. Interview, Kazbek, youth activist, Bishkek, May 10, 2005.

123. On the breadth and depth of NGOs in Kyrgyzstan, see Kelly M. McMann, "The Civic Realm in Kyrgyzstan," in The Transformation of Central Asia, ed. Pauline Jones Luong (Ithaca: Cornell University Press, 2004), 213–45.

124. Interview, Roza, Kogart District, Jalalabad, April 17, 2005.

125. On the multifaceted nature of Islam and the absence of extensive Islamic mobilization in Kyrgyzstan, see Adeeb Khalid, Islam after Communism (Berkeley: University of California Press, 2007); David W. Montgomery, "Namaz, Wishing Trees, and Vodka: The Diversity of Everyday Religious Life in Central Asia," in Everyday Life in Central Asia, ed. Jeff Sahadeo and Russell Zanca (Bloomington: Indiana University Press, 2007), 339–70.

126. Alisher Khamidov and Alisher Saipov, "Islamic Radical Group Bides Time on Sidelines of Kyrgyzstan's Revolution," eurasianet.org, April 14, 2005.

a network of oppositionists in the form of the PMK, possible in Kyrgyzstan's relatively permissive political environment, was the fatal thrust for Akaev. Its constituent parties did not have large followings and made little effort to develop ideological or programmatic appeals. Yet the role played by the PMK in linking the *elites* who were leading protests was the critical component necessary to forge a national movement and resist the regime's attempts to divide and rule. By harmonizing demands and tactics and providing a structure through which local elites could coordinate, the PMK enabled national mobilization. The PMK's leaders worked with a common purpose just long enough to topple Akaev's government, before dissolving into petty squabbling.[127]

In this chapter I analyzed mass mobilization in Kyrgyzstan using the theoretical framework from chapter 1. I emphasized the role of embedded elites, in the guise of candidates for parliament, in bringing about mobilization through subversive clientelist networks. As in the 2002 protests in Aksy, horizontal community networks provided the means to recruit ordinary people to protest and the bonds to maintain their cohesiveness. An omnibus elite network, the PMK, provided a structure that helped transform numerous localized outbreaks into a movement of national scale. In the end, poor farmers and pensioners unwittingly became part of a national upheaval that had major political ramifications not only for Kyrgyzstan but for all of Central Asia.[128]

The groundwork that eventually gave rise to the Tulip Revolution was laid in the early 1990s. Kyrgyzstan, unlike Uzbekistan, established the preconditions for mass mobilization through clientelist ties as a result of early reforms and the adaptation of independent elites to increasing authoritarianism. President Akaev, who was confident like other observers that, even following other revolutions, Central Asia was "different," could not have predicted the circumstances of his ouster. This unexpected turn of events in a small, obscure post-Soviet country raises the following questions: Can the same conditions for elite-led mobilization be found outside Kyrgyzstan, and if so, do they lead to similar outcomes? The next chapter applies the model in other contexts to show how it can help explain the dynamics of mobilization more broadly.

---

127. For an analysis of the consequences of the improvisational nature of the opposition movement regarding governance in the aftermath of Akaev's overthrow, see Erica Marat, *The Tulip Revolution: Kyrgyzstan One Year After* (Washington, D.C.: Jamestown Foundation, 2006); Scott Radnitz, "A Horse of a Different Color: Revolution and Regression in Kyrgyzstan," in *Democracy and Authoritarianism in the Postcommunist World*, ed. Valerie Bunce, Michael A. McFaul, and Kathryn Stoner-Weiss (New York: Cambridge University Press, 2010).

128. Fiona Hill and Kevin Jones, "Fear of Democracy or Revolution," *Washington Quarterly* 29, no. 3 (2006): 111–25.

# 7

# ASSESSING THE DYNAMICS OF MOBILIZATION IN DIVERSE CONTEXTS

In earlier chapters of this book, I laid out a framework for understanding the origins of mobilization through clientelist ties and showed its variation in two Central Asian countries. The root cause of this form of political contestation— present only in Kyrgyzstan—was a set of early postindependence reforms made by President Akaev that enabled the decentralized generation of wealth. Mobilization was not inevitable, but it did not emerge out of thin air either. Evidence that the groundwork had been laid in advance is starkly illustrated by the contrast with Uzbekistan. The two countries were culturally similar, shared a common legacy of Russian and Soviet rule, and began the 1990s with comparable prospects. Yet early decisions resulted in a divergence of fortunes: Kyrgyzstan experienced a significant redistribution of power from the state to society, whereas in Uzbekistan power remained concentrated in the state. Kyrgyzstan did not become a democracy, but instead entered a phase of pluralistic competition in which politics would become fluid and unpredictable. This set it apart from other countries in Central Asia.

Kyrgyzstan's transformation and the informal modes of opposition that resulted raise the question of whether its experience was unique, or whether the events described in earlier chapters have analogies in other contexts. The theory elaborated in this book will be more powerful to the extent that it can elucidate important social and political processes beyond the cases already described. To that end, in this chapter I apply the theory in several diverse geographic and historical contexts in order to uncover common dynamics and "deep causal analogies" between cases.[1] I do this by examining cases exhibiting differing values on the independent variables specified in the theory. In particular, because the events covered in chapters 5 and 6 are "positive" cases, in which subversive clientelist ties and elite networks were present, thus resulting in clientelist mobilization, it can be useful to analyze cases in which one or both independent variables is absent. According to the theory, altering the independent variables should produce different social and political configurations, which in turn should have an effect on the scale and form of mobilization.

For example, what if, unlike Kyrgyzstan, the institutional context is forbidding, so that power and influence emanate from the state alone and are difficult to acquire autonomously? This setting is unlikely to stifle all forms of protest, but it should preclude mobilization through subversive clientelist ties—since such ties would be unlikely to develop in the first place. Instead, mobilization would tend to occur spontaneously and remain localized. This outcome corresponds to the counterfactual case from earlier chapters—Uzbekistan.

If economic opportunities were favorable but the political context was restrictive, then we would expect to find incidences of subversive clientelism, but few cross-cutting elite networks. It is likely that mobilization would occur with independent elite involvement, but the scale would remain relatively small because elites would have difficulty overcoming their collective action problems. This scenario is illustrated by contemporary rural China.

Another possibility is regional variation within a polity in terms of public goods, economic opportunities, and cross-regional collaboration. In this case, mobilization structures would vary according to the institutional configuration in the region. Where elites are constrained, mobilization should be from the bottom up and localized. If elites can create subversive clientelist networks, then top-down mobilization will be possible in the regions where they are present. Finally, if there are cross-cutting institutions on the elite level, then mobilization can spread across regional boundaries as far as the elite networks extend. I illustrate these scenarios by analyzing the dynamics of rebellion in early modern France and England, and in the Mexican War of Independence (1810–21). In both contexts, a central state that lacked full control over its territory engaged in drawn-out struggles with various regional elites for the prerogative to rule over the populace and command the country's resources.

---

1. Arthur Stinchcombe, *Theoretical Methods in Social History* (New York: Academic Press, 1978); Charles Tilly, "To Explain Political Processes," *American Journal of Sociology* 100, no. 6 (1995): 1602; Doug McAdam, Sidney G. Tarrow, and Charles Tilly, *Dynamics of Contention* (New York: Cambridge University Press, 2001).

The non–Central Asian cases described in this chapter offer a productive basis for comparison because they represent a wide range of geographic, historical, and cultural contexts. Specific characteristics of the actors and institutions involved in mobilization vary whereas the underlying dynamics of their interaction are similar. The cases all evince a rough balance of power between rulers and unincorporated elites, and an institutional setting in which informal rules prevail over the rule of law as a means to settle conflicts, but they differ in terms of the how they arrived at that point. The cases of contentious state formation, Europe and Mexico, can be seen as a mirror image of social processes that occurred in Kyrgyzstan—what might be called state erosion. In both sets of cases, the determination of whether a state continued on a path toward consolidation or began to lose control depended on the resources each side could muster and, ultimately, on who could win the allegiance of the population. In contemporary China, economic liberalization and decentralization have created space for the mobilization of social forces, but the regime's repressive tactics and cooptation of elites have limited the potential for major political change. Investigating and comparing the dynamics of distinct, though historically common, processes can yield fruitful insights about the interaction of states and societies and suggest how far the theory can "travel."

To clarify the objectives of this chapter, table 7.1, reproduced from part of table 0.2, summarizes variation among the cases covered in this chapter and shows the mobilization outcomes predicted by the theory. I also represent the relevant characteristics of the selected cases graphically. Figure 7.1 reproduces the diagram of Uzbekistan's incomplete mass-mobilization infrastructure from figure 3.1. Figure 7.2 shows the mobilizing structure corresponding to rural China, and figure 7.3 depicts early nineteenth-century Mexico. I do not depict the European case here, as it is structurally similar to that of Kyrgyzstan, previously shown in figures 1.1 and 3.1.

# The "Negative Case"?
# Uzbekistan since Independence

What was the upshot of Uzbekistan's failure to develop an independent elite class? The political development of Uzbekistan, in contrast with Kyrgyzstan, had an impact on future mobilization. Through 2005, there was mobilization in Uzbekistan, occurring with increasing frequency in the early 2000s, but it was predominantly localized. Protests often broke out spontaneously, in response to pressing local problems, such as restrictive regulations on trade, unexpected price increases, power outages, and, occasionally, family members unfairly persecuted

**Table 7.1**  Cases for extending the theory

| CASE | CLIENTELISM | CHALLENGE TO MULTIPLE NETWORKED ELITES | PREDICTED GREATEST SCALE OF MOBILIZATION | PREDICTED FORM OF MOBILIZATION |
|---|---|---|---|---|
| Uzbekistan: Andijan | No | No | Localized | Spontaneous |
| Rural China | Some | No | Localized/ regional | Possibly elite-led, possibly extending to regional level |
| Early modern Europe | Yes | Yes | Regional/ national | Elite-led, possibly extending to national level |
| Nineteenth-century Mexico | Yes | Some | Regional | Elite-led, possibly extending to regional level |

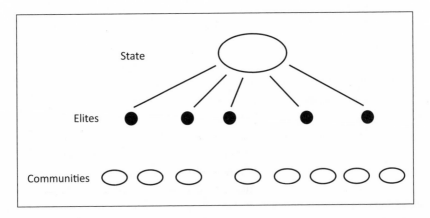

**FIGURE 7.1.**  Mobilization structure with low public goods, low economic opportunities, and low political openness (Uzbekistan)

by the government.[2] Such protests usually involved up to a hundred people and did not diffuse beyond those who were directly affected. They also failed to inspire "copycat" actions in other communities, despite the similarity of people's

---

2. Protests have occurred in most oblasts of Uzbekistan, including Kashkadaryo, Jizzakh, Tashkent, Andijan, Kokand, and Margilon. See "Uzbekistan: The Andijan Uprising," International Crisis Group (ICG), May 25, 2005; and "Uzbekistan: A Year of Disturbances," Institute of War and Peace Reporting (IWPR), May 13, 2005. Due to the limited access of foreign journalists in Uzbekistan, these represent only a sample of protests in the country in recent years.

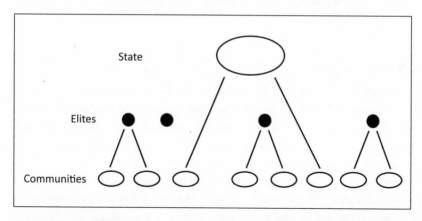

**FIGURE 7.2.** Mobilization structure with moderate public goods, high economic opportunities, and low political openness (rural China)

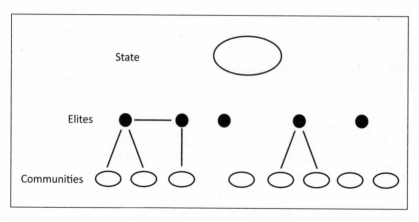

**FIGURE 7.3.** Mobilization structure with regional variation: low public goods, variable economic and political opportunities (nineteenth-century Mexico)

hardships across the country and occasional expressions of solidarity from human rights activists and NGOs in the capital.[3] Demonstrations usually ended without bloodshed, as local government officials would respond by negotiating with protesters and often conceding to their demands, although putative protest leaders could be detained for a short time. In only one case did mobilization

---

3. Galima Bukharbaeva, "Rights Crackdown Mars Uzbek Independence Day," IWPR, September 8, 2003.

occur that approached the magnitude and political significance of the cases in Kyrgyzstan—the events in Andijan.

## Anger in Andijan

The Andijan events of May 2005, in which several thousand people demonstrated on behalf of persecuted local businessmen and several hundred were killed, constitute the event most similar to mobilization in more permissive institutional environments. The roots of protest lay in the arrest of local benefactors who had been providing surrogate collective goods to residents and were therefore perceived by the regime as subversive. As in Kyrgyzstan, the loss of a source of resources motivated people to demonstrate, and they did so through preexisting social ties in contiguous neighborhoods.

Yet, despite surface similarities with the earlier protests in Kyrgyzstan, there was a difference. The businessmen appeared to provide jobs and charity out of financial interest and civic duty rather than from a desire to defend their interests from the government or advance their political fortunes. That is, they were not investing to create clienteles, a fact reflected in the nature of the protests, which were bottom up and spontaneous rather than top down and organized. This did not diminish their size or intensity, however. Spontaneous, bottom-up mobilization can be equally, if not more, effective in revealing flaws and exposing dissatisfaction with the regime. Yet it is also unlikely to spread beyond its original locale, barring a rare spark that can catalyze unassociated people to act similarly bravely.

Mobilization in Andijan began when the state cut off a highly popular source of income and employment for the population. In June–July 2004, twenty-three Andijan businessmen were arrested and charged with membership in an extremist organization called Akramiya.[4] Some of the accused men had emphasized community self-help and redistribution based on Islamic precepts, but there was no credible evidence that they had political ambitions or even that they collaborated as a group. Residents of Andijan reported that the accused, whose businesses included "food, textile, and goods production and merchandise,"[5] acted as community benefactors, by providing jobs, donating money to the poor, and building schools and orphanages.[6] This instance of private charity was a rare exception in Uzbekistan, and its cessation provoked an equally unusual response. When their

---

4. This organization was named after its reputed originator, Akram Yuldashev. Yusuf Rasulov and Matluba Azamatova, "Uzbekistan: Not the Usual Suspects," IWPR, February 18, 2005.

5. "Report of the Mission to Kyrgyzstan by the Office of the High Commissioner for Human Rights (OHCHR) Concerning the Killings in Andijan of 13–14 May 2005," Office of the High Commissioner for Human Rights.

6. ICG, "Uzbekistan: The Andijan Uprising."

trial began in February 2005, friends, relatives, and neighbors showed their support by demonstrating in front of the courthouse in the center of Andijan.

The protests in Andijan represented an outburst of anger by ordinary people in response to a perceived transgression by the government—similar to previous neighborhood protests in Uzbekistan, but on a larger scale. It was not an Islamist uprising, as the government later claimed. The crowd was diverse, encompassing children as well as the elderly, with a high proportion of women. Participants were reported to be local, supporting the claim that they were neighbors or acquaintances of the accused.[7] The protests were peaceful, orderly, and focused on the specific demand of releasing the prisoners.

The character of the protests changed when, on May 13, a group of unidentified armed men stormed the prison holding the businessmen, released many of the occupants, and seized Andijan's regional administration building. News of this development traveled quickly by word of mouth and drew many more people to the rally, if only out of curiosity.[8] While city employees were being held hostage inside the regional headquarters, demonstrators set up a public microphone and began complaining about poverty, unemployment, and corruption. After a rumor emerged that President Karimov would arrive from Tashkent to address the crowd's grievances, more people gathered in anticipation.

The hopes of the protesters were dashed when Uzbek special forces troops opened fire on the crowd, killing several hundred and scattering the rest.[9] The government quickly closed off access to Andijan, expelled journalists, and concentrated soldiers on the border with the neighboring oblast of Namangan. Many protesters fled across the border to Kyrgyzstan. Several skirmishes with police along the way caused more casualties, but no more protests followed. Thus, the Karimov regime abruptly put an end to talk—mostly by outside observers—of a "revolution" along the lines of what Kyrgyzstan had experienced two months earlier.

Due to its tragic outcome, more information has come to light about this event than from any other protest episode in Uzbekistan, permitting an investigation of its causes.[10] The decline in state services and general impoverishment

---

7. Photographs of the crowds in fact show few grown men among the demonstrators. Many were presumably working abroad, as was much of Uzbekistan's adult male population.

8. Numbers reportedly reached ten thousand. "Bullets Were Falling Like Rain: The Andijan Massacre, May 13, 2005," Human Rights Watch, June 6, 2005, 19.

9. Most independent analyses do not dispute that the military fired at unarmed civilians, and place the number of deaths at between five hundred and 750, while the government claimed that fewer than two hundred were killed.

10. Organizations that conducted first-hand interviews and released reports included the UN High Commission for Human Rights, the Organization for Security and Cooperation in Europe, Human Rights Watch, the International Crisis Group, and the Central Asia-Caucasus Institute.

in Andijan in years past had left communities vulnerable and eager to obtain aid from alternative sources to the state. Whereas economic opportunities and political competition allowed elites to fill the void in Kyrgyzstan as described earlier, Uzbekistan's institutional setting prevented the emergence of such elites—or did it? Andijan turned out to be the exception that proved the rule.

As the biggest cotton-producing region of Uzbekistan, Andijan had a unique relationship with the center, receiving more resources and somewhat more autonomy than other oblasts. Its *hokim* (governor), Kobiljon Obidov, headed the region from 1993 to 2004, whereas the average tenure of an Uzbek *hokim* between 1991 and 2002 was only three years.[11] Obidov was rumored to be well liked by Karimov and, as long as the *hokim* fulfilled cotton quotas and maintained order, the president left him in power. Thus, even while enforcing state policies that strangled cross-border trade,[12] Obidov may have enjoyed the rare opportunity to relax the usual curtailment of private economic activity in order to boost employment and conciliate the population. It was in this relatively permissive climate that the twenty-three businessmen were able to open value-producing firms, accumulate capital, and deliver needed services to the local citizenry. However, by neglecting to squeeze entrepreneurs as hard as officials in other regions, Obidov inadvertently allowed social assistance to progress to the point where the central government perceived a political threat.

The arrests that ignited the demonstrations also had origins in political rivalries. Despite enjoying unusual autonomy from the center, Obidov was eventually removed in May 2004 after facing demonstrations reacting to wage arrears and power shortages. Obidov's successor, Saydullo Begaliev, who was considered a confidant of Karimov's, was intent on "purging" Obidov's networks in order to strengthen central control and install his own associates. The arrests of the businessmen were part of this effort.[13] The "new sheriff" in Andijan would put back in place the government's informal restrictions on the private accumulation of capital and increase supervision of the extracurricular activities of entrepreneurs.

---

11. Alisher Ilkhamov, "The Limits of Centralization: Regional Challenges in Uzbekistan," in *The Transformation of Central Asia,* ed. Pauline Jones Luong (Ithaca: Cornell University Press, 2004), 169.

12. In 2003, the government limited Andijan traders' access to markets in neighboring Kyrgyzstan by destroying a makeshift bridge that had been used for smuggling goods to sell at the Kara-su bazaar. "At Least 80 Kyrgyz Drowned since Uzbekistan Destroyed Cross-border Bridge," Agence France-Presse, November 4, 2003.

13. Kudrat Sharipov, "Deistviya novogo hokima Andijanskoi oblasti Begalieva poka privetstvuyutsya nasileniem" [The actions of the new hokim of Andijan Oblast Begaliev are welcomed by the population for now], http://www.ferghana.ru/article.php?id=3004, July 12, 2004. "Andijan Massacre Linked to Local Power Struggle—Source," www.eurasianet.org, September 29, 2005.

However, the businessmen's activities had apparently given locals a taste of what life could have been like under a different system.

Residents of Andijan thus reacted to the arrests with indignation, beginning with those most directly affected. As in Aksy, there were several layers of participants. The first group consisted of families of the entrepreneurs and people who were directly affected by the closure of their firms.[14] Once an invisible line of defiance had been crossed, they were joined by a set of people who were not directly related to the businessmen or affected by the trial, but may have been linked to the first group through network ties. In early May, this cohort took advantage of the anonymity of increasingly large numbers of demonstrators to express their economic and political grievances.[15]

Interviews by journalists with people from the square who had fled to Kyrgyzstan after the shootings revealed that recruitment had spread informally though *mahallas* by word-of-mouth rather than through structures such as civil society, Islamic, or other organizations.[16] The brother of one of the businessmen was reported to be a "protest leader."[17] Meanwhile, salaried community leaders actively tried to suppress mobilization by warning people and propagating the government's version of events. Yet, as the rallies persisted over a number of weeks, sympathy for the detained men spread around Andijan, and joining the demonstrations was increasingly seen as safe. Relatives of those who were shot claimed that the victims included unaffiliated bystanders who had come to observe out of simple curiosity.[18]

Despite the large number of participants who gathered in a single locale, and the fact that many of their grievances were likely shared by many people throughout Uzbekistan, protests did not break out outside Andijan. They were unlikely to spread further through direct personal ties, as networks were dense within neighborhoods of Andijan but sparse outside them. Limits on autonomous association meant it was unlikely the businessmen would have had many professional

14. "Preliminary Findings on the Events in Andijan, Uzbekistan, 13 May, 2005," OSCE/ODIHR, 11. During trials of accused extremists, families of the victims were usually the only ones sufficiently motivated to break the law that prohibited unauthorized protests. See "Uzbekistan: Human Rights Developments 2003," Human Rights Watch.

15. Human Rights Watch reports the leader at the microphone asking the crowd, "Have you invited people from the mahallas?" "Bullets Were Falling," 19. Here, as in previous cases, a critical mass appeared to have been achieved. See Timur Kuran, "Now Out of Never: The Element of Surprise in the East European Revolution of 1989," *World Politics* 44 (1991): 7–48; Rasma Karklins and Roger Petersen, "Decision Calculus of Protesters and Regimes: Eastern Europe 1989," *Journal of Politics* 55, no. 3 (1993): 588–64; Karen Rasler, "Concessions, Repression, and Political Protest in the Iranian Revolution," *American Sociological Review* 61, no. 1 (1996): 132–52.

16. Human Rights Watch, "Bullets Were Falling," 16.

17. Ibid., 10.

18. Ibid., 17.

contacts in other regions who would support them. A possible means of expansion was for sympathetic people in their own localities to launch spontaneous rebellions, but they lacked an immediate motivation equivalent to that of Andijan's residents to do so, and open political opposition was still justifiably seen as dangerous.[19] The dramatic armed attack on the prison may have been intended to provide a spark to overcome those fears, by signaling that the regime was vulnerable. Though this turn of events was unlikely in any case, the regime, which was certainly concerned about losing control, decided that violence was necessary to raise the anticipated future costs of participation in antigovernment protests, and to lay to rest the fanciful stirrings of another "color revolution."

## Political Opportunities and Grievances in Rural China

Unlike Uzbekistan, China in recent years has taken the risk of encouraging independent economic activity for the sake of growth and stability. Following economic reforms in the late 1970s, new entrepreneurs have been able to amass significant wealth and the middle class has grown rapidly. At the same time, rising expectations in the countryside have often not been met, and peasants have shown a willingness to protest against abuses by state officials. Yet despite significant unrest in the countryside (reflected in eighty-seven thousand documented protests in 2005[20]), the vast majority of protests have remained localized, and the regime has managed to successfully co-opt or neutralize most agitators of the opposition.

What has prevented people from uniting and increasing the scale of protests to extract greater concessions from the government? As with Uzbekistan, repression alone cannot be the answer, since that would have the same deterrent effect on mobilization at all levels, which plainly it has not. China's growing number of economically independent elites, whose interests can sometimes be at odds with those of the regime, might be expected to present the greatest threat to the regime, yet they have rarely coalesced to pool their resources.

Instead, a major cause of rural China's (relatively) small-scale mobilization is the restriction of association autonomous from the state and across provinces.

---

19. On the mechanism of emulation: "Connections are also made between actors on the basis of analogy—that is, on a sense of similarity in the nature of issues, situations, or mobilization targets. It is here that mobilization gains its power to travel…across vast distances between communities with seemingly little in common with one another." Mark R. Beissinger, *Nationalist Mobilization and the Collapse of the Soviet State* (New York: Cambridge University Press, 2002), 75.

20. Anthony Kuhn, "Inside China's Angry Villages," *Los Angeles Times,* February 11, 2006.

Following the frustrated pro-democracy demonstrations in 1989, China sought to reaffirm the Chinese Communist Party's (CCP) monopoly of power and the prohibition of independent political activity. By limiting the formation of cross-regional networks, the regime has made it difficult for rural citizens to coordinate autonomously and ensured that the increasingly frequent protests in the countryside are manageable.

In the early twentieth century, China lacked encompassing organizations that could aid in collective action across a vast country. The CCP overcame this weakness by infiltrating cadres into villages, railing against tyrannical landlords and promising to redistribute land, and establishing a national network of rural bases from existing village militias.[21] After its victory in 1949, the CCP used its network of villages to organize production and carry out mass mobilization campaigns.[22]

Opportunities for independent elites outside the structure of the CCP emerged in the 1980s as a result of several major reforms, including the decollectivization of agriculture, experimentation with a market economy, and devolution of decision making to the local level. Most significantly, the state provided incentives for local governments to attract investment or engage in business themselves.[23] Team leaders who managed work brigades acted as liaisons between the state and the village and were strategically positioned to benefit.[24] When land was decollectivized and market reforms were implemented, team leaders-turned-entrepreneurs earned revenues as enterprise managers and from the side payments that came from granting licenses, designating land, and awarding preferential tax rates.[25]

Village leaders, who have been empowered by mandated local elections, manage or distribute a substantial amount of their village's resources and have accrued wealth and power from the growth of private enterprise.[26] In some areas,

---

21. Ian F. W. Beckett, *Modern Insurgencies and Counterinsurgencies* (New York: Routledge, 2001), 74; Tetsuya Kataoka, *Resistance and Revolution in China* (Berkeley: University of California Press, 1974), 104.

22. Jonathan Unger, *The Transformation of Rural China* (Armonk, N.Y.: M. E. Sharpe, 2003), 11.

23. The central state ceased providing financing for health care, welfare, schools, and public security, relying instead on privatization and the initiative of village leaders to compensate. See Anne F. Thurston, "Muddling toward Democracy: Political Change in Grassroots China," United States Institute of Peace, August 1998, 8; Jean C. Oi, "The Role of the Local State in China's Transitional Economy," *China Quarterly* 144 (1995): 1137; Jean C. Oi, *Rural China Takes Off: Institutional Foundations of Economic Reform* (Berkeley: University of California Press, 1999), 62.

24. Jean Oi, "Communism and Clientelism: Rural Politics in China," *World Politics* 37, no. 2 (1985): 256.

25. Unger, *Transformation*, 143–46.

26. As of 1998, twenty million village enterprises employed 130 million people and produced one-third of China's GDP. Bruce Gilley, *Model Rebels: The Rise and Fall of China's Richest Village* (Berkeley: University of California Press, 2001), 149.

local officials have shifted the balance of power from the central government to localities by accumulating resources.[27] The Party in the late 1990s warned of "'a new power class' that was forming in rural areas, which was forming 'independent interest groups' that openly challenged central policies."[28]

At the same time, the new stratum of Chinese capitalists faces tremendous difficulty in collective action.[29] The CCP is the sole legal political party and the only organizational network that spans the entire country.[30] It has brooked no opposition to its rule, as its treatment of dissidents, control of the media, and crackdowns on foreign and domestic NGOs have shown.[31] Several mechanisms for monitoring local officials, including investigations by the Ministry of Supervision, regular inspections by higher officials, and official encouragement to report the "misdeeds" of local leaders, discourage disobedience and impede collective action.[32]

At the same time as new opportunities have been created for a lucky few, rapid development, unresponsive governance, and a weak social safety net have contributed to discontent in the countryside. Despite local elections that were supposed to introduce a mechanism of accountability, corruption among village leaders is rampant. Village leaders have abused their authority by arbitrarily seizing land and selling it to outside investors, retaining rents from the sale of village property, and pocketing bribes for providing basic services.[33] Rising unemployment (or underemployment) has forced many rural citizens to migrate to cities and has contributed to rising crime and alcoholism.[34] Massive development projects such as the Three Gorges Dam have displaced millions from their ancestral

---

27. "Local leaders in rural China use firm resources to increase their status, enhance their promotion possibilities, develop the economic and social foundations of their village, and increase their own personal wealth." Jean C. Oi and Scott Rozelle, "Elections and Power: The Locus of Decision-Making in Chinese Villages," *China Quarterly* 162 (2000): 529.

28. Gilley, *Model Rebels,* 161.

29. It has been argued that entrepreneurs have diverse interests and should not be seen as a coherent class. Kellee Tsai, "Capitalists without a Class: Political Diversity among Private Entrepreneurs in China," *Comparative Political Studies* 38, no. 9 (2005): 1130–58.

30. Elizabeth J. Perry and Mark Selden, "Introduction: Reform and Resistance in Contemporary China," in *Chinese Society: Change, Conflict, and Resistance,* ed. Elizabeth J. Perry and Mark Selden (New York: Routledge, 2000), 7.

31. In particular, the government fears foreign NGOs can broker coalitions of the opposition, especially of urban and rural discontents. See "Democracy, Chinese-Style," *Economist,* October 13, 2005, 19; "The Cauldron Boils," *Economist,* September 29, 2005.

32. Yang Zhong, *Local Government and Politics in China: Challenges from Below* (Armonk, N.Y.: M. E. Sharpe, 2003), 146–53.

33. Kathy Wilhelm, "China's Peasants Angered by Economic, Political Abuses," *Associated Press,* July 21, 1993.

34. "Misery Behind the Migration," *Economist,* November 16, 2000.

homes with insufficient compensation.[35] The proliferation of industry without adequate regulation has caused massive air and water pollution.

## Mobilization in Rural China

The losers from China's economic transformation have articulated their grievances in various ways, including "collective petitioning, demonstrations, besieging government compounds, sacking offices and the homes of local bureaucrats, destroying official vehicles, and rioting."[36] The majority of claims involve local issues, as opposed to ideological or rights-based grievances.[37] The frequency of mobilization has been staggering: there were an estimated 120,000 protests in 2008.[38] The Chinese government estimated in 2004 that there were 74,000 protests involving 3.4 million people in 337 cities and in 1,955 out of 2,861 counties.[39] Most protests last for only a few days, ending when the grievance is satisfactorily addressed or forcibly suppressed, although the government has used force only on rare occasions.[40]

The organizers of protests in rural China come from various social strata. Some are from the rural intelligentsia, possessing education, organizational skills, and local prestige.[41] Some are "organizing outsiders," including "prosperous peasants, lower middle-class city dwellers, taxi drivers, small businessmen, and an array of new social groups."[42] Another cohort of mobilization leaders is "long-time public figures," including incumbent party secretaries and former cadres, who frame grievances, recruit participants, decide on tactics, and build cross-community organizations.[43] In cases where a complaint is directed against a higher level of

---

35. "Dam Shame," *Economist*, July 4, 2002.

36. Kevin J. O'Brien, "Collective Action in the Chinese Countryside," *China Journal* 48 (July 2002): 146.

37. Ibid., 144.

38. Vivian Wai-yin Kwok, "China Tells Courts: Curb Protests," Forbes.com, June 9, 2009, http://www.forbes.com/2009/06/09/china-court-protests-business-markets-legal.html.

39. *Economist*, "Cauldron Boils," September 29, 2005.

40. Exceptions include a protest in December 2005 against the appropriation of land for an electricity plant in the relatively wealthy region of Dongzhou, when police opened fire and killed at least three people. In a sign of the government's concern about appearing heavy-handed, it subsequently arrested the commander reputedly responsible for the violence. "As the Economy Booms, So Does Unrest," *Economist*, December 13, 2005.

41. Thomas P. Bernstein and Xiaobo Lu, *Taxation without Representation in Contemporary Rural China* (New York: Cambridge, 2003), 148–49.

42. Bruce Gilley, "Civil Society: China's Organizing Outsiders," *Asian Wall Street Journal*, February 15, 2001.

43. Influential leaders "are the first to stand up on behalf of other villagers, partly because they share the same grievance, partly to demonstrate their high moral standards, and partly to confirm

government than the village, protest leaders are often village Party cadres, who may sympathize with the heavy tax burdens faced by peasants or resent the lack of support from above.[44] There have also been cases in which (elected) village leaders have themselves initiated and financed mobilization against government policies, since they are prone to identify with the populations they serve and have an electoral incentive to support them.[45]

When newly empowered village leaders have failed to comply with state edicts or shown too much independence of thought, they have attracted the attention of the state—and used or threatened mobilization to defend themselves. In an unusual but well-documented case, the Party secretary of the poor village of Daqiu, taking advantage of early reforms, used his connections to build several factories producing industrial materials.[46] The factories were later expanded into conglomerates that reinvested earnings to spawn over two hundred smaller village firms. Exploiting demand from across the country, the village became the wealthiest in China and saw the construction of new schools, hospitals, and brick houses. Having gained national notoriety through his success, Yu Zuomin, the village head, began challenging some the central government's policies. He articulated a philosophy at odds with the party line, advocating less meddling by the bureaucracy and more conspicuous consumption by peasants. When the government attempted to arrest Yu for a murder for which he was indirectly responsible, he ordered the village to mobilize to defend itself with arms. The Politburo declared that Yu had flaunted party doctrine and had him arrested two months later.

The Daqiu case, though unusual, illustrates how new elites may convert wealth into political allegiance. The enrichment of a village through manufacturing was a common occurrence throughout China in the 1980s and 1990s. Only the decision of the local Party secretary to openly advocate heterodox positions, including criticizing China's leadership, was unusual. Whereas village leaders and farmers who protest about concrete issues such as pollution or land

their status as community leaders." Kevin J. O'Brien and Lianjiang Li, "Protest Leadership in Rural China." Paper presented at the 2007 Annual Meeting of the American Political Science Association, Chicago, August 30–September 2, 2007, 19.

44. Bernstein and Lu, *Taxation*, 153.

45. In one such case, leaders of several villages along the Chaushui River in central China united against Party authorities to protest against pollution from upstream mines. After demonstrators destroyed several mine sites and police did not intervene, sixty village leaders, maintaining contact by cellular phone, threatened to resign if the pollution did not cease. They then conducted a sit-in in the county center. After threatening to mobilize one hundred thousand villagers, county officials promised to close the factories. No village leaders were punished. Edward Cody, "China's Rising Tide of Protest Sweeping Up Party Officials," *Washington Post,* September 12, 2005.

46. This summary is taken from Gilley, *Model Rebels.*

expropriation are usually tolerated, those who challenge the political order are more likely to be met with force. The residents of Daqiu supported Yu not because they necessarily agreed with his opposition to CCP ideology but because their interests aligned with his.

Although protests in China usually remain localized, when an issue has affected many people simultaneously, mobilization on a greater scale has also occurred, albeit usually within contiguous areas. In 1997, two hundred thousand peasants, along with township and village cadres, from eighty-seven villages and towns in fifteen counties of Jiangxi Province protested high taxes, grain prices, and wage arrears. In an unrelated incident, two hundred thousand farmers from all twelve counties in Hubei Province protested against corrupt Party cadres. After a week in which protesters rioted, burned buildings, and took hostages, the government relented by agreeing to the protestors' demands and granting amnesties to those arrested.[47] These examples indicate that, where an issue simultaneously affects numerous communities, protesters are capable of pooling their resources. However, events of such large scale are the exception rather than the rule.[48]

Post-Mao reforms have facilitated local mobilization even while making large-scale action more difficult. Chinese village leaders, like Kyrgyz autonomous elites, sometimes maintain pseudo-clientelistic relationships with communities, along with access to resources and the ability to organize collective action within their domain. They have used their influence on numerous occasions to mobilize villagers against the government, yet have not often coordinated across regions as in Kyrgyzstan, for two reasons.

First, most grievances that lead to protest are parochial and do not reflect a fundamental rejection of the political system. By their very nature, then, the roots of protest in one community are unlikely to be of concern to other communities at any given time. Multiple unconnected locales or regions could mobilize together if an unpopular decision made at a higher level had effects that were widely felt. A second factor hindering coordination is the absence of strong horizontal networks such as parties, interest groups, or independent business associations that could help elites build trust and identify common interests. This structural deficiency is a direct result of China's development strategy— economic reform without political liberalization.

Thus, one explanation—though not the only one—for the difference between outcomes in China and Kyrgyzstan is the extent of political reform. Whereas

---

47. "Thousands of Peasants Reportedly Protest Against Local Party Levies," *BBC Monitoring: Asia-Pacific,* October 13, 1997.

48. O'Brien, "Collective Action," 141.

Kyrgyzstan's early political opening (which later closed somewhat) allowed elites to associate and develop opposition networks that turned out to be crucial in uniting regions against the government, China's Communist Party has maintained a monopoly on political power and hindered autonomous network formation. As localities have demonstrated their ability to mobilize large numbers on their own, the Party has worked to prevent protest leaders from confederating across regions, and, like Uzbekistan, has made examples of those who do, especially after the advent of popular revolutions not far from its borders.[49]

# State Formation and Mobilization in Early Modern England and France

Though not an obvious comparison on its face, early modern Europe and post-Soviet Central Asia have several analogous structural characteristics. First, localism and limited mobility prevailed in preindustrial Europe, as in Central Asia. The major rebellions of seventeenth-century Europe occurred in an era prior to the advent of nationalism and consolidated statehood. Local and provincial ties predominated until the eighteenth century, when technology and warfare conspired to create national identities and facilitate cross-regional communication.[50]

Second and relatedly, the most common networks that were mobilized in early modern Europe were located within villages. Solidarity and local institutions facilitated collective action against the state.

Third, a power struggle was taking place that pitted centralizing monarchies against traditional landowners who were defending their autonomy and privileges. Although European states were expanding rather than weakening as in Kyrgyzstan, the structural configuration is similar: autonomous elites sometimes allied with the sovereign and at other times collaborated with the masses to increase their leverage against the center.

This section examines the causes of both localized revolts and those of greater scale in England and France between 1500 and 1660.[51] Applying the logic of

49. Yongding, "China's Color-Coded Crackdown," *Foreign Policy*, October 18, 2005; Thomas Carothers, "The Backlash against Democracy Promotion," *Foreign Affairs* 85, no. 2 (2006): 55–68.

50. Ernest Gellner, *Nations and Nationalism* (Ithaca: Cornell University Press, 1983); Charles Tilly, *Coercion, Capital and European States, AD 990–1990* (Malden, Mass.: Blackwell, 1990).

51. Scholars agree that these years roughly delimit a transition period characterized by struggles between the crown, landlords, and capitalists; efforts by monarchs to centralize and strengthen the state; and numerous peasant revolts, which subsided after the state consolidated its control of the provinces. Yves-Marie Berce, *History of Peasant Revolts: The Social Origins of Rebellion in Early Modern France* (Oxford: Polity Press, 1990), 326. Tilly dates the century as being from 1598 to 1715.

the theory elaborated in this book, major rebellions should occur in regions where elites and masses are bound by patron-client ties or have common interests in opposing the state. When a greater number of elites participate, the scale should increase accordingly. We should also see larger-scale mobilizations where institutions exist for regional elites to exchange information, collaborate, and build trust, and at times when the sovereign is perceived as unable or unwilling to use repression, that is, when bandwagoning appears profitable.

The states that ultimately developed in Western Europe were a product of frequent contention stemming from struggles for power. England and France experienced a greater amount of large-scale mobilization in the sixteenth and seventeenth centuries than in any other period because the dispersion of wealth stemming from industrialization, along with technological advances in weaponry, had empowered local notables.[52] Localized peasant rebellions or *jacqueries* were so frequent that individual rebellions rarely merit close study by historians. By one count, there were 47 uprisings in France between 1590 and 1635, 282 between 1635 and 1660, and 130 from 1660 to 1715.[53] The last major rebellion of the period, the Fronde (1648–53), which was brutally put down, began a period of relative passivity until the French Revolution over one hundred years later. England experienced a smaller amount of localized peasant uprisings—most over the issue of enclosure[54]—but compensated for this with its major struggles over dynastic succession and religion. The majority of uprisings in both countries were contained within a province, and many incidents in which people from several regions rose up were in fact spontaneous reactions to similar provocations that erupted in an uncoordinated manner.[55]

In this period, the overarching struggle was over the degree of centralization of the state, which played out differently in England and France, and which shaped the form and scale of contention. In England, where trade was more developed and agricultural capitalism predominated over feudal structures, middle-level elites were relatively more powerful vis-à-vis the monarch than in France, where regional power brokers had fewer resources.[56] In England, monarchical overreach

---

Charles Tilly, *The Contentious French: Four Centuries of Popular Struggle* (Cambridge: Harvard University Press, 1986), 11.

52. In the Middle Ages, peasant revolts had been more parochial, directed primarily against their landlords and not against the state. In the seventeenth century, by contrast, local lords often collaborated with peasants against central authority. Berce, *History of Peasant Revolts*, 338.

53. Ibid., 327. Tilly counts thirty-one "revolutionary situations" in the same period, primarily fought over tax burdens or rejection of Catholicism. Charles Tilly, *European Revolutions, 1492–1992* (Oxford: Blackwell, 1993), 151.

54. Perez Zagorin, *Rebels and Rulers, 1500–1660* (New York: Cambridge University Press, 1982), 178.

55. Berce, *History of Peasant Revolts*, 322; ibid., 177.

56. Margaret Levi, *Of Rule and Revenue* (Berkeley: University of California Press, 1988), 111.

in extracting resources led to rebellions by those with capital, and resulted in the creation of a parliament as a permanent counterweight to royal authority. France, by contrast, developed a stronger bureaucracy to implement a uniform tax system, and was able to extract resources from the population without the intervention of provincial elites.[57]

The people occupying the middle rung between the monarchy and the masses played a critical role in determining the course of state-building and the ability of the monarch to act. Charles Tilly describes this cohort as "powerful intermediaries who enjoyed significant autonomy, hindered state demands that were not in their interest, and profited on their own accounts from the delegated exercise of state power. The intermediaries were often privileged members of subordinate populations, and made their way by assuring rulers of tribute and acquiescence from these populations."[58] The political allegiance of lords and nobles, nominally directed toward the crown, was conditional and limited by strong ties to people in their region. Interests and identity often coincided as "local solidarities created paternalistic bonds between peasants and seigneurs, who were impelled to protect as well as to exploit their peasant subjects and who had their own interests in resisting fiscality [taxation]."[59] Distinctive provincial identities, values, and family attachments often outweighed obedience to the state, especially in France,[60] and more commonly in subsistence regions where survival was dependent on cooperation between classes.[61]

The major contentious issue stemming from state centralization was taxation. As rulers began raising standing armies to cope with the increasing costs of war in the sixteenth century, both England and France took on large public debts and developed national tax systems.[62] As tax rates became increasingly burdensome—Tilly estimates that they increased from two days' wages in 1620 to twelve days' wages in 1640[63]—to cover the state's ever-growing debts, impoverished peasants sometimes fought back. Tax rebellions, which involved passing around petitions to repeal the tax and attacking collectors sent out to enforce compliance, usually continued without the aid of outsiders until the rebels relented.[64] The ability of villages in seventeenth-century Europe to collaborate and unite was impeded by isolation: "Geographic distance was of great physical

---

57. Ibid., 119
58. Tilly, *Coercion, Capital*, 104.
59. Zagorin, *Rebels and Rulers*, 218.
60. Ibid., 110.
61. William Brustein and Margaret Levi, "The Geography of Rebellion: Rulers, Rebels, and Regions, 1500–1700," *Theory and Society* 16, no. 4 (1987): 480.
62. Tilly, *Coercion, Capital*, 74.
63. Ibid., 157.
64. Tilly, *Contentious French*, 87–88.

and psychological importance, and while each community held no secrets from its members, it was often isolated from the wider world to a degree unthinkable today."[65] Most protests would thus end when the local governor promised concessions or crushed the revolt forcibly, or the peasants' improvised militia dissolved out of frustration or the need to return to the fields.[66]

In contrast to peasant revolts, Tilly argues that "the great rebellions of the seventeenth century all built on the complicity or active support of local authorities and regional magnates."[67] Although peasants on their own could muster enough forces to alarm local governors, it was only when a movement found a wealthy patron or "major rivals to the crown" who could unite local rebellions that opposition took on alarming proportions.[68] Nobles could provide protection, organization, arms, and even the use of their castle to support rebels against tax collectors.[69]

Alliances between peasants and their landlords were variable yet critical in determining scale. William Brustein argues that cross-class collaborative rebellions against the state were more likely in regions based on sharecropping than on commercial agriculture. Where the former prevailed, cultivators were dependent on landlords for resources and landlords relied on cultivators' labor.[70] This economic interdependence often aligned the two classes' interests regarding enclosures and taxes, producing more frequent collaboration against the state than in commercial agricultural regimes or where there was more frequent interaction with third parties.[71] William Brustein and Margaret Levi add several factors to explain the variation in the scale of rebellion, including access to resources, religious homogeneity, communal (i.e., village) institutions, and regional parliaments that facilitate collective action among nobles.[72]

In the Croquant rebellion of the 1630s, an ordinary tax revolt became a fledgling war when the residents of the communes of Perigord created a peasant army

---

65. Thomas Munck, *Seventeenth-Century Europe: State, Conflict and the Social Order in Europe, 1598–1700,* 2nd ed. (New York: Palgrave Macmillan, 2005), 287.

66. Berce, *History of Peasant Revolts,* 324. When new taxes threatened the interests of mayors, councils, and lords by diverting to the crown part of their anticipated revenue, these elites could join with aggrieved peasants or lead revolts themselves to protest the policy. Ibid., 86.

67. Tilly, *Contentious French,* 40.

68. Tilly, *European Revolutions,* 158.

69. Karen Barkey, "Rebellious Alliances: The State and Peasant Unrest in Early Seventeenth-Century France and the Ottoman Empire," *American Sociological Review* 56, no. 6 (1991): 702.

70. Subsistence agriculture predominated in western and southwestern France, northwestern and southwestern England, and northern Spain. William Brustein, "Class Conflict and Class Collaboration in Regional Rebellions 1500 to 1700," *Theory and Society* 14, no. 4 (1985): 450.

71. Brustein, "Class Conflict," 447.

72. Brustein and Levi, "Geography of Rebellion," 481.

of six thousand men.[73] Several prominent noblemen led the rebellion, and lower-level seigneurs were compelled by peasants to support the rebels' aims, though many already sympathized with their demands and used the pretext of coercion to join in opposing the crown.[74] In the subsequent months, even though the initial uprising was suppressed, neighboring provinces also rebelled, spurred on by contact with rebels and a manifesto making claims on the crown. Yet although rebellious activity took place in many villages throughout western and central France in response to the same general grievance, the outbreaks remained isolated and did not coalesce into a unified movement.[75]

Mobilization occurred on a broader scale in regions that were less integrated into the state. In southwestern France, a region that had been fought over by English and French monarchs, localities enjoyed greater autonomy from the center than regions that had submitted to French rule in the more distant past. Residents of the region were more sensitive to new taxes and capitalists were able to amass greater resources without paying tribute to the crown.[76] Brustein also notes that low population growth and density led landlords to offer peasants favorable contracts, for example, by stipulating that landlords share the burden of paying state taxes.[77] Thus, with elites inclined to join the masses, the region from the Pyrenees to the Loire saw not only more frequent revolts but also greater numbers of participants, and the majority of rebellions in that period reached regional scale.[78]

When an issue was sufficiently general so as to provoke the interests of nobles and magnates from multiple regions who shared grievances with peasants, mobilization would be even broader in scope. Two examples, one from each country, illustrate how elite brokerage was the critical factor in achieving national mobilization.

Major rebellions in England were often outgrowths of the Protestant Reformation, as religion often coincided with dynastic struggles and generated new grievances that could be used to rally the masses. The so-called Pilgrimage of Grace (1536) in northern England was nominally a protest against Henry VIII's attacks on Catholicism, but it also was seized upon by opportunistic aristocrats with the intention of curbing absolutist rule.[79] The region was especially prone to rebellion due to two factors: the relative independence of nobles due to the

---

73. Berce, *History of Peasant Revolts,* 130.

74. Zagorin, *Rebels and Rulers,* 221; Robin Briggs, *Early Modern France: 1560–1715* (New York: Oxford University Press, 1977), 117.

75. Berce writes that "there was never any question of a general, concerted rebellion. The idea was inconceivable. These scattered manifestations of an inchoate uprising took place on their own accord in different parts of the country, and no single model or incident was needed to spark them off." Berce, *History of Peasant Revolts,* 144. See also Zagorin, *Rebels and Rulers,* 222.

76. Berce, *History of Peasant Revolts,* 333.

77. Brustein, "Class Conflict," 454.

78. Berce, *History of Peasant Revolts,* 322.

79. Brustein, "Class Conflict," 459–60.

proximity of the Scottish border, and the extreme poverty of the population, which was dependent on the clergy for survival.[80] Local outbreaks of indignation occurred when the king began expropriating monasteries, which had provided peasants with benefits such as "charity, hospitality, the provision of tenancies, or other benefits."[81] For reasons ranging from ideology to the desire for power, elites from across the region joined in; "this involvement of men in the governing class was crucial" to mobilizing the peasantry and sustaining an insurgency.[82] A "council of pilgrims" was created that comprised lords, knights, and commoners and united mobilizing towns in a single movement. The council submitted petitions to the king demanding not only to restore the authority of the Catholic Church but also to reform parliament and rein in the power of the monarchy.[83] Ultimately the Pilgrimage, which amassed an army of thirty-six thousand men but never expanded beyond the northern counties, ended its resistance after the king promised to make concessions (which he later repudiated).[84]

In the Fronde, the final gasp of resistance to state centralization in France, "shifting alliances of urban power-holders and great warlords opposed royal demands for greater subordination and financial support in connection with the enormous expenses of wars against Habsburg power."[85] In contrast to previous French rebellions that primarily revolved around peasant grievances, the Fronde represented a wider array of regional actors and communities that were able to coordinate action over great distances and, to a greater extent than before, unite in pursuit of common goals. It was also different from ordinary peasant uprisings because "the masses became involved only as followers of other social groups."[86] The Fronde began as the confluence of an antitax rebellion in Paris and demands by Parisian judges to reverse the fiscal policies of King Louis XIV and his chief minister.[87] Participation by nobles, who, like their dependents had an interest in curtailing royal authority, expanded the movement throughout most of western France.[88] Governors with clienteles mobilized provincial nobles, who, in turn, used their patronage ties to raise peasant armies.[89] Regional parliaments, which

80. Yves-Marie Berce, *Revolt and Revolution in Early Modern Europe* (Manchester: Manchester University Press, 1987), 167.

81. Zagorin, *Rebels and Rulers*, 23; Wayne te Brake, *Shaping History: Ordinary People in European Politics, 1500–1700* (Berkeley: University of California Press, 1998), 57.

82. Zagorin, *Rebels and Rulers*, 25.

83. Ibid., 27–28; te Brake, *Shaping History*, 60.

84. Ibid., 25; Berce, *Revolt and Revolution*, 168.

85. Tilly, *European Revolutions*, 129.

86. Berce, *History of Peasant Revolts*, 320.

87. Tilly, *European Revolutions*, 159.

88. Brustein, "Class Conflict," 461.

89. Sharon Kettering, "Patronage and Politics during the Fronde," *French Historical Studies* 14, no. 3 (1986): 412 (citing Roland Mousnier, "Recherches sur le soulevements populaires en France avant la Fronde," *Revue d'histoire moderne et contemporaine* 5 [1958]).

Brustein and Levi contend facilitate rebellion by providing a forum in which elites can exchange information and cooperate, enabled elites to broker between mobilizing locales and unite localized protests into provincial movements.[90]

Over time, structural transformations in society altered the balance of power between the center and the regions, first lowering the barriers to cooperation among regional elites, then strengthening the capacity of the state to put down resistance. Daniel Nexon describes a process of increasing opportunities for widespread collective action fostered by heterodox religious ideologies in the Reformation. New religious identities undercut the power of monarchs to control their subjects and isolate them from other regions, giving rise to "movements involving both common identities and cross-cutting ties, both of which brought together social groups that, in the early modern context, often shared few concerns and interests."[91] The result weakened dynastic control over imperial peripheries and laid the foundations for the modern nation-state.

Yet in the long run, the central state prevailed. In the eighteenth century, the king and parliament in England reached an understanding that reduced the likelihood that their disagreements would degenerate into war. Parliament became seen as a reliable conduit through which to communicate grievances, and popular revolts declined accordingly. In France, after suppressing the Fronde, the state regularized a system of agents serving in the provinces, usurping the power of some local notables and co-opting others, and shifting people's loyalties from the provinces to the center.[92] The advance of capitalism further reduced the influence of rural elites, who "deserted popular rebellion."[93]

As the French state extended its rule, local revolts increasingly targeted the seigneurial regime rather than the state. In the French Revolution, instead of allying with their lords, peasants mobilized against them. The National Assembly in Paris advanced antiseigneurial legislation, news of which made its way to the provinces and encouraged further local insurrections. Repertoires of protest actions took on a regional character as they spread across proximate villages.[94] The Revolution furthered the state's imposition of direct rule, which in turn altered the dominant mode of contention. By the nineteenth century, interest groups

---

90. The first parliaments to rebel after a change of power in Paris were those in Aix, Rouen, and Bordeaux. Ibid.

91. Daniel H. Nexon, *The Struggle for Power in Early Modern Europe: Religious Conflict, Dynastic Empires, and International Change* (Princeton: Princeton University Press, 2009), 131.

92. Tilly, *European Revolutions,* 129, Tilly, *Contentious French,* 40.

93. Tilly, *European Revolutions,* 160; Edgar Kiser and April Linton, "The Hinges of History: State-making and Revolt in Early Modern France," *American Sociological Review* 67, no. 6 (2002): 889–910.

94. John Markoff, *The Abolition of Feudalism: Peasants, Lords, and Legislators in the French Revolution* (University Park: Pennsylvania State University Press, 1996).

replaced communities as the dominant basis of mobilization, which enabled people to coalesce and articulate their grievances on a wider scale than in previous eras and without relying on elites.[95]

## Mexico's Abortive War for Independence

Like seventeenth-century Europe, Mexico—or New Spain—in the early nineteenth century was largely rural and poor, divided by ethnicity, class, and region, and characterized by intense localism. Also like early modern Europe, the state maintained only tenuous control over large parts of its nominal territory. Where the state was unable to extend its authority, local *caciques* (landowners) acted as brokers between the government and the mass populace.[96] At the turn of the century, opposition to Spanish rule was percolating among the educated classes, who were largely creole (descendants of European settlers born in Mexico), but the prospect of independence meant little to the mass of indigenous peasants. When the war for independence finally came in 1810, its outcome would be determined by a "three-way struggle among peasant villages, creole insurgent directorate, and colonial state."[97] As in Europe, the middle stratum of autonomous elites acted as a crucial pivot that could stimulate resistance against the regime from below, or cooperate with the top echelons of society to maintain the status quo.

New Spain, like early modern France, was a scene of frequent and fierce—but localized—rebellions over issues such as taxation, tribute, land, and administrative abuses.[98] Villages were a source of identity and solidarity and therefore also the basis for mobilization, although they were sometimes stratified internally.[99] Localized rebellions did not typically involve political or ideological objectives. They were inherently self-limiting due to the parochial nature of the grievances and the barriers to collective action. As a result, "Only rarely, and certainly not in

---

95. Tilly, *Contentious French*, 74.

96. Eric R. Wolf, "Aspects of Group Relations in a Complex Society: Mexico," *American Anthropologist*, n.s., 58, no. 6 (1956): 1076; Brian R. Hamnett, *Roots of Insurgency: Mexican Regions, 1750–1824* (New York: Cambridge University Press, 1986), 55.

97. Eric Van Young, "Agrarian Rebellion and Defense of Community: Meaning and Collective Violence in Late Colonial and Independence-Era Mexico," *Journal of Social History* 27, no. 2 (1993): 248.

98. Hamnett, *Roots of Insurgency*, 74, 84. Is it estimated that Mexico experienced 137 "small scale village riots and uprisings" between 1700 and 1820. See John H. Coatsworth, "Patterns of Rural Rebellion in Latin America: Mexico in Comparative Perspective," in *Riot, Rebellion, and Revolution: Rural Social Conflict in Mexico*, ed. Frederich Katz (Princeton: Princeton University Press, 1988), 31.

99. Michael T. Ducey, *A Nation of Villages: Riot and Rebellion in the Mexican Huasteca, 1750–1850* (Tucson: University of Arizona Press, 2004), 72.

New Spain until 1810, did a broad enough spectrum of rural and urban discontent provide sufficient manpower for a generalized insurrection."[100]

The uprising against Spanish rule led by Miguel Hidalgo, a priest and intellectual from central Mexico, marked a rupture with past rebellions by uniting people from several regions, albeit loosely, under a single banner.[101] The rebellion declared its opposition to Spanish rule and the political dominance of the European elite class and demanded autonomy under the king and, later, outright independence. The driving forces behind the rebellion were not the mass poor—although many participated—but rather a group of marginal elites from a single region. Two colonial practices generated resentment among creoles: the appointment of European-born Spaniards to high administrative positions in the church and government;[102] and a Spanish decree during the Napoleonic Wars requiring churches to call in the loans previously made to estate owners, in order to repay the Crown. The order fell especially hard on creoles, whereas European landowners used their connections to the mother country to avoid full compliance.[103] When Napoleon's invasion of Spain forced the abdication of King Charles IV in 1808, latent grievances against the colonial government broke out into the open. A conspiracy launched by Hidalgo and a group of frustrated regional elites to overthrow Spanish rule was exposed, forcing the plotters to begin their uprising prematurely.[104]

Hidalgo tapped into insecurity and anger among peasants and quickly raised a militia in his home region of Bajio, a step he hoped would encourage other disgruntled creoles to join him.[105] To appeal to potential allies of this cohort, Hidalgo recruited through local networks of midlevel elites—"wealthy landowners, hacienda majordomos, lawyers, and priests"—who supervised farmers and peasants.[106] Initially the (provincial) urban conspirators managed to convince mar-

---

100. Hamnett, *Roots of Insurgency,* 75.

101. Ducey, *Nation of Villages,* 60. Hidalgo's army numbered one hundred thousand men at its peak. Eric Van Young, "Moving toward Revolt: Agrarian Origins of the Hidalgo Rebellion in the Guadalajara Region," in Katz, *Riot, Rebellion, and Revolution,* 178.

102. Hugh M. Hamill, *The Hidalgo Revolt: Prelude to Mexican Independence* (Gainesville: University of Florida Press, 1966), 21.

103. John Tutino, *From Insurrection to Revolution in Mexico: Social Bases of Agrarian Violence, 1750–1940* (Princeton: Princeton University Press, 1986), 107–08; Peter F. Guardino, *Peasants, Politics, and the Formation of Mexico's National State: Guerrero, 1800–1857* (Stanford: Stanford University Press, 1996), 18.

104. Hamnett, *Roots of Insurgency,* 56.

105. Peasants in Bajio may have been especially susceptible to antigovernment appeals, since they had recently suffered drought, famine, and population growth that put pressure on their land. Anthony McFarlane, "Rebellions in Late Colonial Spanish America," *Bulletin of Latin American Research* 14, no. 3 (1995): 325–26. But see also Simon Miller, "Land and Labour in Mexican Rural Insurrections," *Bulletin of Latin American Research* 10, no. 1 (1991): 55–79.

106. Hamnett, *Roots of Insurgency,* 125; Guardino, *Peasants, Politics,* 57.

ginal rural elites in the surrounding areas to join the revolt by appealing to their desire for greater local autonomy, whereas better established elites supported the status quo. Yet after successfully capturing the Bajio, the rebel army had difficulty recruiting influential actors outside it. As the insurgency advanced on Mexico City, the leaders hoped to appeal to landowners and peasants in the surrounding towns to increase their ranks. Instead, it was unable to generate the support of either class—landlords were predisposed to support the government and prohibited their subordinates from joining the rebels.[107] The militia was beaten back by Royalist forces only four months after the revolt began.

When it became clear that rebellion was not attracting fellow creole elites, the insurgents focused increasingly on recruiting among the peasantry through class-based appeals. Yet this strategy backfired: when word got out of the brutal killing of Spanish elites by Hidalgo's forces, the prospect of armed Indian peasants roaming the countryside alarmed both landed elites and the middle class, driving them into the arms of the state.[108] Without the support of the elite, the rebels found it difficult to recruit their natural allies, the mass poor, and the insurgency stalled. After several defeats, Hidalgo was captured in March and executed in July 1811.

Following the failed advance on Mexico City, Hidalgo's anointed successor, José Maria Morelos, also a priest, pursued a different strategy and began a second—and more successful—phase of the insurgency that continued for the next decade. He concentrated on winning over disgruntled provincial notables, or caciques, in the weakly penetrated "hot country" south and west of the capital. Facing a less imposing government presence than in central Mexico, caciques joined the rebellion out of self-interest, whether to defend against the encroachment of Spanish merchants and investors or to extend their economic operations.[109] They contributed by mobilizing their extended families along with villages and workers under their control who "lent themselves readily to transformation into insurgent bands."[110] The army succeeded in controlling a belt extending from Acapulco to Oaxaca, before Morelos was captured and killed in 1815. Militia commanders (caudillos) continued to battle Royalist forces until 1821.

---

107. It has been argued that recruitment stalled because economic conditions in the central highlands made the peasantry less vulnerable and therefore less revolutionary. Relative autonomy from landlords gave peasants leverage in obtaining work and procuring food in difficult times, causing peasants to view their interests as aligned both with their conservative landlords and the regime. Tutino, *Insurrection*, 139–51.

108. Hamill, *Hidalgo Revolt*, 176; Tutino, *Insurrection*, 133.

109. Hamnett, *Roots of Insurgency*, 138–45.

110. Ibid., 55.

Both the first and second phases of the insurrection were jury-rigged assemblages consisting of disparate groups, which prevented unification around a set of principles and made it difficult to maintain discipline. Some rebel leaders acted opportunistically, claiming solidarity with the leadership of the movement, but in fact sought to redress local grievances and pursue their own social or political objectives.[111] This heterogeneity undermined cohesiveness and gave rise to looting and banditry, which pushed potential allies into the arms of the government in the interest of self-preservation.

The contrast between Hidalgo's failure to expand the scale of his uprising and Morelos's relative success in carrying out a regional insurgency confirms a lesson from the other cases in this chapter. Because of the social and economic structure of colonial Mexico, it was difficult to raise a peasant army in regions where elites did not also support the movement. The conspirators thus faced a paradox: a successful rebellion would need to involve a critical mass of creole elites, yet in trying to win them over with a show of early victories, Hidalgo's peasant army made this impossible. Whatever antipathy creoles held toward Spanish rule was outweighed by their interest in maintaining their social and economic position vis-à-vis the (mostly Indian) peasantry, and their fear of social revolution. Unable to win the support of influential elites outside their regions, the rebels "failed to build a consensus broad enough to displace the existing regime."[112] Only where the state was weak and elites already enjoyed substantial autonomy did Morelos build a cross-regional movement by appealing to the self-interest of independently inclined caciques.

Ironically, Mexico secured its independence in 1821 not through violence but through a pact negotiated between the conservative upper classes—which had opposed Hidalgo's struggle for independence—and a newly installed liberal regime in Spain. The peasantry played no role in the achievement, which served the interests of creole elites by entrenching social and economic inequalities. Political reformers thus won a victory without violence, but it was only a partial resolution of Mexico's problems. It would be another century before the underclass developed sufficient mobilizational capacity to bring about the social revolution that elites had managed to avert in the 1810s.

This chapter has examined cases beyond Kyrgyzstan in order to shed light on the relationship between the configuration of actors and the distribution of resources on one hand, and the scale and dynamics of mobilization on the other. Contemporaneous with Kyrgyzstan's "revolution," a large protest occurred in

---

111. Tutino, *Insurrection*, 211; Van Young, "Moving toward Revolt," 180.
112. Hamnett, *Roots of Insurgency*, 208.

Uzbekistan but, because of its restrictive political system and centralized economy, it occurred spontaneously and remained localized. In rural China, where there were economic opportunities but political institutions were not responsive to the public, local elites of various stripes were likely to take part in mobilization, but had difficulty coordinating across larger regions. In early modern Europe and colonial Mexico, where the state had yet to consolidate control over its territory, autonomous elites had both the ability and—at times—the incentive to rebel against the center and collaborate across regions.

Contrary to popular perceptions about the ability of grassroots activists to mobilize ordinary people to effect political change, this chapter has highlighted the role that strategically placed elites play in activating and expanding rebellion. Brokers occupying an ambivalent niche between the state and the mass populace played a pivotal role as "gatekeepers" of information and stewards of important resources.[113] If challenged, they could defend their interests by activating their ties to communities and preexisting contacts with other elites. "Bottom-up" mobilization that was not elite-driven was unlikely to spread far where villages faced social and geographic barriers.

When structural forces produced a rough balance of power between the state and regional elites, as in England and France, the process of state formation could be a fitful and wrenching process. The state's perceived violation of long-standing local traditions and privileges often provoked bloody cross-class and cross-regional rebellions. Yet Western Europe's experience of state formation and the conflict it engendered were not inevitable. In fact, rulers facing similar center-periphery dynamics and with access to the same technologies could produce different outcomes by varying their strategies of rule. Karen Barkey argues that, in contrast to Western Europe, the Ottoman Empire in the seventeenth century never faced significant coordinated rebellion due to tenuous ties between elites and the peasantry, and the center's divide-and-rule tactics. First, elites were dependent on the sultanate for their authority, and were frequently rotated to prevent the formation of strong cross-class alliances. Second, when the central leadership extended its authority, it would attack some notables while rewarding others, rather than challenge the whole landlord class at once, reducing their opportunities to collaborate. Thus, the peasantry was deprived of influential allies, and elites lacked horizontal networks. Consequently, mobilization against Ottoman rule was localized and contained, and it did not reach the large scale of revolts in seventeenth-century France.[114]

---

113. Roger V. Gould and Roberto M. Fernandez, "Structures of Mediation: A Formal Approach to Brokerage in Transaction Networks," *Sociological Methodology* 19 (1989): 89–126.

114. Barkey, "Rebellious Alliances"; Karen Barkey, *Bandits and Bureaucrats: The Ottoman Route to State Centralization* (Ithaca: Cornell University Press, 1994).

Today, many hybrid regimes, which possess elements of both democracy and authoritarianism, face similar dilemmas to European and Ottoman state-builders. They retain power by selectively rewarding loyalists and constituents, and threatening (and sometimes using) repression against opponents. Rival economic and political actors often agree to be "bought" and have an interest in maintaining stability. But they also have an incentive in preserving their independence and leveraging their position, lest they fall out of favor. Aware of the danger of cross-class alliances, autocrats must work hard to hold their coalition together and deter independent elites from going into opposition. An opportunity for regime change occurs when an event pushes elites of different stripes together, and unites elites and masses in an antiregime coalition. The final chapter pursues this point with an eye toward furthering our understanding of the interaction between these three sets of actors.

# POLITICAL ECONOMIES, HYBRID REGIMES, AND CHALLENGES TO DEMOCRATIZATION

Mass mobilization is one of the most dramatic and inspiring of all political phenomena. The sight of thousands of impassioned citizens taking to the streets to demand their rights can be a great leveling force in the face of powerful and repressive governments, which have recourse to police, armies, and the state-run media to maintain their power. "People power" is one of the great innovations of the post–World War II era, capable of producing monumental and lasting political change through peaceful means, and paralleling the worldwide rise in democracies.[1] Sometimes it occurs in the most unlikely of places, where ordinary people appear to have little recourse but put their lives at risk. Protest events that result in the overthrow of a nondemocratic government are rare yet consequential for the future political trajectory of a nation, and therefore of great significance to social scientists and policy makers alike.

In this book I introduced an important caveat to the conventional narrative of grassroots political change, by delving into the structural and organizational bases of movements that appear on the surface to be expressions of the popular will. I approached the issue by tying mobilization to the informal means that nonstate actors use to ensure their interests and contest power where formal institutions are weak or highly politicized. In such systems, the ruling elite typically exploits access to state resources to maintain control. Antiregime mobilization in

---

1. Peter Ackerman and Jack DuVall, *A Force More Powerful: A Century of Nonviolent Conflict* (New York: St. Martin's Press, 2000); Kurt Schock, *Unarmed Insurrections: People Power Movements in Nondemocracies* (Minneapolis: University of Minnesota Press, 2005).

this context can transpire as a defensive response by actors lacking other means to secure their interests—protecting power and property, in the case of independent elites; defending those elites' interests, for the masses.

In this chapter I explore some of the implications that stem from the theoretical and empirical claims of this book. The link between mass protest and informal strategies of adaptation can shed light on the forces that determine the survival or demise of authoritarian and hybrid regimes, which today constitute the majority of the world's states and population.[2] In particular, I note the importance of economic dispersion as an enabling condition for the success of opposition movements in nondemocratic states. I discuss the implications of subversive clientelism and other informal strategies that hybrid regimes tend to engender. Then, based on the experience of Kyrgyzstan and other recent cases of regime change by mass mobilization in Eurasia, I speculate on the book's implications for democracy and governance in the aftermath of "revolutionary" political change.

## Mass Mobilization as Elite Self-defense

This book began with the puzzle of how ordinary villagers in Kyrgyzstan, preoccupied with making ends meet and not politically active, came to take part in a peaceful mass uprising that overthrew their president. I described how the evolving institutional structure of Kyrgyzstan following independence shaped the behavior of actors in ways that made mass mobilization feasible. The bulk of the population sought security by investing time and energy in informal community networks, which helped solve pressing collective action problems. At the same time, however, the capacity of community networks to serve the needs of their members was fundamentally limited by their homogeneity and the poverty of resources to which they had access.

The next piece of the puzzle was the cohort of elites whose interests increasingly diverged from those of a detached and unpopular regime. Elites who enjoyed autonomy from the state were relatively scarce in Uzbekistan due to its suffocating economic environment and repressive political institutions, but were a fixture of politics in Kyrgyzstan as a result of its early policies that dispersed power from the state. In a system that, despite its freedoms, was characterized by weak institutions and uncertain property rights, these elites sought out various means to preserve and advance their interests.

In some cases the interests of autonomous elites converged with those of the (more numerous) losers from postcommunist reform. A mutually beneficial

---

2. According to Freedom House, 104 countries, containing 54% of the world's population, are "not free" or "partly free." http://www.freedomhouse.org/template.cfm?page=70&release=756.

relationship could result when elites offered needed assistance—or made appeals demonstrating their solicitousness—to local communities, a process I called subversive clientelism. Material and symbolic investments increased the probability that ordinary people would develop a stake in the well-being of their patron, and they gave the latter a latent reserve of social and political support. To hedge their bets, elites could also enter into informal cross-regional alliances with other elites based on common economic or political interests.

When elites who embedded themselves in society faced a threat to their power or property, influence over communities could be a valuable asset. Using their financial, organizational, and human resources, embedded elites could activate ordinary people to mobilize on their behalf, as occurred in the Aksy protests. If multiple elites were threatened and believed mobilization to be advantageous, they could act as brokers between otherwise unaffiliated communities and construct a mass movement, an undertaking that led to the overthrow of President Akaev in Kyrgyzstan in 2005. Although protests were initiated by elites for instrumental reasons, participation was not coerced; demonstrators by and large shared their patron's grievance or were closely associated with someone who did. In the final analysis, people's participation stemmed from their willingness to embrace patrons in pursuit of material security. This mundane objective, and the exigencies of elite-level political struggles, inadvertently drew them into national-level political activism.

## The Political Economy of Political Contention

The events described in this book highlight the crucial link between political economy and political opposition. By implementing liberal reforms in the early 1990s, President Akaev inadvertently provided the means for his opponents to overthrow him over a decade later. Privatization and limited barriers to wealth accumulation outside the state created opportunities for a wide array of actors to aspire to prosperity, while official toleration of civil society allowed new elites to strengthen their autonomy through unfettered association. Akaev's later manipulation of the constitution and attempts to claw back freedoms he had previously granted drove unaffiliated elites and some former supporters to coalesce against him. Akaev thus followed in the footsteps of other leaders whose policies inadvertently empowered critical actors in society who would later come to oppose or topple them.[3]

---

3. Kenneth Medhurst, "Spain's Evolutionary Pathway from Dictatorship to Democracy," *West European Politics* 7, no. 2 (1984): 30–49; Samuel P. Huntington, *The Third Wave: Democratization in the Late Twentieth Century* (Norman: University of Oklahoma Press, 1991), 59–72; Robert E. Bedeski,

That the unraveling of a regime can emanate from its own policies is an insight not lost on insecure autocrats. A nondemocratic ruler who seeks to retain power must always maintain a balance of policies intended primarily to maintain popular support and ones intended to undermine putative opponents. He can tolerate isolated expressions of dissent, which may even be useful as a way for aggrieved citizens to "let off steam." If grievances are widely shared, he can prevent a broad-based revolt by selectively employing coercive and financial resources to keep the opposition weak and divided. However, in the long run, political power is in large part a function of economic might, and a regime's ability to endure depends on its ability to control, and deprive its putative opponents of access to, resources. The autocrat's dilemma is that good governance, which facilitates economic growth and increases his legitimacy, can also hasten his downfall if opponents of authoritarianism are empowered in the process.[4] Where a regime and its allies enjoy a preponderance of resources, the political economy favors the status quo. If resources become dispersed—through economic growth and the rise of a middle class, for example—independent centers of power can emerge, putting pressure on a regime to liberalize politically.[5] In the extreme, a regime may be faced with a choice of making drastic concessions or unleashing repression, which risks provoking a backlash that hastens the regime's demise. This is a dilemma authoritarians have struggled to resolve, sometimes successfully, at other times, less so.[6]

The relationship between the concentration of wealth and the durability of authoritarianism finds expression in states subject to the "resource curse." Regimes that control natural monopolies can use the resulting revenues to build up their coercive apparatus and distribute patronage to society. Oppositions, for

---

The Transformation of South Korea: Reform and Reconstitution in the Sixth Republic under Roh Tae Woo, 1987–1992 (London: Routledge, 1994); Carles Boix and Susan C. Stokes "Endogenous Democratization," World Politics 55, no. 4 (2003): 517–49.

4. The idea that a society that is prosperous is also one that can overthrow a regime is the obverse of the aphorism that "a government that is strong enough to protect property and enforce contracts is also strong enough to confiscate the wealth of its citizens." Barry R. Weingast, "Constitutions as Governance Structures: The Political Foundations of Secure Markets," Journal of International and Theoretical Economics 149 (1993): 287.

5. This is the classical argument of modernization theory. See Seymour Martin Lipset, Political Man: The Social Bases of Politics (Baltimore: Johns Hopkins University Press, 1981); Ross E. Burkhart and Michael S. Lewis-Beck, "Comparative Democracy: The Economic Development Thesis," American Political Science Review 88 (Dec. 1994): 903–10. Other works on economic change and the loss of political control include Dietrich Rueschemeyer, Evelyne Huber Stephens, and John D. Stephens, Capitalist Development and Democracy (Chicago: University of Chicago Press, 1992); Kenneth F. Greene, Why Dominant Parties Lose: Mexico's Democratization in Comparative Perspective (New York: Cambridge University Press, 2007).

6. Huntington, Third Wave; Kellee Tsai, Capitalism without Democracy (Ithaca: Cornell University Press, 2007).

their part, are cut off from receiving state spoils and find themselves at a financial and organizational disadvantage. Energy-rich states are therefore able to resist democratization even at high levels of income per capita, a pattern typified by the Gulf states.[7] In the former Soviet Union, as well, energy-rich states such as Russia, Azerbaijan, and Kazakhstan have been able to effectively hold together their ruling coalitions and marginalize opposition forces thanks in part to the regime's disproportionate control of resources. Nondemocratic regimes are often loath to privatize those assets precisely because their loss of revenue can become someone else's gain.[8] Likewise, nondemocratic governments that succeed economic liberals have sometimes tried to reassert control over natural resources, a more difficult task than preventing an initial dispersion.[9]

The dispersion of resources plays a role in social movements that is often overlooked. One of the most commonly cited factors that influences the success of social movements is the political opportunity structure, which usually includes the openness of political institutions, the presence of elite allies, the stability of political alignments, and conflicts among elites.[10] In Kyrgyzstan, early regime defections made allies available to potential protesters, joining elites who had emerged from society. However, taking regime splintering as a given misses part of the story: elite defections can themselves be a function of other variables, such as the presence of economic opportunities outside the state. The ability to maintain a livelihood independent of the state affords potential activists political autonomy by weakening the executive's ability to exert leverage through the threat of material deprivation,[11] while also increasing the temptation for

---

7. On the "resource curse," see Terry Lynn Karl, *The Paradox of Plenty: Oil Booms and Petro-States* (Berkeley: University of California Press, 1997); Michael L. Ross, "Does Oil Hinder Democracy?" *World Politics* 53 (April 2001): 325–61.

8. Pauline Jones Luong and Erika Weinthal, "Prelude to the Resource Curse: Explaining Oil and Gas Development Strategies in the Soviet Successor States and Beyond," *Comparative Political Studies* 34, no. 4 (2001): 367–99.

9. Harley Balzer, "The Putin Thesis and Russian Energy Policy," *Post-Soviet Affairs* 21, no. 3 (2005): 210–25; Paul Domjan and Matt Stone, "A Comparative Study of Resource Nationalism in Russia and Kazakhstan 2004–2008," *Europe-Asia Studies* 61, no. 1 (2010): 35–62; Frank Jack Daniel, "Chavez to Expand Venezuela Oil Nationalizations," Reuters, January 6, 2009, http://www.reuters.com/article/reutersComService_3_MOLT/idUSTRE55519L20090606.

10. Sidney G. Tarrow, *Democracy and Disorder: Protest and Politics in Italy, 1965–1975* (Oxford: Clarendon Press, 1989); Hanspeter Kriesi, "The Political Opportunity Structure of New Social Movements," in *The Politics of Social Protest: Comparative Perspectives on States and Social Movements,* ed. Craig Jenkins and Bert Klandermans (Minneapolis: University of Minnesota Press, 1995), 167–98. For criticism of the concept, see William A. Gamson and David S. Meyer, "Framing Political Opportunity," in *Comparative Perspectives on Social Movements,* ed. Doug McAdam, John D. McCarthy, and Mayer D. Zald (New York: Cambridge University Press, 1996), 275.

11. Kelly M. McMann, *Economic Autonomy and Democracy: Hybrid Regimes in Russia and Kyrgyzstan* (Cambridge: University Press, 2006).

disgruntled regime officials to defect to existing oppositions. The regime will still retain the threat of coercion, but threats will yield diminishing returns as the balance of resources turns toward antiregime forces.[12] Thus, the political opportunity structure is endogenous to political-economic forces, and protest may be only the most visible manifestation of the advantages the opposition has already secured.

## Subversive Clientelism and Other Informal Strategies in Hybrid Regimes

Many polities in which resources are fairly dispersed fall into the category of hybrid or semiauthoritarian regimes, in which leaders vitiate the formal democratic rules of the game but allow a modicum of pluralism. No longer seen as being "in transition" to democracy, they are laboratories for innovative politics, with a menu of both formal and informal institutions, and legal and illegal tools, from which to select.[13] Rulers in hybrid regimes, intent on maintaining cohesion within the ruling coalition and neutralizing challengers from outside it, have been described as Machiavellian manipulators, careful managers, and cunning strategists.[14] Yet the tendency of observers to see politics from the regime's point of view overstates the ruler's ability to acquire undistorted information and neglects the variety of tools available to nonregime forces. The uncertainty engendered by hybrid regimes creates fertile soil for the development of strategies by other actors to compensate for the failure of formal institutions to protect rights and property. The adaptive responses by both independent and oppositional actors constantly threaten to undermine regime hegemony. The rulers who endure are not omnipotent; they are better seen as quick learners and clever improvisers.

Significant attention has been paid to elections in hybrid and authoritarian regimes—for good reason—yet scholars should also be attuned to the give-and-take of ordinary politics, which can give rise to creative solutions and insti-

---

12. Scott Radnitz, "The Color of Money: Privatization, Economic Dispersion and the Post-Soviet 'Revolutions,'" *Comparative Politics* 43, no. 1 (2010): 127–46. See also Barbara Junisbai, "Reform Regimes, Elite Defections, and Political Opposition in the Post-Soviet States: Evidence from Belarus, Kazakhstan, and Kyrgyzstan," paper presented at the annual meeting of the Midwest Political Science Association, Chicago, April 2–5, 2009.

13. Thomas Carothers, "The End of the Transition Paradigm," *Journal of Democracy* 13, no. 1 (2002): 5–21.

14. Andreas Schedler, "The Menu of Manipulation," *Journal of Democracy* 13, no. 1 (2002): 36–50; Harley Balzer, "Managed Pluralism: Vladimir Putin's Emerging Regime," *Post-Soviet Affairs* 19, no. 3 (2003): 189–226; Jason Brownlee, *Authoritarianism in an Age of Democratization* (New York: Cambridge University Press, 2007).

tutional forms not likely to be found in consolidated democracies. I have identified (subversive) clientelism as one such strategy utilized for self-preservation in hybrid regimes.

Scholars have recently made great strides in the study of political clientelism, a strategy used by politicians to advance their electoral prospects by providing targeted benefits to their constituents. Clientelism tends to appear where institutions of accountability are weak and levels of inequality are high. Politicians in such systems find it more cost effective to solicit votes through particularistic rather than through programmatic appeals.[15] This research program has yielded crucial insights into the political development of emerging democracies.

Yet scholars of clientelism have often neglected to incorporate insights from the study of authoritarianism, which details the (subtly) coercive tools that regimes use to remain in power and the ever-present threat of predation they pose to their opponents. In this milieu, clientelism is not only a means for politicians to purchase votes but can also be a way for them to invest in security. Unlike politicians who are backed by political machines or ruling parties, those who engage in subversive clientelism may do so because they lack the support of a powerful patron and therefore seek other means to compensate for their position of relative weakness.

The logic of subversive clientelism expands the scope for investigation of the roots and consequences of clientelism. First, modern clientelism need not be studied only in the context of elections. Subversive clientelism occurs as a product of daily struggles over power, property, and prestige. Elections may momentarily bring latent conflicts out into the open, but the efforts of insecure elites to win societal allegiance are ongoing. Scholars should therefore be attuned to the activities of aspiring patrons in everyday life, which may have important implications for state-society relations and political legitimacy.

Second, clients can offer their patrons more than votes and attendance at political rallies. If a politician succeeds in winning mass allegiances, he may be able to elicit a more fervent commitment from his supporters, including protest or even the use of violence against his opponents.[16] In some cases, the investments a politician makes for the purpose of winning votes may be fungible to these more contentious forms of support.

---

15. Susan C. Stokes, "Political Clientelism," in *Handbook of Comparative Politics*, ed. Carles Boix and Susan C. Stokes (Oxford: Oxford University Press, 2007); Philip Keefer, "Clientelism, Credibility, and the Policy Choices of Young Democracies," *American Journal of Political Science* 51, no. 4 (2007): 804–21.

16. Guilain Denoeux, *Urban Unrest in the Middle East: A Comparative Study of Informal Networks in Egypt, Iran, and Lebanon* (Albany: State University of New York Press, 1993); John T. Sidel, *Capital, Coercion, and Crime: Bossism in the Philippines* (Stanford: Stanford University Press, 1999).

Third, subversive and conventional political clientelism may have different implications for democracy and stability. Where clientelism is used by a ruling party (such as the PRI in Mexico) as a means to channel state resources to supporters, it incorporates the masses into the political system as party members, helping the party consolidate power.[17] If instead clientelism is decentralized and practiced in an entrepreneurial manner, it can enhance pluralism by empowering elites who lack the backing of the regime. It can also reduce inequality by forcing patrons to compete with one another by offering more attractive benefits, and by presenting an alternative source of sustenance to people who reject the incumbent.[18] On the other hand, such competitive clientelism can also hinder the coalescence of politicians into parties and inhibit the development of state capacity.[19]

Some recent works have explored other unexpected and sometimes innovative actions, besides subversive clientelism, taken by political actors in hybrid regimes. For example, Graeme Robertson identifies center-regional struggles as a cause of labor protest in Russia. In regions where the governor was in a weak bargaining position and maintained poor relations with the center, strikes occurred more frequently than in pro-Kremlin regions, suggesting that regional elites mobilized labor to gain concessions from the center.[20] Several studies have noted how political contenders in hybrid regimes collect evidence of corruption against political opponents or subordinates and strategically wield the threat of revealing the evidence in order to gain leverage.[21] A number of studies have identified cases in which incipient opposition movements have taken advantage of

---

17. Alberto Diaz-Cayeros, Beatriz Magaloni, and Barry R. Weingast, "Democratization and the Economy in Mexico: Equilibrium (PRI) Hegemony and Its Demise." Unpublished manuscript (Stanford University, 2001).

18. Luis Medina and Susan Stokes, "Clientelism as Political Monopoly," paper presented at the annual meeting of the American Political Science Association, Boston, August 28, 2002; Beatriz Magaloni, Alberto Diaz-Cayeros, and Federico Estevez, "Clientelism and Portfolio Diversification: A Model of Electoral Investment with Applications to Mexico," in *Patrons, Clients, and Policies: Patterns of Democratic Accountability and Political Competition*, ed. Herbert Kitschelt and Steven I. Wilkinson (New York: Cambridge University Press, 2007), 182–205.

19. Dan Slater, "Can Leviathan be Democratic? Competitive Elections, Robust Mass Politics, and State Infrastructural Power," *Studies in Comparative International Development* 43, no. 3 (2008): 252–72.

20. Graeme Robertson, "Strikes and Labor Organization in Hybrid Regimes," *American Political Science Review* 101, no. 4 (2007): 781–98.

21. Andrew Wilson, *Faking Democracy in the Post-Soviet World* (New Haven: Yale University Press, 2005); Keith Darden, "The Integrity of Corrupt States: Graft as an Informal Political Institution," *Politics and Society* 36, no. 1 (2008): 35–59; Gulnaz Sharafutdinova, "What Explains Corruption Perceptions? The Dark Side of Political Competition in Russia's Regions," *Comparative Politics* 43, no. 1 (2010): 147–66.

pockets of autonomy in apolitical civil society to build up their organizations.[22] Hybrid regimes grant social organizations greater latitude in conducting their activities than expressly political ones, yet rulers may underestimate both the fungibility of social capital and the ability of political entrepreneurs to mobilize it for their own purposes. These examples all illustrate how the fluid and uncertain political circumstances endemic to hybrid regimes can produce unexpected outcomes, as resourceful actors utilize social and political institutions to serve their own ends. Further research in such settings can uncover other informal strategies of political competition in order to better understand how informal institutions emerge and what their role is in regulating power, with the aim of identifying common patterns across cases.

# The Aftermath of Regime Change from Below in Kyrgyzstan

The processes engendered by the dynamics of hybrid regimes can in turn generate new political configurations and institutions that can push a polity in various directions. We can gain insight into some possible outcomes by examining the political trajectories of a subset of hybrid regimes—those that experienced "color revolutions." What does the future hold for those states? This book has focused on the informal political processes in Kyrgyzstan that led up to its "revolution"; the aftermath of a revolution can be just as instructive as a demonstration of the stubbornness of informal politics across the post-Soviet world and the challenges that the residue of the past presents to democratization.

After the initial euphoria surrounding the Tulip Revolution, subsequent developments in Kyrgyzstan disappointed those hoping the event would mark a decisive break with the past. Most immediately, the abrupt and chaotic nature of the government's collapse created a breakdown in authority that both criminals and politicians hastened to exploit. The weeks after the collapse saw a scramble for property and a spate of business-related violence that a fragile state and a feckless police force were incapable of preventing.[23] The mode of regime change

---

22. Diane Singerman, *Avenues of Participation: Family, Politics, and Networks in Urban Quarters of Cairo* (Princeton: Princeton University Press, 1995); Roger D. Petersen, *Resistance and Rebellion* (New York: Cambridge University Press, 2001); Carrie Rosefsky Wickham, *Mobilizing Islam: Religion, Activism, and Political Change in Egypt* (New York: Columbia University Press, 2002).

23. Erica Marat, *The State-Crime Nexus in Central Asia: State Weakness, Organized Crime, and Corruption in Kyrgyzstan and Tajikistan* (Washington, D.C.: Central Asia-Caucasus Institute, October 2006); Regine A. Spector, "Securing Property in Contemporary Kyrgyzstan," *Post-Soviet Affairs* 24, no. 2 (2008): 149–76.

suggested to politicians that the best (and perhaps only) means of extracting concessions from the new regime—without being part of it—was to take to the streets. Embedded elites who had not joined in the mass mobilization tested this hypothesis in the months after the revolution by mobilizing their supporters in order to secure parliamentary seats or demand the resignation of objectionable government officials.[24] This spate of power grabs and protests ushered in a new phase in Kyrgyz politics in which intimidation trumped negotiation as means of resolving conflicts. The adversarial posture of the regime and those vying for a share of the spoils stunted, rather than encouraged, civil society, increased the gap between the state and its citizens, and increased the potential for a violent escalation.

Eventually, order was restored and crime was brought back to manageable levels, but the reemergence several months later of familiar patterns of autocratic control—only in an intensified form—was just as troubling. The irony of the March 2005 events was that the "revolutionary" movement, once in power, demonstrated a striking propensity to continue old practices. The movement's leader, Kurmanbek Bakiev, promised improvements in governance as president. Yet after edging aside tactical allies in his government and neutralizing the reform-minded opposition, Bakiev worked to consolidate his power in the form of a new presidential party. After forcing through a constitution that instituted a new electoral system heavily favoring large, omnibus parties—especially ones enjoying state resources—Bakiev's Ak Jol (New Way) Party captured seventy-one out of the ninety seats in parliament.[25]

The new president's actions took some observers by surprise, as he and other Tulip Revolution leaders had staked their claim of legitimacy on the basis of reform in opposition to Akaev-era corruption. Yet the change in government did not alter the fundamental nature of Kyrgyz politics. Bakiev, regardless of his initial intentions, did not change the informal rules of governance. He was beholden to interest groups and relatives and proved willing to use the levers of state power for his and his family's benefit. He made few replacements below the top level of officials, while new appointees showed themselves to be less interested in clean, competent governance than in availing themselves of their new privileges.[26] Despite the participation of thousands of ordinary citizens, the aftermath

---

24. Leila Saralaeva and Sultan Jumagulov, "Kyrgyzstan: Protesting About Everything," Institute of War and Peace Reporting, April 29, 2005.

25. To gain seats, parties had to win at least 5% of the overall vote and 0.5% of total registered voters (13,500) in each of Kyrgyzstan's seven provinces and two largest cities. See "The Kyrgyz Republic—Pre-term Parliamentary Elections, 16 December 2007," OSCE Observation Mission, December 17, 2007, http://www.osce.org/documents/odihr/2007/12/28916_en.pdf.

26. For a more detailed analysis of the post–March 24 events, see Scott Radnitz, "A Horse of a Different Color: Revolution and Regression in Kyrgyzstan," in *Democracy and Authoritarianism in the*

of "revolution" saw the ascendance of elites who were interested not in systemic change, but in maintaining the status quo—only with themselves in charge. In 2009, although still deemed better off than Uzbekistan, Kyrgyzstan was considered less democratic than it was during the Akaev era.[27] A series of mysterious deaths of opposition politicians and journalists in 2009 and 2010 signaled an alarming breach of the previous rules of the game, even by the bare-knuckle standards of Kyrgyz politics. Bakiev's landslide reelection victory in July 2009, severely criticized by impartial observers, underscored the point—the country had turned a dark corner.

So it was that Bakiev received his ironic comeuppance on April 7, 2010, when crowds of demonstrators overran the White House and overthrew his government. An opposition coalition led by Roza Otunbaeva, Omurbek Tekebaev, Almaz Atambaev, and Temir Sariev had periodically held protests against the regime over the previous two years and planned more for spring 2010.[28] After weeks of localized protests against rising utility prices in several regions, on April 6 protesters stormed and occupied the regional government headquarters in Talas. The following day, protesters in Bishkek were met by riot police and snipers. After several hours of clashes, the crowds stormed into the White House, Bakiev and his associates fled, and the opposition declared itself the new government. After the smoke had cleared, eighty-six people were dead.

Following this unexpected uprising, few analysts invoked the notion of people power or color revolutions, mostly due to its violent nature and the absence of elections as a catalyst, but there was still an implicit assumption that the protests were spontaneous. Commentators variously attributed the event to lack of democracy, economic hardship, Russian customs duties on refined petroleum exports to Kyrgyzstan, anti-Bakiev propaganda in the Russian media to punish Bakiev for allowing the U.S. Manas airbase to remain open, and Bakiev's nepotistic practices, in particular his appointment of his son Maksim as the head an agency managing funds entering the country.[29] In retrospect, these aggravating

*Postcommunist World*, ed. Valerie Bunce, Michael A. McFaul, and Kathryn Stoner-Weiss (New York: Cambridge University Press, 2010).

27. Kyrgyzstan received a rating of "not free" from the nonpartisan Freedom House. "Freedom in the World 2010," http://www.freedomhouse.org/template.cfm?page=505.

28. As some commentators have pointed out, considering how frequently politicians in Kyrgyzstan change sides, the term "opposition," implying a relatively fixed, principled separation from the government, is misleading. See Eric McGlinchey, "Running in Circles in Kyrgyzstan," *New York Times*, April 10, 2010.

29. For example, Stephen Blank, "Moscow's Fingerprints in Kyrgyzstan's Storm," *Central Asia-Caucasus Analyst*, April 14, 2010; Peter Leonard, "Ousting a Kyrgyz Leaer Means Ousting a Family," *Associated Press*, April 14, 2010; "Kyrgyzstan: A Hollow Regime Collapses," International Crisis Group, April 27, 2010.

factors appear to have made a coup all but certain, yet disaffection does not guarantee mass protests, much less topple a regime. The spontaneity hypothesis is contradicted by a closer look at the events, which reveal some of the same underlying characteristics as the Tulip Revolution.

One notable feature reminiscent of 2005 was the ability of opposition elites to mobilize citizens to press their claims, indicating that pockets of pluralism remained even after Bakiev had nearly consolidated control over formal political institutions. In January 2009, the major protagonists coalesced into the United People's Movement (UPM), a vehicle that would continue to coordinate opposition demands into the following year. In March 2010, the UPM held an assembly at which it put forward several demands short of calling for Bakiev's resignation.[30] Those demands were not met, and the UPM planned nationwide protests for April 7.

As in previous cases of rapidly occurring large-scale demonstrations, the regime's challenge to elites acted as the trigger for the uprising. On this occasion, the critical event leading to the government's collapse took place in a northern, rather than southern, oblast, reflecting the prominence of northern politicians in the anti-Bakiev opposition. When Bolot Sherniyazov, a former deputy parliamentary speaker close to Tekebaev, was arrested in his native Talas on April 6, residents came out in his defense in larger numbers than in any event since the Tulip Revolution.[31] The protesters overpowered the police and seized the Talas government headquarters. That night other opposition leaders, including Tekebaev, Atambaev, and Sariev, were arrested in an attempt by the Bakiev regime to decapitate the opposition. This tactic inadvertently added fuel to the fire, especially as protests were already scheduled for the following day in Bishkek.

It is also noteworthy how closely the sequence of mobilization hewed to the script of previous protest events. Conforming to the existing "repertoire of contention," protests involved mass gatherings at the central squares of the regional capitals (this time Talas and Naryn), the capture of the administrative headquarters, and the proclamation of a new government.[32] Following the script, once control of the regions had changed hands, crowds formed in Bishkek. Last, as in 2005, less than twenty-four hours passed between the appearance of the first

30. Farangis Najibullah, "Thousands Air Grievances at Kyrgyz Rallies," Radio Free Europe/Radio Liberty (RFE/RL), March 17, 2010. Parallel with this, people in Alai demonstrated throughout the winter for the release of co-villager Ismail Isakov, who had been Bakiev's defense minister but was convicted of corruption after joining the opposition.

31. Human Rights Watch reported that up to 15,000 people arrived to "demand the release of Sherniyazov." "Recommendations to the Interim Government of Kyrgyzstan," Human Rights Watch, April 15, 2010.

32. Charles Tilly, *From Mobilization to Revolution* (New York: Random House, 1978).

demonstrators in Bishkek and the collapse of the government. Five years after the fall of Akaev, the Kyrgyz state was still so weak that a protester could drive a truck through the front gates of the White House, opening the way for mobs to flood into the building.

A third commonality with previous events was the strength of locally based elite-mass ties—which were again revealed as critical—and the relative weakness of regional (north-south) identity. Just as opposition politicians appealed to their social bases for support, Bakiev headed to his family's native village of Teyit, outside Jalalabad, after fleeing the capital. Over the next week, he attempted to negotiate with the interim government under the protection of armed guards and unarmed co-villagers. He orchestrated public rallies in the village in front of television cameras, intending to convey popular support in the south of the country. Yet when he attempted to organize a rally in Osh, detractors far outnumbered supporters. When some people from the crowd rushed the stage as he began speak, security guards whisked him away. This traumatic event perhaps laid bare to the deposed president that the unconditional support he enjoyed in his village did not extend far beyond it; he immediately submitted his resignation and departed the country.

Why, despite his efforts, was Bakiev unable to mobilize a wider base of support based on regional identity? The fact was that southerners did not benefit from his rule. They were as cognizant as northerners that their own quality of life continued to deteriorate while the Bakiev family had availed itself of the spoils of office. Simply invoking "southernness" was not sufficient to rally people of the region to Bakiev's side. Even those who were sympathetic feared that playing on regional tensions risked provoking a civil war, and acted in the interest of restraint.

This is not to say that the 2010 events proceeded exactly like the events in 2005—events can alter structure and actors can learn from the past.[33] The most striking and disturbing aspect of the turmoil of 2010 was its violent character. The clashes occurred in part because the security forces were better prepared than in 2005 and were willing to fire on demonstrators. Yet this was not the only cause of violence. Photographs of the crowds from April 7 show young and middle-age men, some of them armed, and almost no women, in contrast to the more peaceful protests of 2005 and demonstrations held by UPM over the previous months. Some men threw fire bombs at riot police and fired automatic weapons at armed

---

33. William H. Sewell, Jr., "Historical Events as Transformations of Structures: Inventing Revolution at the Bastille," *Theory and Society* 25, no. 6 (1996): 841-881; Mark R. Beissinger, "Structure and Example in Modular Political Phenomena: The Diffusion of Bulldozer/Rose/Orange/Tulip Revolutions," *Perspectives on Politics* 5, no. 2 (2007): 259-276.

presidential guards. This group of impetuous men undeterred by tear gas or bullets was probably necessary to overcome the president's defenses.

These scenes did not come out of the Tulip Revolution playbook; instead they were reminiscent of incidents that occurred *after* the Tulip Revolution, when young, tough members of "sport clubs" occupied the streets in the absence of police, and when opportunistic elites bused in and sometimes paid people to use confrontational tactics to advance their interests. In the five years between coups, challengers asserting power on the streets adopted new—and more aggressive— tactics, while political institutions that could have resolved disputes through peaceful means rotted. It remains to be seen whether Kyrgyzstan can escape the cycle of authoritarian power grabs and reactive coups.

## Postrevolutionary Politics in Light of the Kyrgyz Case

The experience of Kyrgyzstan since 2005 provides a cautionary lesson to champions of bottom-up political change as a panacea for years of deficient postcommunist rule. The "color revolutions" in Serbia, Georgia, and Ukraine initially heartened observers of the region and reawakened interest in people power as a force for positive change. The wave of peaceful protests challenging decrepit autocrats was widely viewed as a delayed but necessary shove back onto a more promising transition path, seemingly vindicating efforts of the democracy promotion community, which had been unable to effect change through gradual reform.[34] These events were initially portrayed as "democratic breakthroughs."[35] The Bush administration even saw them as evidence of the success of its "freedom agenda."[36] (It is no coincidence that the road from Tbilisi's airport to the city center is named George W. Bush Avenue.)

Initially, the jubilation appeared justified, as Ukraine celebrated the election of a pro-Western reformer and the defeat of a corrupt candidate with a sordid history and backed by Vladimir Putin; and Georgia saw the installation of a Western-educated and charismatic exemplar of the NGO sector. Both leaders

---

34. Valerie Bunce and Sharon Wolchik, "Bringing Down Dictators: American Democracy Promotion and Electoral Revolutions in Postcommunist Eurasia." Working Paper, Cornell University, 2007.

35. McFaul, "Transitions from Postcommunism," *Journal of Democracy* 16, no. 3 (July 2005): 5–19; Anders Åslund and Michael McFaul, eds., *Revolution in Orange: The Origins of Ukraine's Democratic Breakthrough* (Washington, D.C.: Carnegie Endowment for International Peace, 2006); Taras Kuzio, "Democratic Breakthroughs and Revolutions in Five Postcommunist Countries: Comparative Perspectives on the Fourth Wave," *Demokratizatsiya* 16, no. 1 (2008): 97–112.

36. Kathleen T. Rhem, "Bush: 'Freedom on the March' Throughout World," Armed Forces Press Service, http://www.defenselink.mil/news/newsarticle.aspx?id=24241.

promised closer ties with the West and embarked on ambitious reform agendas. The initial euphoria in the West was based not only on their new foreign policy orientations but also on a deep-seated belief that mass involvement in politics would help prevent the reemergence of the old guard and ensure that the countries would return to a democratic trajectory, following in the path of the Eastern European revolutions of 1989.[37]

Yet, even while clearing away some troublesome obstacles, first among them corrupt authoritarian leaders, the color revolutions also gave rise to new difficulties once the euphoria subsided. As scholars of political transitions remind us, the breakdown of an authoritarian regime does not necessarily herald the installation of a democratic one.[38] In fact, depending on the baggage of the past, the interests and capabilities of the new leaders, and the deals they are compelled to make, democracy is far from the only possible outcome.

Not long after taking power, the postrevolutionary leaderships of Ukraine and Georgia encountered resistance to their respective programs. In Ukraine, Viktor Yushchenko and Yulia Tymoshenko of the victorious Orange bloc had to contend with the country's cultural, linguistic, and social divides, which gave the Russia-backed loser Viktor Yanukovich significant support in the East. Changes to the constitution negotiated during the disputed election weakened the executive and granted the president and prime minister overlapping powers, which led to factional struggles within the government.[39] Political stalemate had negative consequences for economic reform and growth, and public opinion has reflected severe disillusionment with the revolutionary coalition and the progress of the country since 2004.[40] It was no surprise that Yanukovich recaptured the presidency in 2010, putting the final nail in the coffin of the Orange coalition.

In Georgia, Mikheil Saakashvili did not have to contend with rival elites within the government. Entering office with widespread support, he took measures to strengthen the state and reduce corruption, a move that involved

---

37. Jeffrey Kopstein, "The Transatlantic Divide over Democracy Promotion," *Washington Quarterly* 29, no. 2 (2006): 85–98.

38. Guillermo O'Donnell and Philippe Schmitter, *Transitions from Authoritarian Rule: Tentative Conclusions about Uncertain Democracies* (Baltimore: Johns Hopkins University Press, 1986); Guillermo O'Donnell, "In Partial Defense of an Evanescent 'Paradigm,'" *Journal of Democracy* 13, no. 3 (2002): 6–12.

39. Paul D'Anieri. "What Has Changed in Ukrainian Politics? Assessing the Implications of the Orange Revolution," *Problems of Post-Communism* 52, no. 5 (2005): 82–91.

40. Ivan Katchanovski, "The Orange Evolution? The 'Orange Revolution' and Political Changes in Ukraine," *Post-Soviet Affairs* 24, no. 4 (2008): 351–82; David Lane, "The Orange Revolution: 'People's Revolution' or Revolutionary Coup?" *British Journal of Politics and International Relations* 10, no. 4 (2008): 525–49.

purging the bureaucracy of old-guard civil servants and their patrons.[41] He also undertook economic reforms to qualify for international assistance. Yet a new opposition eventually coalesced, objecting both to the president's policies and his leadership style.

More troubling, both Yushchenko and Saakashvili—who had previously been associates of their disgraced predecessors—responded to adversity less than magnanimously, resorting to underhanded tactics associated with the previous regime. Ukraine was plagued by incessant factional infighting among three national rivals, all of whom engaged in intimidation, abuse of power, and self-serving interpretations of laws in order to increase their power at the expense of others. In Georgia, Saakashvili concentrated power around himself to a degree reminiscent of his predecessor. He strengthened the presidency, changed electoral rules to secure 119 out of 150 seats in parliament for his party, and used force against peaceful demonstrators, injuring over five hundred.[42] Although none of these examples are meant to imply that Georgia and Ukraine are destined to regress back to authoritarianism, they do highlight some of the difficulties facing both leaders and citizens after the rapid collapse of the previous government.

These troubled members of the "second wave" of postcommunist transitions pose problems for theorizing about the relationship between the mode of transition and the regime that follows. Whereas early democratization theorists, studying southern European and Latin American transitions, argued that pacting was the most reliable route to stable democracy, scholars of transitions from state socialism maintained that transitions *from below* were the most assured path to democracy because they allowed reform-minded leaders to set the agenda.[43] The aftermaths of the color revolutions should, at the very least, lead scholars to qualify the latter view. There are several reasons why the odds are stacked against democracy following regime overthrow from mass mobilization.

41. Jonathan Wheatley, *Georgia from National Awakening to Rose Revolution* (London: Ashgate Press, 2005).

42. Clifford J. Levy, "Georgia's Future Looks Like More of the Past," *New York Times,* November 15, 2007; Miriam Lanskoy and Giorgi Areshidze, "Georgia's Year of Turmoil," *Journal of Democracy* 19, no. 4 (2008): 154–68; Vicken Cheterian, "Georgia's Rose Revolution: Change or Repetition? Tension between State-building and Modernization Projects," *Nationalities Papers* 36, no. 4 (2008): 689–712.

43. On pacted transitions, see Guillermo O'Donnell, Philippe C. Schmitter, and Laurence Whitehead, eds., *Transitions from Authoritarian Rule: Prospects for Democracy* (Baltimore: Johns Hopkins University Press, 1986); Terry Lynn Karl, "Dilemmas of Democratization in Latin America," *Comparative Politics* 23, no. 1 (1990): 1–21; Giuseppe Di Palma, *To Craft Democracies: An Essay on Democratic Transitions* (Berkeley: University of California Press, 1990); Adam Przeworski, *Democracy and the Market* (New York: Cambridge University Press, 1991). On postsocialist transitions, see Michael McFaul, "The Fourth Wave of Democracy *and* Dictatorship," *World Politics* 54, no. 2 (2002): 212–44; Valerie Bunce, "Rethinking Recent Democratization: Lessons from the Postcommunist Experience," *World Politics* 55, no. 2 (2003): 167–92.

First, mass mobilization produces instability and weakens the state. Kyrgyzstan, a weak state even before the revolution, is a case in point. The period following Akaev's downfall saw looting in the capital and several months of sometimes violent struggles over control of property. Local claimants for power, including "revolutionary" activists, also took advantage of the change at the top, by installing themselves or their allies in provincial posts. It took the Bakiev government several months to build enough support to replace them. Yet even after Bakiev consolidated political control, it was not clear that the Kyrgyz state was any more capable of enforcing laws and performing everyday tasks than it had been under Akaev.[44]

Kyrgyzstan also illustrates a second perverse effect of bottom-up regime change: as a result of the instability that revolutions engender, the new elite's efforts to quickly regain control often entail concentrating power and marginalizing dissenting voices, which is counterproductive to democracy. The temporary breakdown of authority and the threat of resurgence by supporters of the old regime empower authoritarian leaders and radical populists at the expense of moderates, who favor gradual steps and coalition building to advance reform. History has shown that revolutionary leaders use instability as a pretext for repressing actual or suspected opponents of the revolution. The result is the consolidation of a new, and perhaps more repressive, regime that uses state power to advance its agenda and tends to generate its own radical opposition.[45]

Even if the new leaders do not intend to use their power for malevolent purposes, there is no guarantee that they will act in pursuit of the common good. One reason relates to the background of the leaders. The protagonists of the color revolutions were elites who had held influential positions in the previous government, and brought with them baggage from the preceding era. This can be seen in their style of governing and the boundaries of acceptable political practices; and in their networks of associates, which included both old-regime officials and the revolution's financial backers—businessmen who were less interested in democracy than in placing their patrons in high office to protect their economic interests.[46]

---

44. "Kyrgyzstan: A Deceptive Calm," International Crisis Group, August 14, 2008.

45. According to Theda Skocpol, writing of the French, Russian, and Chinese revolutions, "new state organizations forged during the Revolutions were more centralized and rationalized than those of the Old Regime." Theda Skocpol, *States and Social Revolutions: A Comparative Analysis of France, Russia, and China* (New York: Cambridge University Press, 1979), 161.

46. Anders Åslund, "The Ancien Regime: Kuchma and the Oligarchs," in *Revolution in Orange: The Origins of Ukraine's Democratic Breakthrough,* ed. Anders Åslund and Michael McFaul (Washington, D.C.: Carnegie Endowment, 2006). For arguments that focus on the role of elites in the color revolutions, see Paul D'Anieri, "Explaining the Success and Failure of Post-Communist Revolutions," *Communist and Post-Communist Studies* 39 (2006); Radnitz, "Color of Money."

A second impediment to effective governance following the color revolutions is the legacy of the previous regime. Henry Hale argues that new leaders in post-Soviet countries inherit the old system of informal "patronal politics," which pushes potential reformers to continue the practices of their discredited predecessors. In particular, the levers of punishment and reward remain intact, albeit in new hands. As a result, even a presumptive democrat can find himself adopting authoritarian characteristics in the face of pervasive corruption and minimal legal constraints, much as Eduard Shevardnadze and Akaev succumbed in their day.[47] Whatever the intentions of Saakashvili, Yushchenko, and Bakiev, in order to remain in power, not to mention to implement any desired policies, they were forced to play the (inauspicious) hand they were dealt.

An additional problem common to corrupt, informal systems is that reform may not be a rational strategy for new leaders to pursue. The transition from authoritarian to democratic governance is a formidable task, requiring that the players overcome two collective action problems. The first comes in the coordination game played by elites (and perhaps masses), who must unite to oppose a sitting autocrat. Yet this is only the first, and easiest, step. The autocrat's successor faces a second collective action problem. Challenging entrenched informal politics and establishing formal and binding democratic institutions requires resolving a prisoners' dilemma, in which rival elites must cooperate to achieve an outcome that benefits society, but each has an incentive to deviate by continuing to exploit the state for their own benefit, lest they be made a "sucker."[48] Unable to overcome the collective action problem, leaders will exhibit short time horizons and take advantage of their (perhaps short) tenure in office by acting first and foremost to advance their own interests.

The solution to this problem brings us back to one of the themes of this book: it is not the fact of mass mobilization that matters, but its character. When elites initiate mobilization and the masses play a subordinate role, elites will subsequently be in a position to trample the grassroots. If the masses are brought into the political system through the dependence relationships of clientelism rather than through autonomous organizations of civil society, they will be not be able to put pressure on elites to rein in corrupt informal practices, and governing will revert to a division of spoils.[49] Conversely, a protest movement that developed primarily through bottom-up organization and brought nonelites to power

---

47. Henry E. Hale, "Democracy or Autocracy on the March? The Colored Revolutions as Normal Dynamics of Patronal Presidentialism," *Communist and Post-Communist Studies* 39 (2006): 305–29.

48. Barbara Geddes, *The Politician's Dilemma* (Berkeley: University of California Press, 1994).

49. Lane calls this a "revolutionary coup d'etat." David Lane, "Coloured Revolution as a Political Phenomenon," *Journal of Communist Studies and Transition Politics* 25, no. 2 (2009): 113–35.

might secure a more significant role for the masses and improve accountability. Closer scrutiny by a broader swath of society could push leaders to adopt longer time horizons and raise the costs of perpetuating the status quo, thus enabling a genuine break with the past—a *ruptura*.[50] However, the conditions for such an outcome in most post-Soviet (and many hybrid) regimes are lacking due to the weakness of autonomous grassroots expression.

This insight has implications for policy makers intent on furthering democracy in the post-Soviet world. A substantial amount of support for building democracy has gone to NGOs that participate in civic education, election monitoring, media development, or other activities that focus primarily on elections. In most cases, the beneficiaries, who must navigate the process of writing and winning grants from international development agencies, are members of the intelligentsia, who are usually located in major urban centers.[51] This cohort has at times proved a useful partner in advancing democracy, as it played a significant supporting role in the critical elections in Ukraine and Georgia, albeit a lesser one in Kyrgyzstan. Yet the disappointments that occurred in the transition from opposition to government have exposed limits in what they can accomplish.

First, NGOs are often detached from the broader society they claim to represent, a fact that is especially striking in rural societies. Once mobilization ends, NGOs are likely to be edged aside by other, more powerful members of the coalition, who enjoy a mass base of support and can convert it into political power. Thus, in Ukraine and Kyrgyzstan, NGO leaders took a back seat to quarreling politicians who were less committed to democratic principles than to prevailing over their political rivals. Unlike politicians, NGOs could not rely on any constituency in society to assert their influence and advance their ideas.

Second, even if NGO activists come to power, as they did in Georgia to an unprecedented extent, their lack of ties to the broader society raise questions about democratic legitimacy. A talented politician such as Saakashvili could win support for controversial reforms initially by relying on charisma, and by enjoying the legitimacy that came with not being Shevardnadze. However, when his initial support declined, he could not fall back on a natural constituency and was forced to resort to undemocratic methods to stay in power and continue implementing reforms.

Disappointments in the wake of regime change point to a larger challenge for advocates of democracy. The crucial developments that determine the course of politics following the breakdown of a regime take place long before mobilization

---

50. Juan J. Linz, "Transitions to Democracy," *Washington Quarterly* 2 (Summer 1990): 145–59.

51. Lisa McIntosh Sundstrom, *Funding Civil Society: Foreign Assistance and NGO Development in Russia* (Stanford: Stanford University Press, 2006).

begins. The tendency of the poor to support, whether through voting or mobilization, politicians who do not represent their interests suggests why democratic practice has not usually translated into substantive democratic outcomes. The high levels of inequality present in all post-Soviet countries have given the economic elite an advantageous position in society and inhibited the ability of the poor to shape the political process.[52] To achieve democratic outcomes, whether through gradual or rapid change, conditions in society must change to give the masses greater capacity to organize and articulate their interests. Thus, a more viable strategy for democratization is to approach it through the lens of development.

The evidence presented in this book demonstrates how economic insecurity can have political ramifications, in ways that do not benefit the poor and unorganized. Individual and collective strategies to improve their well-being can push people into clientelist relationships that, while mitigating problems of subsistence, severely limit their ability to influence political outcomes. Societies that have overcome clientelist politics first developed the capacity to access alternative sources of goods, organize as social movements, and act collectively on a large enough scale to reshape politics.[53] Fortunately, in Central Asia as in other post-Soviet states, institutions that can help strengthen the organizational capacity of society already exist—in personal networks and communities. Unlike NGOs, these informal networks already generate trust and elicit long-term commitments from their members. Their potential is limited by members' lack of access to outside resources, as a product of asymmetric vertical ties and weak horizontal ties.[54]

A developmental approach can begin to remedy these weaknesses. External actors can aid in increasing the well-being and political autonomy of the poor by first weaning them off the largesse of self-interested political actors. Programs such as microcredit and support for rural infrastructure can make people less dependent on elites. Small-business development can reduce the relative power

---

52. Sebastian Leitner and Mario Holzner, "Economic Inequality in Central, East and Southeast Europe," *Intervention: European Journal of Economics and Economic Policies* 5, no. 1: 159–60.

53. Robert Gay, *Popular Organization and Democracy in Rio de Janeiro: A Tale of Two Favelas* (Philadelphia: Temple University Press, 1994); Jonathan Fox, "The Difficult Transition from Clientelism to Citizenship: Lessons from Mexico," *World Politics* 46 (1994): 151–84.

54. The absence of cross-cutting ties is thought to be detrimental because primary groups "reinforce pre-existing social stratification, prevent mobility of excluded groups, minorities or poor people, and become the bases of corruption and co-optation of power by the dominant social groups." Deepa Narayan, "Bonds and Bridges: Social Capital and Poverty" (Washington, D.C.: World Bank, 1999), 13. See also Mark Granovetter, "The Strength of Weak Ties," *American Journal of Sociology* 78, no. 6 (1973): 1360–80; Geof Wood, "Staying Secure, Staying Poor: The Faustian Bargain," *World Development* (2003): 455–71; Aaron Schneider and Rebeca Zúniga-Hamlin, "A Strategic Approach to Rights: Lessons from Clientelism in Rural Peru," *Development Policy Review* 23, no. 5 (2005): 567–84.

of wealthier businessmen by cultivating self-sustaining proprietors from among the poor, leading eventually to local economic competition. Although this will not eradicate poverty, new entrepreneurs can at least compete with existing patrons and offer people a greater choice of benefactors, leading to greater levels of redistribution.[55] In the longer term clientelism will not erode until enough people are self-sufficient that politicians come to favor programmatic over clientelist appeals.

A second reason to take a development-oriented approach to democratization is that a strong civil society can only come about through improvements in social capital. Insofar as communities are internally cohesive but effectively isolated from one another, increasing the scope and diversity of social networks would give a necessary boost to people's ability to articulate and aggregate their interests.[56] Assistance in the form of infrastructural projects such as paved roads and affordable public transportation can help individuals become more mobile and expand the reach of their horizontal networks. Aid to lower the costs and increase the availability of mobile phones can help in areas of deteriorating telecommunications infrastructure. Assistance to farmers to reach centrally located markets and interact with traders from disparate networks can increase both economic and social capital in rural areas. For these projects to be effective, they must incorporate existing community networks but also give people new options outside them.

A comprehensive approach that centers on strengthening the autonomy of the poor may take another generation or more, but it stands a better chance of achieving meaningful economic and political results than efforts focused on an unrepresentative sliver of target populations. As the events in this book have shown, mass mobilization may provide the impetus necessary to chase out a president and his coterie, but it is not sufficient to address the deeply rooted structural problems and informal politics of resource distribution that evolved over decades of Soviet and post-Soviet political development.

---

55. Herbert Kitschelt and Steven I. Wilkinson, "Citizen-Politician Linkages: An Introduction," in *Patrons, Clients, and Policies: Patterns of Democratic Accountability and Political Competition*, ed. Herbert Kitschelt and Steven I. Wilkinson (New York: Cambridge University Press, 2007), 33.
56. Narayan, "Bonds and Bridges."

# METHODOLOGICAL APPENDIX

## Notes on Fieldwork

To conduct research for this book, I relied heavily on interviews to gather micro-level data. Working at this level of analysis was necessary to establish the mechanisms behind community involvement used in chapter 2, and to reconstruct how protests unfolded, in chapters 5 and 6. Overall, I spent approximately eight months in Kyrgyzstan and six months in Uzbekistan conducting fieldwork, not including an additional six months of language study and exploratory research in the region. Social science research in Central Asia by Westerners became possible only in the early 1990s, so existing work on the region, both qualitative and quantitative, is relatively sparse. Yet the challenges of conducting fieldwork, including cultural differences, logistical barriers, and political constraints, are similar to those faced by ethnographers in other regions.

My research strategy varied depending on whether I was doing ethnographies of communities or gathering data on mobilization events. For the former, my objective was to understand how people faced the challenges of deprivation and to detail the mechanisms of community interaction. Two particular challenges were ensuring representativeness and collecting unbiased information. I selected areas of both countries that varied in terms of geography, primary economic mode, and, where applicable (i.e., multiethnic Kyrgyzstan), ethnicity. At every site, I lived with a local family, which allowed me to closely observe and understand individual and collective actions, and to earn trust within the community. My field notes from observing everyday encounters, attending community events, and engaging in spontaneous discussions were an invaluable source of information for understanding the intangibles of social interaction.

In addition, I conducted semistructured interviews in my research sites, speaking in Russian or Uzbek, whichever informants were more comfortable speaking.[1] I was almost always accompanied by a local assistant who would either translate during the interview (from the Central Asian language into Russian) or simply introduce me to the informant as a way of vouching for me and earning the subject's trust. My assistant was usually a university or graduate student who had some training in social science research and methodology, and whom I identified with the help of a local professor who understood my research objectives. When living in an urban area, I also made several trips to rural areas together with either my assistant or another local person who was from the village.

In conducting research about community networks, at each site I sought to interview a diverse spectrum of informants to understand the degree of variation in community networks and relations with elites. I asked respondents about the major changes in their communities since independence, how they dealt with everyday problems, why they did or did not participate in community activities, and where they turned for material and other assistance. I would adapt the interview template to suit my informant's social status, profession, and other characteristics such as gender, ethnicity, and age. Interviews lasted forty-five to seventy-five minutes on average, and I conducted follow-up interviews on numerous occasions.

Because this part of my research dealt with social, rather than political, issues, people rarely declined to speak with me, despite the authoritarian political setting, which was more of a risk in Uzbekistan. Living with a local family and being accompanied by a student helped to allay concerns. In addition, I always took written notes rather than use a voice recorder, which could cause informants to self-censor. After my assistant explained the purpose of my interview, he or she offered anonymity for the interview, an option the vast majority of my informants waived. However, in cases in which my writing might embarrass informants or place them in a compromising situation, as a precaution I used an alias to protect their identities. I insisted on interviewing informants one-on-one (plus my translator) so as to prevent conformity of opinions and to encourage informants to speak candidly, especially when discussing their neighbors and other acquaintances.[2]

Gathering information on elites was more difficult, as I was often unable to speak with them directly since they were either busy or unwilling to speak with

---

1. Most Kyrgyz were comfortable speaking in Russian.

2. On the drawbacks of using focus groups in social movement research, see Kathleen M. Blee and Verta Taylor, "Semi-structured Interviewing in Social Movement Research," in *Methods of Social Movement Research,* ed. Bert Klandermans and Suzanne Staggenborg (Minneapolis: University of Minnesota Press, 2002), 108.

me. When I did obtain access, their statements were often self-serving and un-reliable. For this reason, I developed a strategy of identifying and interviewing elites' assistants, who were both knowledgeable about the elite's activities and more likely to speak candidly. As representatives of the urban or rural intelli-gentsia, they were articulate and well organized. When the assistants provided information about elite charitable activities, I verified it with community resi-dents. When elite parliamentary candidates were involved in mobilization, it was their assistants, who had also often worked as trusted agents (*doverennye litsa*) in their political campaigns, who worked in communities to plan and coordinate protests. Protest organizers proudly shared their achievements.[3]

Fieldwork on mobilization presented a different set of opportunities and challenges. It was not difficult to elicit information from respondents on their participation in mobilization. People in general enthusiastically shared their sto-ries because they perceived the outcomes of both Aksy and the Tulip Revolu-tions to have been successful and were eager to highlight their contributions. Additionally, I conducted fieldwork not long after these events occurred, so their memories were still fresh. I worked in Aksy two years after the protests but before the Tulip Revolution; and I worked on the Tulip Revolution one month after it occurred, and made a follow-up visit one year later. Informants could recall specific details and were still bullish about the future course of the country post-revolution. On the other hand, even the passage of a short time does not prevent a convergence of people's narratives or their selective elimination or emphasis of particular details.

Thus, one challenge of research on mobilization is to separate the "why and "how" of the events in question. There is often a tendency for media and popular accounts of dramatic events to emphasize their ideological aspects and take the claims of protest leaders at face value.[4] To test my hypotheses about the causes of, and mechanisms behind, mobilization, it was necessary to probe beneath the surface and reconstruct the process. When conducting interviews on mobiliza-tion[5], my objective was to ascertain the sequence of events through which my informants came to participate, in order to piece together the larger picture.

---

3. On the benefits of an ethnographic approach when gathering data on political topics in con-texts where important decisions are often made informally, see Jessica Allina-Pisano, "How to Tell an Axe Murderer: An Essay on Ethnography, Truth, and Lies," in *Political Ethnography: What Immersion Contributes to the Study of Power,* ed. Edward Schatz (Chicago: University of Chicago Press, 2009).

4. Kalyvas argues in discussing civil wars that a focus solely on the macro- or meso-level requires analytic shortcuts that lead the researcher to mistakenly reify groups and take ideological framing at face value. Stathis N. Kalyvas, *The Logic of Violence in Civil War* (New York: Cambridge University Press, 2006), 10.

5. I conducted forty-eight interviews on Aksy and eighty-one on the Tulip Revolution, which do not include interviews from bazaars—described below—or data on the frequency of participation by district in Jalalabad used in figure 6.2.

Although my strategy was to inquire *how* they came to join the movement in order to test my hypotheses as to *why* they did so, some of the protagonists nonetheless evaded the question, initially proclaiming that they protested for "justice" or "democracy." Yet such statements clearly did not explain the variation in participation by village or individual.

A second challenge comes from the tendency of participants in emotionally resonant events to harmonize their recollection of their actions through common narratives, leading to a risk of bias. Oftentimes familiar tropes appeared in interviews, such as Aksy protesters' assertions that they refrained even from picking fruit from trees while on long marches, in order to emphasize the discipline and peaceful character of the movement.[6] Informants who protested also had a tendency to frame the protests as spontaneous and lacking in organization.

I addressed these challenges in several ways. First, before interviewing protest participants, I read all existing published accounts of the event in question and spoke with observers, such as journalists and the staff of local or international NGOs, who did not participate. I used their accounts as a starting point, as hypotheses to be tested in the field. Having a rough chronology of events in hand, I could break the inquiry into smaller increments and ask concrete questions that forced my informant to recall her state of mind and social surroundings on a given day, that is, to explain *how* she arrived at a march or demonstration, rather than *why* she joined. In general, I placed the most weight on the evidence given by direct participants—those who could say, "I did…." If those informants were unavailable or unreliable, then the second best informants were direct eyewitnesses ("I saw…"). I gave the least credence to those with only indirect knowledge of an event ("I heard…"), but their testimony was useful for generating hypotheses. Knowing the actions of specific individuals enabled me to reconstruct the social ties that led to their participation, from individuals to informal leaders within the community, to candidates' assistants, to the candidates themselves.

Second, I sought out a diversity of perspectives in the field, which involved traveling to regions with little mobilization activity, and speaking with people who did not participate in protests as well as ones who did. I decided to work in Bishkek in the north and the oblasts of Osh and Jalalabad in the south. Each region experienced mobilization but also exhibited wide variation on lower levels of analysis, enabling me to hold a number of variables constant as I compared otherwise similar locales that had experienced differing levels of participation.

---

6. On the use of narratives in social movements, see Francesca Polletta, "Contending Stories: Narrative in Social Movements," *Qualitative Sociology* 21, no. 4 (1998): 419–46; Charles Tilly, "The Trouble with Stories," in *The Social Worlds of Higher Education: Handbook for Teaching in a New Century,* ed. Ronald Aminzade and Bernice Pescosolido (Thousand Oaks: Pine Forge Press, 1999).

As with interviews on community networks, I worked with a local assistant who helped me identify protest organizers, participants, and nonparticipants; or who accompanied me as I randomly selected people to interview who were unacquainted with my assistant. Traveling to villages that had experienced little protest enabled me to test whether the interests of (losing) candidates explained the variation. Interviews with nonparticipants in otherwise active communities revealed the importance of social networks and people's support for a winning or losing candidate in the decision to protest.

While "horizontal" variation among ordinary people was useful in gathering data on individual motivations, I also sought out informants to allow for "vertical" variation: leaders, community organizers, and rank-and-file protesters. By asking the same questions of actors at different levels—especially elite assistants and ordinary protesters, who rarely had direct contact—I was able to cross-check different accounts and construct an accurate sequence of events. I could then ascertain the circumstances surrounding those actors' decision to participate in order to explain variation on the individual, community, and district levels. Elite assistants proved to be valuable resources, as they were directly involved in organizing protests, coordinating with both the losing candidate and informal community leaders. Their "bird's-eye" perspective provided the crucial link between the political origins (defending the challenged elite) and the social content (subversive clientelism and community networks) of the protests. Additionally, candidates' assistants in the Tulip Revolution, who were charged with coordinating with demonstration organizers in other regions, could recount how localized protests expanded to national scale.

As an additional test of hypotheses on mobilization, I conducted interviews in the central bazaars in Jalalabad, Osh, and Bishkek. Traditional markets have often been the source of protests, given the ease of collective action through social and commercial networks, and the likelihood that merchants share common grievances. In Iran, the bazaar was a focal point of revolutionary activity.[7] To ascertain the extent to which bazaar merchants joined protests, I interviewed a random but not representative sample of ten to twelve merchants, to ascertain how many times they participated in protests before the city was captured by the opposition, whether ties to fellow villagers played a role in their decision, and whether they joined on the final day of demonstrations. The results from the three cities confirmed other findings: merchants were more likely to join if they were from outlying villages rather than from the city center, to participate on the

---

7. Theda Skocpol, "Rentier State and Shi'a Islam in the Iranian Revolution," *Theory and Society* 11, no. 3 (1982): 265–83; Misagh Parsa, *Social Origins of the Iranian Revolution* (Rutgers University Press, 1989).

last day rather than earlier, and to merge with co-villagers rather than with the crowd as a whole. A higher proportion of informants reported participating in Jalalabad than in Osh or Bishkek.

## Note on Protest Numbers

The figures on protest numbers cited throughout the text are based on my best estimates from multiple sources. Previous research has noted the difficulties in estimating the size of crowds.[8] As a rule, I assumed that numbers reported by pro-testers were inflated, while the government's figures were low. When interviewing community organizers, who were in charge of a group of protesters, usually from one neighborhood or village, I asked how many people they could personally ac-count for. I also spoke with journalists who observed the protests (while taking their probable biases into account) and, where possible, corroborated my figures with reports from the Kyrgyz wire service, Akipress; Radio Liberty; and other news sources. The figures I report are rough estimates, but they are comparable to the most widely circulated numbers and can be relied on to make inferences on the comparative size of protests among locales cited in the text.

## Survey Methodology

The survey, drafted by Jonathan Wheatley, Christoph Zuercher, and myself, was conducted under the auspices of the Free University of Berlin. It was carried out in July and August 2005 by a research firm based in Tashkent and a partner firm in Bishkek. After a pilot phase interviewing thirty respondents in each country, one thousand respondents were selected in each country by three-stage stratified clustered sampling. All thirteen oblasts in Uzbekistan were covered, while six out of Kyrgyzstan's seven oblasts were surveyed, excluding Batken for logistical reasons.

The sampling scheme was designed to capture a representative sample in each country of permanent residents eighteen years or older. A three-stage stratified clustered sampling procedure was used. First, provinces were proportionally stratified by population, then by their share of urban and rural populations.

---

8. Eric Swank and John D. Clapp, "Some Methodological Concerns When Estimating the Size of Organizing Activities," *Journal of Community Practice* 6 (1999): 49–71; Jennifer Earl, Andrew Martin, John D. McCarthy, and Sarah A. Soule, "The Use of Newspaper Data in the Study of Collective Action," *Annual Review of Sociology* 30 (2004): 65–80.

Within each stratum, primary sampling units were selected according to the population. In cities, such units were neighborhood-based administrative units (*mahallinskie komitety*) in Uzbekistan and city subdivisions in Kyrgyzstan, with populations ranging from four thousand to five thousand residents. In rural areas in both countries, primary sampling units were village councils—formerly, village soviets—which are the lowest level of government. Within primary sampling units, households (including individual apartments in high-rise buildings) were sequentially numbered from household registration books and drawn by a random-number scheme. Individual respondents were chosen via Kish grid. The sample was weighted to correct for discrepancies from the sampled population by sex and age, based on the most recent census (2002 in Uzbekistan; 1998 for Kyrgyzstan) and in the population of the primary sampling units.

The questionnaire consisted of thirty-six questions in Uzbekistan and thirty-nine questions in Kyrgyzstan (of which thirty-six were the same as the Uzbek version), translated into the local languages (Russian, Uzbek, and Kyrgyz). Local employees of the research firm administered the survey. The average response rate was about 70 percent (with 428 nonresponses) in Uzbekistan and 85 percent (117 nonresponses) in Kyrgyzstan. The process took forty-five to sixty minutes per interview on average. Supervisors hand-checked the completed questionnaires and verified the accuracy of interviews by making in-person follow-up visits to 23 percent of respondents in Uzbekistan and 11 percent in Kyrgyzstan. I personally accompanied and observed several interviewers during the pilot phase in Tashkent.

The questionnaire covered four main issue areas: the (mostly unofficial) networks people rely on for everyday survival; characteristics of official and unofficial leaders and people's perceptions of the qualities a leader should possess; measurement of social capital in communities (how often people exchange information, where and with whom people interact, and measures of trust); and the institutions that govern social interaction in communities, especially as they elicit participation in community events. In addition, questions were added to the Kyrgyz version of the questionnaire inquiring about the ways people self-identify and whether they own a car or a telephone.[9]

---

9. For an analysis using the survey data, see Scott Radnitz, Jonathan Wheatley, and Christoph Zuercher, "The Origins of Social Capital: Evidence from a Survey of Post-Soviet Central Asia," *Comparative Political Studies* 42, no. 6 (2009): 707–32.

# Index